SQL: Practical Guide for Developers

The Morgan Kaufmann Practical Guides Series
Series Editor, Michael J. Donahoo

For further information on these books and for a list of forthcoming titles, please visit our Web site at http://www.mkp.com/practical

Critical Acclaim for

SQL: Practical Guid

UNIVERSITY OF
GLOUCESTERSHIRE

The book lives up to its title: it is a very practical guide. The authors clearly know their SQL and manage to write about the language in a step-by-step style that progresses smoothly from the simple to the more difficult aspects of the language. The profuse use of examples, each with an accompanying motivation and explanation of the results, lets the reader follow even complex topics without a constant struggle. The authors have even included examples that illustrate common errors programmers make, explaining the right way to perform the task. It doesn't hurt that the sample application is based on something everybody uses every day: food.

I especially enjoyed the manner in which the authors explained the rationale behind most of the SQL facilities. Even though they have not been an active part of the standard's development efforts, their insight into the underlying reasons for a feature's inclusion is spot on. They also do an excellent job of explaining complex sets of rules in easily understood language—I learned new ways of understanding some of the very rules that I personally wrote into the standard!

Each chapter ends with a summary of the principle points, and most of them include practical advice for programmers who intend to use the SQL language features described in the chapter. The inclusion at every chapter's end of a set of questions and exercises—all directly relevant to the chapter's material—makes this book an excellent candidate for use in the classroom.
– **Jim Melton**, Oracle Corporation, Editor of ISO/IEC 9075-* (SQL) and Co-Chair, W3C XML Query Working Group

This book provides a succinct yet complete introduction to the fundamental aspects of the SQL language. It is not just another SQL text. The authors' use of simple yet clear examples to illustrate difficult concepts throughout the text makes this a perfect book for use in an introductory database systems class as a supplement or as an introductory reference for the novice practitioner.
– **Paul Fortier**, University of Massachusetts, Dartmouth

SQL: Practical Guide for Developers

Michael J. Donahoo

Gregory D. Speegle

PARK LEARNING CENTRE
UNIVERSITY OF GLOUCESTERSHIRE
P.O. Box 220, The Park
Cheltenham GL50 2RH
Tel: 01242 532721

AMSTERDAM • BOSTON • HEIDELBERG • LONDON
NEW YORK • OXFORD • PARIS • SAN DIEGO
SAN FRANCISCO • SINGAPORE • SYDNEY • TOKYO

ELSEVIER

Morgan Kaufmann Publishers is an imprint of Elsevier

MORGAN KAUFMANN PUBLISHERS

Publisher	Diane Cerra
Publishing Services Manager	Simon Crump
Project Manager	Brandy Lilly
Editorial Assistant	Asma Stephan
Cover Design	Yvo Riezebos
Cover Image	Getty Images
Composition	Cepha Imaging Pvt. Ltd.
Technical Illustration	Dartmouth Publishing, Inc.
Copyeditor	Graphic World Inc.
Proofreader	Graphic World Inc.
Interior printer	The Maple-Vail Book Manufacturing Group
Cover printer	Phoenix Color Corp.

Morgan Kaufmann Publishers is an imprint of Elsevier.
500 Sansome Street, Suite 400, San Francisco, CA 94111

This book is printed on acid-free paper. ∞

Library of Congress Cataloging-in-Publication Data
Application submitted

ISBN-13: 978-0-1222-0531-6
ISBN-10: 0-12-220531-6

For information on all Morgan Kaufmann publications,
visit our Web site at www.mkp.com or www.books.elsevier.com

Printed in the United States of America
05 06 07 08 09   5 4 3 2 1

Contents

Preface

The value of the relational database is indisputable. It is by far the most commonly used, modern database system. The primary language for relational databases is SQL, making it the gateway to the data of the small business and corporate enterprise. Many of the applications that you see on the Internet, in your local library, and so on, access and manipulate their data using SQL.

Intended Audience

We wrote this book for technically competent readers who want a short, focused, and inexpensive introduction to the main features of SQL. Our general approach revolves around creating the resource *we* have wished for in our classes. We believe that this book is appropriate for both students and professionals.

This is not a guide to using a specific database product. We assume that you have a database system installed and sufficient access privileges to perform the operations described in this book. There are many database products readily available if you do not have access to an existing one. Many such systems are available for download from the Internet for trial or even free use. See the book Web site (http://www.mkp.com/practical/sql) for a partial list of products.

Approach

Chapter 1 provides a general overview of basic relational database and SQL concepts. It is not a comprehensive introduction to the database area; instead, it is intended to introduce the terminology and concepts used in the book. Chapters 2 through 7 cover querying data. After reading these chapters, you should be able to answer a broad range of queries on an existing database. Chapter 8 describes data creation and manipulation. Chapters 9 and 10 deal with creation of the structures to represent stored data. Finally, Chapters 11 through 13 address advanced database features such as transactions, security, and database application development.

You may wish to begin your exploration of SQL with database creation instead of querying an existing database. To take this approach in our book, begin by reading the relational database and SQL introduction in Chapter 1. Next, read Chapter 9 on creating database tables, followed by Chapter 8 on manipulating data. Skim over the creation and population of tables from existing tables as these assume an understanding of database querying. It will be easy to read these sections later. At this point, you should be able to create a database and fill it with data. Next, read Chapters 2 through 7 on querying your new database. Finally, read Chapters 11 through 13 to understand some advanced database features.

Acknowledgments

We would like to thank all the people who helped make this book a reality. Despite the book's brevity, many hours went into reviewing the original proposal and the draft, and the reviewers' input has significantly shaped the final result.

We thank those who reviewed the original proposal and offered advice on what to put in and what to leave out. We especially thank those who meticulously reviewed the various drafts of the text and made suggestions for improvement. Any errors that remain are, of course, our responsibility. We are very interested in weeding out such errors in future printings, so if you find one, please send an email to either of us. We will maintain an errata list on the book's Web site.

We are also grateful to the folks at Morgan Kaufmann. They take a hands-on approach to development that contributes significantly to the ultimate text quality. Diane Cerra, our editor, worked hard to provide valuable guidance throughout this process. We are also grateful to Lisa Royse, our production editor from Graphic World Publishing Services, who has been very willing to work with us on the design and "look and feel" of the text; we hope you like the result.

Feedback

We invite your suggestions for improvement of any aspect of this book. You can send feedback via the book's Web site (http://www.mkp.com/practical/sql), or you can send us an email to the addresses below.

Michael J. Donahoo
Jeff_Donahoo@baylor.edu

Gregory D. Speegle
Greg_Speegle@baylor.edu

SQL: Practical Guide
for Developers

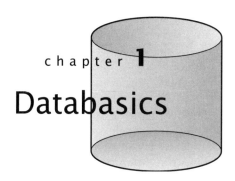

chapter 1

Databasics

A *database* is a repository designed for organizing and accessing information. For simple data, management is easy. For example, a grocery list may be written on scratch paper, and contact information may be kept in an address book. Both the scratch paper and address book are examples of databases.

Grocery List

Milk
Bread
Coffee
SQL book

Name_____Bob Feakins_____

Business
address_____123 Pine St_____

City_Dallas___State_TX__Zip_78909

Address_____

Home phone:_____

Work phone:_(25)7892-1361_____

Fax:_____

Mobile:_(25)7892-8193_____

(25)7881-2391 (pager)

Basic lists may work for very simple databases. However, the limitations of this approach can make even simple tasks difficult. Let's look at our address book example again. One problem is that it has space for information we don't know/need (e.g., home address), whereas it does not have space for information we need to know (e.g., pager number). Searching presents another problem. An address book is typically organized alphabetically by name. What if we want to search using some other criteria? Finding all of our friends who live in a particular city requires an exhaustive search. Data entry and maintenance can also be problematic. Paper-based address books are fine for a small set of people; however, it would be very time-consuming to add all of the people in your company. Keeping up with the changes quickly becomes unmanageable. Another problem is relating our paper-based address book with other databases. If we wanted to call all of the individuals on our softball team, we would need to combine the information from our team roster with our address book. Clearly, additional complexity makes it harder and harder to effectively represent the various data relationships. Likewise, as the volume of data increases, the complexity of managing and querying information grows.

Lucky for us, computers are especially adept at managing and quickly accessing information. Software designed to store, manipulate, and retrieve data in a database is called a *Database management system* (DBMS). Here, we focus exclusively on a specific (and by far the most common) type of DBMS, the *relational DBMS*. There are many relational DBMSs (see the book Web site for pointers to some examples). Fortunately, relational DBMSs speak a common language called SQL. Using SQL, we can define, manipulate, and query our data. SQL is correctly pronounced as S-Q-L; however, many people also pronounce it *see-kwel.*

This text is based on the ANSI 2003 SQL standard. **NOTE:** Each DBMS does things differently, and no major DBMS follows the specification exactly. The specifics of a particular DBMS can be found in its documentation. There are many reasons a DBMS may vary from the standard, including performance, legacy, or marketing. Fortunately, the basic syntax of SQL is the same for all DBMS. See the book Web site for information on DBMS-specific syntax.

SQL is divided into three major parts. *Data manipulation language* (DML) is used to store and retrieve data from the database. The majority of this book is on SQL DML, and that will be the part of SQL used by the most people. *Data description language* (DDL) is used to define the structure of the data. Chapters 9 and 10 cover the basics in SQL DDL. *Data control language* (DCL) is used to restrict access to data by certain users. We introduce DCL in Chapter 12.

We assume that you have a DBMS already installed and are able to enter SQL commands. Consult your DBMS documentation for instructions on how to do this. If you do not have a DBMS, consider downloading one from the Internet. There are some free relational databases, and several commercial DBMSs provide a free version of their product for experimentation. See the book Web site for suggestions of DBMSs.

The best way to understand how a relational database works is to consider a specific application. Imagine that you are the proud owner of a restaurant named *Garden Variety Salads.* You need to manage information about a variety of real-world entities to run your establishment. For example, you need to maintain a list of food items so your customers will have something to purchase. Each food item is made from one or more different ingredients, such as lettuce, tomatoes, and so on. You also want to track how much each ingredient costs so you can determine how much to charge and how much profit you're making. If you don't want to grow the ingredients yourself, you should keep a list of vendors.

Let's look at representing this information in a relational database called the Restaurant Database. Our design is contrived solely for the purpose of teaching SQL, not database design. Proper database design is a difficult problem, well beyond the scope of this text. Most introductory database texts address design.

1.1 Tables

In the relational model, a database contains a set of tables. A *table* is made up of *rows* and *columns.* Each table has a name, which is unique within the database. Each column has a name and a data type. We discuss data types in the next section. The name of a column need only be unique within a table so other tables in the same database can have columns of the same name. Each row constitutes one *record* in the table. A table may contain zero or more rows. A row is subdivided into *fields,* one per column. Tables may be used to model real-world objects and relationships.

Let's look at an example table. In our Restaurant Database, we record information about the suppliers of our ingredients in a table named *vendors.*

vendorid	companyname	repfname	replname	referredby FK
VGRUS	Veggies_R_Us	Candy	Corn	NULL
DNDRY	Don's Dairy	Marla	Milker	VGRUS
FLVCR	Flavorful Creams	Sherman	Sherbert	VGRUS
FRTFR	"Fruit Eating" Friends	Gilbert	Grape	FLVCR
EDDRS	Ed's Dressings	Sam	Sauce	FRTFR
SPWTR	Spring Water Supply	Gus	Hing	EDDRS

Each row in the *vendors* table records information about a particular vendor. For example, the row with a *vendorid* of VGRUS is a record representing the vendor named Veggies_R_Us. The attributes that we wish to record for each vendor are represented by the five columns of the *vendors* table: a unique vendor identifier (*vendorid*), the name of the vendor (*companyname*), the first and last name of the vendor representative (*repfname* and *replname*), and an identifier for the vendor (*referredby*) who recommended this vendor.

Not everybody uses the same terminology. A table may also be called a *relation.* Technically, a table and a relation are not exactly the same thing. Unlike a table, a relation cannot contain duplicate rows. A row is sometimes called a *tuple.* Finally, a column may also be called an *attribute* of the relation. A table may be represented by its name followed by a comma-delimited list of columns:

vendors(vendorid, companyname, repfname, replname, referredby)

We refer to individual columns of a table using the *tablename.columnname* notation (e.g., *vendors.vendorid*).

1.2 Data Types

Every column has a declared data type, which specifies what kind (e.g., characters, numbers, time, etc.) of information may be contained in the column. Your DBMS may not support all of these types, and it may have some additional types as well. Consult your DBMS documentation for details. We divide the SQL data types into five categories: character string, numeric, temporal, binary, and boolean.

1.2.1 Character String

Attributes such as names and addresses are typically represented by strings of characters (e.g., 'Bob Smith'). There are many database types for character strings. The most common are as follows:

CHARACTER[(L)] specifies a fixed-length character string containing exactly L characters. If the length is not specified, SQL uses a length of 1. If the string contains fewer than L characters, the remaining characters contain padding characters (usually spaces). CHARACTER may be abbreviated as CHAR.

CHARACTER VARYING(L) specifies a variable-length character string that may hold up to L characters. Only the specified characters are stored so there is no padding. CHARACTER VARYING may be abbreviated as CHAR VARYING or, most often, VARCHAR.

String literals are enclosed in single quotes (e.g., 'Bob'). A single quote within a literal is indicated by two single quotes (e.g., 'Bob''s Car').

The inclusion of trailing spaces is the primary difference between CHAR and VARCHAR. For example, *vendorid* is defined as CHAR(5) and *repfname* is defined as VARCHAR(20). Assume we add a row such as the following:

BOB	Bob's Bakery	Bob	Bobson	VGRUS

to *vendors.* Because *vendorid* is CHAR(5), two extra spaces are stored. However, *repfname* is VARCHAR(20), so no extra spaces are added. This also makes a difference when we retrieve data from the database. The *vendorid* 'BOB␣␣' will match 'BOB' or 'BOB␣␣', but the *repfname* 'Bob' will not match 'Bob␣␣'.

The default character set for your DBMS may be limited in the kinds of characters it can represent. For example, if your DBMS uses the ASCII (American Standard Code for Information Interchange) character encoding, it can only represent English characters. Unfortunately, this doesn't work well for internationalization. The national character string type can represent internationalized character sets such as Unicode. The fixed-length national character string type is NATIONAL CHARACTER (abbreviated NATIONAL CHAR or NCHAR). The variable-length national character string type is NATIONAL CHARACTER VARYING (abbreviated NATIONAL CHAR VARYING or NCHAR VARYING). String literals for NATIONAL CHARACTER types are prefixed with an N (e.g., N'Bob').

Most DBMSs place an upper limit on the size of a character string. To store large strings, SQL provides the CHARACTER LARGE OBJECT data type (abbreviated as CHAR LARGE OBJECT or CLOB). SQL allows the use of the national character string encoding with NATIONAL CHARACTER LARGE OBJECT (abbreviated NCHAR LARGE OBJECT or NCLOB).

1.2.2   Numeric

SQL includes several different types to store numeric information, such as age and salary. In specifying a numeric type, we need to consider three questions: 1) Are our data limited to whole numbers, 2) What range of values do we wish to support, and 3) How much control do we need over precision?

INTEGER, SMALLINT, and BIGINT—INTEGER, SMALLINT, and BIGINT store signed whole numbers. The range of possible values is DBMS dependent; however, the range of values for SMALLINT is less than or equal to the range of value for INTEGER, which is less than or equal to the range of values for BIGINT. INTEGER may be abbreviated as INT.

NUMERIC[(P [, S])] and DECIMAL[(P [, S])]—NUMERIC(P, S) specifies a signed, fixed-point number where P (precision) specifies the total number (to the left and right of the decimal) of digits in the number and S (scale) specifies the number of digits to the right of the decimal place. For example, NUMERIC(5, 2) specifies a type ranging from −999.99 to 999.99. DECIMAL(P, S) is the same as NUMERIC(P, S) except that the actual precision may exceed the specification. For both NUMERIC and DECIMAL, if P or S are not specified, default values will be used. DECIMAL may be abbreviated as DEC.

REAL and DOUBLE PRECISION—REAL specifies a signed, single-precision, floating-point number. The range is DBMS specific. DOUBLE PRECISION is the same as REAL except it supports a greater range of values.

FLOAT[(P)]—FLOAT(P) specifies a signed, floating-point number with a precision of at least P. Here P specifies the number of *binary* digits.

Numeric literals look like you would expect. For REAL, DOUBLE, and FLOAT, literals may be written in exponential notation as nEp representing $n \times 10^p$ where n is a signed, floating-point number and p is a signed, whole number (e.g., 7.4E-3).

If you try to use a number with an absolute value that is too large for the data type, the database should generate an exception. For example, an exception would be raised if we tried to put −1000 into a NUMERIC(5,2) field. If you use a number with too many digits to the right of the decimal point, the DBMS may either truncate or round the value. So, placing 0.0001 into a NUMERIC(5,2) field results in a value of 0.00. A number with fewer digits than the limit of the data type can be placed into a column without exception or change. For example, 9.9 fits in a NUMERIC(5,2) field.

1.2.3 Temporal

SQL provides several data types specific to storing information about temporal information. Representing and utilizing data and time information can be complicated with considerations of time zone, daylight savings time, and so on. As a result, temporal data tend to be more DBMS specific than other types. If the syntax presented here does not work on your database, check your DBMS documentation. SQL divides its temporal types into two categories: datetime and interval. We begin by looking at the date and time types in SQL.

Datetime

Datetime types store date, time information, or both.

Type	Stores	Literal
DATE	year, month, day	DATE 'YYYY-MM-DD'
TIME	hour, minute, and second	TIME 'HH:MM:SS'
TIMESTAMP	year, month, day, minute, and second	TIMESTAMP 'YYYY-MM-DD HH:MM:SS'

Seconds may contain fractional values (e.g., 32.456 seconds). An optional precision for fractional seconds may be given for TIME and TIMESTAMP. TIME and TIMESTAMP may include time zone information. Consult your DBMS documentation for details on WITH TIMEZONE.

Use DATE for columns where you do not care about the time of an event, only the specific day (e.g., birthday). Use TIME type where you do not care about the date, only the specific time. An example is the time of a college class, which might be at 8 AM on Tuesday and Thursday for a semester. TIMESTAMP covers the other cases. An example of a TIMESTAMP might be the time when an order is placed. In this case, we want to know both the date and the time.

Interval

In addition to dates and times, SQL can represent time intervals. Such a data type might be useful for representing concepts such as a warranty period (e.g., 90 days). Interval data types come in two flavors:

Year–Month—Interval expressed in years and/or months. A Year–Month interval data type can be INTERVAL YEAR, INTERVAL MONTH, or INTERVAL YEAR TO MONTH.

Day–Time—Interval expressed in days, hours, minutes, and/or seconds. A Day–Time interval data type is of the following form:

INTERVAL *<start interval value>* [TO *<stop interval value>*]

where the possible interval values are DAY, HOUR, MINUTE, and SECOND. If the optional *<stop interval value>* is specified, it must be an interval with a *smaller* granularity than the *<start interval value>*. For example, if the *<start interval value>* is HOUR, the only valid values for the *<stop interval value>* are MINUTE and SECOND.

Creating an interval literal is a two-step process. First, determine the interval type (e.g., DAY TO MINUTE). Second, place an interval literal string between INTERVAL and the interval value range specification. Here are some example interval literals:

Type	Example Literal	Description
Year–Month	INTERVAL '5' YEAR	5 years
	INTERVAL '2' MONTH	2 months
	INTERVAL '3-1' YEAR TO MONTH	3 years and 1 month
Day–Time	INTERVAL '5 10:30:22.5' DAY TO SECOND	5 days, 10 hours, 30 minutes, and 22.5 seconds
	INTERVAL '-5' DAY	5 days ago
	INTERVAL '2 18:00' DAY TO MINUTE	2 days and 18 minutes

1.2.4   Binary

Although everything on the computer is ultimately stored as binary data, SQL binary data types are designed to store sequences of binary digits. Binary types differ from character string and numeric types in that they are more limited in the allowable comparisons, searches, and other functions. Common uses for binary types include storage of multimedia, such as photographs, sounds, and movies, and storage of scanned images, as in a document imaging and retrieval system.

BIT[(L)] specifies a fixed-length binary string containing exactly L bits. If the length, L, is not specified, SQL uses a length of 1. The behavior for attempting to insert fewer than L bits is system specific. Some systems will reject the insertion attempt; others will pad with zeros.

BIT VARYING(L) specifies a variable-length binary string that may hold up to L bits.

BINARY LARGE OBJECT[(L)] specifies a large, variable-length binary string that may hold up to L bytes. If the length, L, is not specified, the system default length is used. BINARY LARGE OBJECT may be abbreviated as BLOB.

BIT and BIT VARYING literals may be written either in binary form—a single quote enclosed sequence of 0s and 1s prefixed with a B (e.g., B'10110')—or hexadecimal form—a single quote enclosed sequence of hexadecimal digits prefix with an X (e.g., X'3AF'). Note that the 2003 SQL specification drops both BIT and BIT VARYING so systems supporting these types may exclude them in future releases.

1.2.5 Boolean

Truth gets a category all its own in SQL with the BOOLEAN data type. The BOOLEAN data type has three possible values: true, false, and unknown. The unknown value may surprise those familiar with boolean types in most programming languages. We discuss the unknown value in Section 2.8. BOOLEAN literals are (surprise) TRUE, FALSE, and UNKNOWN. The BOOLEAN type is not widely supported, but it is hoped that it will be in the near future.

1.2.6 Other Data Types

Most DBMSs include a slew of custom data types (e.g., money, network, geometric). Using such data types is convenient but may limit portability. Note that not all SQL standard data types are supported by every DBMS. Consult your DBMS documentation for a list of supported types.

1.3 *NULL*

What if a particular attribute for a row isn't known? A value may be unknown because there is no applicable value, the value is currently missing, or the value is purposefully omitted. Let's look more carefully at the *referredby* column in the *vendors* table. For each vendor, this field contains the identifier of the recommending vendor. Flavorful Creams was recommended to you by Veggies_R_Us so the *referredby* field of the row in *vendors* for Flavorful Creams contains the value VGRUS. What value should *referredby* contain for a vendor without a recommendation? We could try to pick a special identifier value to indicate that the *referredby* identifier is not valid (say, XXXXX); however, we would need to ensure that this identifier could never be a valid vendor identifier. Also, any application using this database would have to know about this special identifier and enforce its special meaning.

To avoid these difficulties, relational databases provide a special value, called *NULL*, indicating that a field's value is unknown. In the *vendors* table, *referredby* is *NULL* for all vendors where we do not have a recommending vendor. Unless explicitly forbidden, *NULL* is a valid value for a column of *any* data type. For example, *NULL* is a valid value for a column of type NUMERIC. This means that *NULL* can be a valid value in a column of type FLOAT. *NULL*s are a sticky subject, and how they are handled may not always be obvious. We address the special status of *NULL*s whenever applicable.

1.4 Primary Key

The *primary key* of a table is a column or set of columns whose values uniquely identify a row. Using the values of the primary key, we can refer to a specific row in a table. In the *vendors* table, each vendor has a unique identifier, *vendorid,* which we use as the primary key. If we declare a primary key on a table, the DBMS will enforce the following rules:

- The value of a primary key for a particular row must be unique.
- None of the primary key column values can be *NULL.*

Why is a primary key so important? Suppose we did not have this unique identity and we wanted to change the company name for a representative named Bob Snitch. If there are multiple representatives with this name, we have no way of knowing which Snitch is which. By having a primary key like *vendorid,* we can tell our Snitches apart.

In this text, we indicate the column(s) of the primary key for a table with the symbol. Note that a relational DBMS may allow tables to be created without primary keys; however, good database design calls for a primary key in virtually all tables.

1.5 Table Relationships

A database typically contains several tables. Each table in a database usually has one or more relationships to other tables in the database. In addition to the *vendors* table, your restaurant application has a separate table of ingredients:

ingredients

ingredientid	name	unit	unitprice	foodgroup	inventory	vendorid FK
CHESE	Cheese	scoop	0.03	Milk	150	DNDRY
CHIKN	Chicken	strip	0.45	Meat	120	DNDRY
CRUTN	Crouton	piece	0.01	Bread	400	EDDRS
GRAPE	Grape	piece	0.01	Fruit	300	FRTFR
LETUS	Lettuce	bowl	0.01	Vegetable	200	VGRUS
PICKL	Pickle	slice	0.04	Vegetable	800	VGRUS
SCTDR	Secret Dressing	ounce	0.03	NULL	120	NULL
TOMTO	Tomato	slice	0.03	Fruit	15	VGRUS
WATER	Water	glass	0.06	NULL	NULL	SPWTR
SODA	Soda	glass	0.69	NULL	5000	SPWTR
WTRML	Watermelon	piece	0.02	Fruit	NULL	FRTFR
ORNG	Orange	slice	0.05	Fruit	10	FRTFR

Each ingredient used in your restaurant has a row in the *ingredients* table, and each ingredient can be uniquely identified by its *ingredientid,* the primary key of *ingredients.* Each row in *ingredients* also contains the identifier of the vendor that supplies it. The *vendorid* in ingredients connects each row with the corresponding row in the *vendors* table. Note that having columns with the same name in different tables doesn't confuse SQL (e.g., *vendorid* in both *vendors* and *ingredients*). SQL does not require that related columns be named the same, nor do columns named the same have to be related.

1.5.1 Foreign Key

A *foreign key* is a column or set of columns in a table that refers to a column or set of columns in some (possibly the same) table. In the Restaurant Database, *ingredients.vendorid* is a foreign key referencing *vendors.vendorid.* Consider the table excerpts in Figure 1.1. The Grape ingredient has a *vendorid* of FRTFR, which refers to the vendor identifier for "Fruit Eating" Friends. Veggies_R_Us provides two of the ingredients in the figure example.

A foreign key depends on the row it is referencing in another table for completeness. In the *ingredients* table, a *vendorid* attribute value makes little sense without a corresponding row in the *vendors* table. For example, the *vendorid* for Cheese in *ingredients* is DNDRY, which has little meaning unless we can find out information about the vendor with that identifier. The table containing the foreign key is called the *child* table, and the table containing the attribute(s) it references is called the *parent* table. The attribute(s) values referenced in the parent table are required to be unique. Usually, these referenced attributes are the primary keys of the parent table, but this is not a requirement. A *foreign key (or referential) integrity constraint* requires that any foreign key value in a child table must have one of the following characteristics:

- Have a matching value in the parent table OR
- Be *NULL*

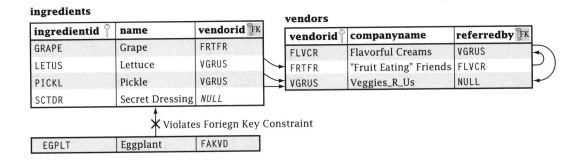

Figure 1.1: Foreign keys.

Consider the tables in Figure 1.1. If we try to add a row for the ingredient eggplant with a vendor identifier of FAKVD, the DBMS will not allow the addition because the *vendorid* value FAKVD does not exist in the *vendors* table. Note that several rows in the child (*ingredients*) table may reference the same row in the parent (*vendors*) table.

If a foreign key is declared, the DBMS will enforce the foreign key integrity constraint by never allowing the existence of a violating row in the child table. Like the primary key, a foreign key may have multiple attributes. Foreign keys can even refer to attributes in the same table. For example, *vendors.referredby* is a foreign key to *vendors.vendorid* (see Figure 1.1). Here the DBMS will not allow a row containing a value for *referredby* that does not already exist in the *vendorid* column of *vendors*.

1.5.2 Relationship Types

There are three basic types of relationships between tables: one-to-many, many-to-many, and one-to-one.

One-to-Many

In a one-to-many relationship between tables *T1* and *T2*, each row from *T1* relates to zero or more rows in *T2*, and each row in *T2* relates to at most one row in *T1*. To model this relationship, *T2* will have a foreign key referencing attributes in *T1*. For the Restaurant Database, the relationship between *vendors* and *ingredients* is one-to-many. Each vendor can supply many different ingredients; however, an ingredient may be supplied by at most one vendor. Figure 1.2 shows the one-to-many relationship between *vendors*

vendors

vendorid 🔑
VGRUS
DNDRY
FLVCR
FRTFR
EDDRS
SPWTR

ingredients

ingredientid 🔑	vendorid 🔑 FK
CHESE	DNDRY
CHIKN	DNDRY
CRUTN	EDDRS
GRAPE	FRTFR
LETUS	VGRUS
PICKL	VGRUS
SCTDR	NULL
TOMTO	VGRUS
WATER	SPWTR
SODA	SPWTR
WTRML	FRTFR
ORNG	FRTFR

Figure 1.2: One-to-many relationship between *vendors* and *ingredients*.

and *ingredients*. Each row from *ingredients* contains the identifier of the supplying vendor (or *NULL*). A particular vendor identifier can show up in multiple *ingredient* rows. For example, you get cheese from the vendor with identifier DNDRY. Looking up DNDRY in the *vendors* table, we see the name of the cheese vendor is Don's Dairy. To find the ingredients provided by Veggies_R_Us, first look up its vendor identifier in the *vendors* table (i.e., VGRUS) and then look up the ingredients for that vendor identifier in the *ingredients* table. We make the *vendorid* attribute in *ingredients* a foreign key to the *vendorid* attribute in *vendors* to enforce this relationship.

A vendor can exist without providing any ingredients. Such a vendor will have a row in the *vendors* table but no matching rows in the *ingredients* table. In the *vendors* table, the Flavorful Creams vendor does not provide any ingredients. Conversely, an ingredient may exist without a vendor. In this case, the *vendorid* attribute in the *ingredients* table will be *NULL*. Your Secret Dressing ingredient doesn't have a vendor because you make it yourself.

The *vendors* table also participates in a one-to-many relationship with *itself*. A vendor may recommend many other vendors; however, a vendor may be recommended by at most one vendor. To represent this one-to-many relationship, *vendors.referredby* is a foreign key that references *vendors.vendorid*.

Many-to-Many

In a many-to-many relationship between tables *T1* and *T2*, each row from *T1* relates to zero or more rows in *T2*, and each row in *T2* relates to zero or more rows in *T1*. To make money, you need some food items to sell to customers. To represent this, our Restaurant Database contains a table of items. Each item is made from many ingredients, and each ingredient can be used in many items. Consequently, we have a *many-to-many relationship* between items and ingredients. Let's first look at the *items* table.

items

itemid	name	price	dateadded
CHKSD	Chicken Salad	2.85	1998-11-13
FRTSD	Fruit Salad	3.45	2000-05-06
GDNSD	Garden Salad	0.99	2001-03-02
MILSD	Millennium Salad	NULL	2002-08-16
SODA	Soda	0.99	2003-02-06
WATER	Water	0.00	2002-05-19
FRPLT	Fruit Plate	3.99	2000-09-02

Each item has an item identifier, *itemid,* the primary key for the *items* table. Each item also has a full name, a menu price, and the date the item was added to the menu. To express the many-to-many relationship, we need some way to match items to ingredients and vice versa. To do this, we create a new table, called a *madewith* table, that pairs ingredients with items.

madewith

itemid ⚷ FK	ingredientid ⚷ FK	quantity
CHKSD	CHESE	2
CHKSD	CHIKN	4
CHKSD	LETUS	1
CHKSD	SCTDR	1
FRTSD	GRAPE	10
FRTSD	WTRML	5
GDNSD	LETUS	4
GDNSD	TOMTO	8
FRPLT	WTRML	10
FRPLT	GRAPE	10
FRPLT	CHESE	10
FRPLT	CRUTN	10
FRPLT	TOMTO	8
WATER	WATER	1
SODA	SODA	1
FRPLT	ORNG	10

For each ingredient in an item, the *madewith* table has a row containing the corresponding item and ingredient identifiers. A table like *madewith* that links rows from one table to another is called a *join* table. Figure 1.3 shows the many-to-many relationship between *ingredients* and *items*. The Chicken Salad item has 4 ingredients, represented by 4 rows in *madewith* with an *itemid* of CHKSD. The Cheese ingredient is used in two items, represented by 2 rows in *madewith* with an *ingredientid* of CHESE.

You can see that the relational model doesn't have explicit many-to-many relationships. It implements a many-to-many relationship using 2 one-to-many relationships. To record how much of each ingredient to include in an item, we add a *quantity* attribute. For example, each fruit salad has 10 grapes and 5 watermelon cubes.

The primary key for *madewith* consists of two attributes: *itemid* and *ingredientid*. As you might suspect, *madewith.ingredientid* is a foreign key referencing *ingredients.ingredientid,* and *madewith.itemid* is a foreign key referencing *items.itemid.* Given these primary and foreign keys, the DBMS will enforce the following constraints for the *madewith* table:

- Every *itemid, ingredientid* pair in a *madewith* must be unique (primary key).

- Neither the *itemid* nor the *ingredientid* column may contain *NULL* (primary key).

- Any *itemid/ingredientid* value must already exist in the *item/ingredient* table (foreign key).

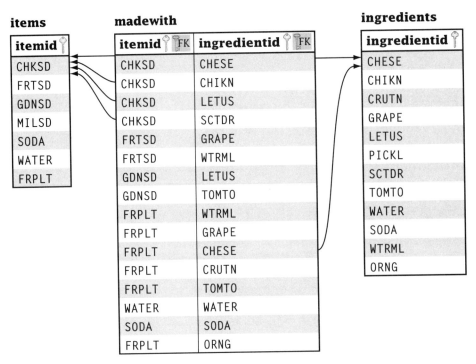

Figure 1.3: Many-to-many relationship between *ingredients* and *items*.

One-to-One

Usually, one-to-one relationships are represented by attributes within a single table. That is, all of the attributes of a table exhibit a natural one-to-one relationship. In the *vendors* table, a row relates one vendor identifier to one company name to one representative.

In a one-to-one relationship between tables *T1* and *T2*, each row from *T1* relates to at most one row in *T2* and vice versa. In reality, a one-to-one relationship between tables is often just a special case of a one-to-many relationship.

1.5.3   Schemas

The collection of tables and other data description objects in a database is called the *schema*. We *populate* the database by adding data to the tables in the schema. Note that the schema does *not* include the data but only the description of the data. Whereas we expect the data to change often (with every insert, update, and delete), the schema of a database should change infrequently.

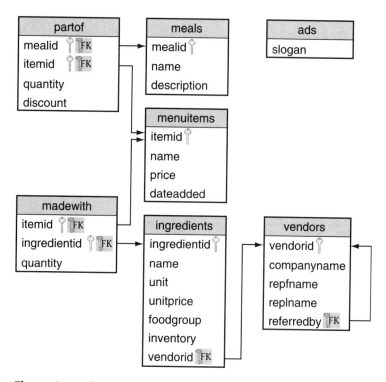

Figure 1.4: Schema for the Restaurant Database.

1.6 Restaurant Database

We present the schema and data for our sample Restaurant Database. Figure 1.4 gives an overview of the Restaurant Database by showing the tables and relationships. This section will be useful as a reference so note where it is. To help find it again, this particular page is 2 microns[1] taller and wider than all of the other pages, which should make it stick out.

vendors—Vendors who supply ingredients for the restaurant.

Column	Type	Description
vendorid	CHAR(5)	Unique vendor identifier
companyname	VARCHAR(30)	Vendor company name
repfname	VARCHAR(20)	Vendor representative first name
replname	VARCHAR(20)	Vendor representative last name
referredby FK	CHAR(5)	Identifier of vendor that referred this vendor to you. Foreign key referencing *vendors.vendorid*

---

[1] Because of variations in the publishing process, page widths may vary up to 125 microns.

vendors

vendorid 🔑	companyname	repfname	replname	referredby 🔑FK
VGRUS	Veggies_R_Us	Candy	Corn	NULL
DNDRY	Don's Dairy	Marla	Milker	VGRUS
FLVCR	Flavorful Creams	Sherman	Sherbert	VGRUS
FRTFR	"Fruit Eating" Friends	Gilbert	Grape	FLVCR
EDDRS	Ed's Dressings	Sam	Sauce	FRTFR
SPWTR	Spring Water Supply	Gus	Hing	EDDRS

ingredients—Ingredients provided by vendors for use in items.

Column	Type	Description
ingredientid 🔑	CHAR(5)	Unique ingredient identifier
name	VARCHAR(30)	Ingredient name
unit	CHAR(10)	Ingredient serving size
unitprice	NUMERIC(5,2)	Cost of an ingredient serving
foodgroup	CHAR(15)	Ingredient food group
inventory	INTEGER	Number of available ingredient servings
vendorid 🔑FK	CHAR(5)	Identifier of vendor supplying ingredient. Foreign key referencing *vendors.vendorid*

ingredients

ingredientid 🔑	name	unit	unitprice	foodgroup	inventory	vendorid 🔑FK
CHESE	Cheese	scoop	0.03	Milk	150	DNDRY
CHIKN	Chicken	strip	0.45	Meat	120	DNDRY
CRUTN	Crouton	piece	0.01	Bread	400	EDDRS
GRAPE	Grape	piece	0.01	Fruit	300	FRTFR
LETUS	Lettuce	bowl	0.01	Vegetable	200	VGRUS
PICKL	Pickle	slice	0.04	Vegetable	800	VGRUS
SCTDR	Secret Dressing	ounce	0.03	NULL	120	NULL
TOMTO	Tomato	slice	0.03	Fruit	15	VGRUS
WATER	Water	glass	0.06	NULL	NULL	SPWTR
SODA	Soda	glass	0.69	NULL	5000	SPWTR
WTRML	Watermelon	piece	0.02	Fruit	NULL	FRTFR
ORNG	Orange	slice	0.05	Fruit	10	FRTFR

items—Basic items for sale to customers.

Column	Type	Description
itemid	CHAR(5)	Unique item identifier
name	VARCHAR(30)	Item name
price	NUMERIC(5,2)	Item price
dateadded	DATE	Date item added to menu

items

itemid	name	price	dateadded
CHKSD	Chicken Salad	2.85	1998-11-13
FRTSD	Fruit Salad	3.45	2000-05-06
GDNSD	Garden Salad	0.99	2001-03-02
MILSD	Millennium Salad	NULL	2002-08-16
SODA	Soda	0.99	2003-02-06
WATER	Water	0.00	2002-05-19
FRPLT	Fruit Plate	3.99	2000-09-02

madewith—Item ingredients: Join table for the many-to-many relationship between *ingredients* and *items*.

Column	Type	Description
itemid FK	CHAR(5)	Identifier of item that uses the ingredient. Foreign key referencing *items.itemid*.
ingredientid FK	CHAR(5)	Identifier of ingredient used in the item. Foreign key referencing *ingredients.ingredientid*.
quantity	INTEGER	Number of units of specified ingredient to use in item.

madewith

itemid FK	ingredientid FK	quantity
CHKSD	CHESE	2
CHKSD	CHIKN	4
CHKSD	LETUS	1
CHKSD	SCTDR	1
FRTSD	GRAPE	10
FRTSD	WTRML	5
GDNSD	LETUS	4
GDNSD	TOMTO	8
FRPLT	WTRML	10
FRPLT	GRAPE	10
FRPLT	CHESE	10
FRPLT	CRUTN	10

Continued on next page

madewith (cont'd)

itemid⚷ FK	ingredientid⚷ FK	quantity
FRPLT	TOMTO	8
WATER	WATER	1
SODA	SODA	1
FRPLT	ORNG	10

meals—A meal is a collection of items. To entice customers to buy more food, you combine items together into a meal and sell it at a discount. For example, our Chicken N Suds meal combines a chicken salad with a soda.

Column	Type	Description
mealid⚷	CHAR(5)	Unique meal identifier
name	CHAR(10)	Meal name

meals

mealid⚷	name
CKSDS	Chicken N Suds
VGNET	Vegan Eatin'

partof—Meal items: Join table for the many-to-many relationship between *meals* and *items*.

Column	Type	Description
mealid⚷ FK	CHAR(5)	Identifier of meal that includes the item. Foreign key referencing *meals.mealid*.
itemid⚷ FK	CHAR(5)	Identifier of item to be used in the meal. Foreign key referencing *items.itemid*.
quantity	INTEGER	Number of specified items to use in meal.
discount	DECIMAL(2,2)	Percentage discount for item when part of this meal. To compute the price of a meal, sum the discounted individual price of all items. For example, *Chicken N Suds* meal costs

$$2.85 * 98\% + 0.99 * 90\% = 3.68.$$

partof

mealid⚷ FK	itemid⚷ FK	quantity	discount
CKSDS	CHKSD	1	0.02
CKSDS	SODA	1	0.10
VGNET	GDNSD	1	0.03
VGNET	FRTSD	1	0.01
VGNET	WATER	1	0.00

ads—Possible advertising slogans for the restaurant.

Column	Type	Description
slogan	CHAR(50)	Advertising slogan

ads

slogan
Grazing in style
NULL
Bovine friendly and heart smart
Where the grazin's good
The grass is greener here
Welcome to the "other side"

menuitems—Combination of both meals and items to go on the restaurant menu. We implement *menuitems* as a view (see Chapter 10).

Column	Type	Description
menuitemid🔑	CHAR(5)	Item or meal identifier
name	VARCHAR(30)	Menu item name
price	NUMERIC(5,2)	Item price

menuitems

menuitemid🔑	name	price
CHKSD	Chicken Salad	2.85
CKSDS	Chicken N Suds	3.68
FRPLT	Fruit Plate	3.99
FRTSD	Fruit Salad	3.45
GDNSD	Garden Salad	0.99
MILSD	Millennium Salad	NULL
SODA	Soda	0.99
VGNET	Vegan Eatin'	4.38
WATER	Water	0.00

stores—Stores franchised across the country.

Column	Type	Description
storeid🔑	CHAR(5)	Unique store identifier
street	VARCHAR(25)	Street address of the store
city	VARCHAR(25)	City of the store
state	CHAR(2)	U.S. state of the store
zip	CHAR(10)	U.S. zip code in XXXXX-XXXX format
operator	VARCHAR(41)	Name of the operator of the store (e.g., owner or the manager)

stores

storeid	address	city	state	zip	manager
FIRST	1111 Main St.	Waco	TX	76798	Jeff Donahoo
#2STR	2222 2nd Ave.	Waco	TX	76798-7356	Greg Speegle
NDSTR	3333 3rd St.	Fargo	ND	58106	Jeff Speegle
CASTR	4444 4th Blvd	San Francsico	CA	94101-4150	Greg Donahoo
NWSTR	NULL	NULL	TX	NULL	Man Ager

orders—Information about each order placed at every store. Each order that a customer places is given a unique order number. Each item within an order is given a line number, which is unique within the order. The *menuitemid* is not declared as a foreign key to allow for future deletion of menu items.

Column	Type	Description
ordernumber	INTEGER	Unique order identifier
linenumber	INTEGER	Order line identifier for orders with multiple items that is unique within an order
storeid FK	CHAR(5)	Identifier of the store where the order is placed. Foreign key referencing *store.storeid*
menuitemid	CHAR(5)	Identifier of menu item ordered for this line number
price	NUMERIC(5,2)	Price of the menu item ordered
time	TIMESTAMP	Time and date the order was placed

orders

ordernumber	linenumber	storeid FK	menuitemid	price	time
1	1	FIRST	FRTSD	3.45	2005-01-26 13:46:04.188
1	2	FIRST	WATER	0.00	2005-01-26 13:46:19.188
1	3	FIRST	WATER	0.00	2005-01-26 13:46:34.188
2	1	FIRST	CHKSD	2.85	2005-01-26 13:47:49.188
3	1	FIRST	SODA	0.99	2005-01-26 13:49:04.188
3	2	FIRST	FRPLT	3.99	2005-01-26 13:49:19.188
3	3	FIRST	VGNET	4.38	2005-01-26 13:49:34.188
1	1	#2STR	CKSDS	3.68	2005-01-26 14:02:04.188
1	2	#2STR	CHKSD	2.85	2005-01-26 14:02:19.188
1	3	#2STR	SODA	0.99	2005-01-26 14:02:34.188
1	4	#2STR	GDNSD	0.99	2005-01-26 14:02:49.188
2	1	#2STR	CHKSD	2.85	2005-01-26 14:04:04.188
2	2	#2STR	SODA	0.99	2005-01-26 14:04:19.188
3	1	#2STR	CHKSD	2.85	2005-01-26 14:05:34.188
3	2	#2STR	FRPLT	3.99	2005-01-26 14:05:49.188
3	3	#2STR	GDNSD	0.99	2005-01-26 14:06:04.188
1	1	NDSTR	WATER	0.00	2005-01-26 14:14:04.188
1	2	NDSTR	FRPLT	3.99	2005-01-26 14:14:19.188

orders (cont'd)

ordernumber	linenumber	storeid FK	menuitemid	price	time
2	1	NDSTR	GDNSD	0.99	2005-01-26 14:15:34.188
3	1	NDSTR	VGNET	4.38	2005-01-26 14:16:49.188
3	2	NDSTR	FRPLT	3.99	2005-01-26 14:17:04.188
3	3	NDSTR	FRTSD	3.45	2005-01-26 14:17:19.188
3	4	NDSTR	SODA	0.99	2005-01-26 14:17:34.188
1	1	CASTR	CHKSD	2.85	2005-01-26 14:22:04.188
1	2	CASTR	GDNSD	0.99	2005-01-26 14:22:19.188
2	1	CASTR	SODA	0.99	2005-01-26 14:23:34.188
2	2	CASTR	FRTSD	3.45	2005-01-26 14:23:49.188
2	3	CASTR	SODA	0.99	2005-01-26 14:24:04.188
2	4	CASTR	VGNET	4.38	2005-01-26 14:24:19.188
3	1	CASTR	VGNET	4.38	2005-01-26 14:25:34.188
3	2	CASTR	FRPLT	3.99	2005-01-26 14:25:49.188
3	3	CASTR	FRTSD	3.45	2005-01-26 14:26:04.188
3	4	CASTR	WATER	0.00	2005-01-26 14:26:19.188
3	5	CASTR	CHKSD	2.85	2005-01-26 14:26:34.188

1.7 Wrap Up

Like any language, the best way to learn is to use it over and over again. The way to try SQL is to create a schema in a DBMS, load some data, and bang out some SQL. We encourage executing each and every SQL statement in this book, experimenting with new queries, and working the exercises at the end of each chapter. Unfortunately, each DBMS is different. Even worse, how something is implemented in a particular DBMS changes with new releases. Given this, we do not include DBMS specifics in this book; however, the book Web site includes materials on the major DBMSs, such as scripts to create and populate the Restaurant Database.

Review Questions

1. A row in a table can be uniquely identified by _____.

2. The _____ includes the set of tables but not the data.

3. What is the difference between the literal 'Bob' stored as a CHAR(5) versus a VARCHAR(5)?

4. Can an attribute of type INTEGER have the value *NULL*? _____

5. In the Restaurant Database, an item may have between _____ and _____ ingredients.

6. If we added a new row to *vendors* in the Restaurant Database with *vendorid* = HMFDS, give the list of all possible values for *referredby*.

7. In the Restaurant Database, would the DBMS allow a row in the *vendors* table with a *vendorid* of *NULL*? Explain.

8. Give a type and an example literal for the following data:

Data	Type	Literal
Weight	NUMERIC(5, 2)	129.3
Street		
Birthday		
Contract Length		
Salary		
Gender		

9. What is the difference between a database and a DBMS?

10. In the Restaurant Database, give the name of all of the ingredients in the *Vegan Eatin'* meal.

11. If a vendor could be recommended by multiple vendors, how would our restaurant schema change?

12. We must call our vendors to place new orders; unfortunately, we don't know their phone numbers. Of course, a vendor may have several phone numbers. For the restaurant schema, how would you add the number and phone type (e.g., office, home, cell, fax, etc.)? Assume that a phone number is assigned to only one vendor.

13. For your restaurant, you need to create a table for customers containing an identifier, name, number of visits, and percent discount. Give the column names and data types of this table. What is the primary key of this new table?

14. In the Restaurant Database, we want to add 2 more scoops of cheese to the Chicken Salad item. We could simply increase the value of the quantity field in the *madewith* table for the row pairing Chicken Salad with cheese. Could we also just add another row to *madewith* containing the values (CHKSD, CHESE, 2)? Explain.

15. In the Restaurant Database, you have a new vendor, "Homemade Foods", that makes a single ingredient, "Homemade Bread". Give the new rows to add to the various tables to add this new information and include two slices of bread in the "Chicken N Suds" meal.

16. Can any of the numeric fields have a negative value?

17. Provide an example of an attribute that would require a time interval.

18. In the Restaurant Database, can FRPLT be the name of an item?

19. Consider the *ads* table in the restaurant schema. Could we make *slogan* the primary key? Explain.

20. Can a table have no rows?

21. Give a data type to represent a number without loss of precision that can range from −1397 to 24892.99.

Practice

To practice SQL, we introduce a new database application. The Employees Database stores information about a business, including employees, departments, and projects. Each employee works for one department and is assigned many projects. Each department has many employees, has many projects, and may be a subdepartment of one department (e.g., Accounting is a subdepartment of Administration). Each project is assigned to one department and is worked on by many employees. Figure 1.5 gives the schema for the Employees Database.

employees—Employees who work for the company.

Column	Type	Description
employeeid	NUMERIC(9)	Unique employee identifier
firstname	VARCHAR(10)	Employee first name
lastname	VARCHAR(20)	Employee last name
deptcode FK	CHAR(5)	Identifier of department the employee works for. Foreign key referencing *departments.code*
salary	NUMERIC(9,2)	Employee salary

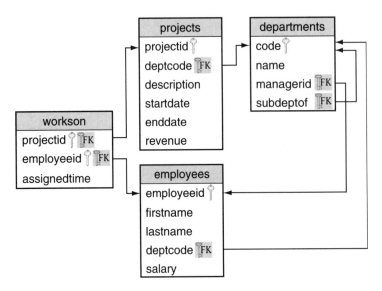

Figure 1.5: Schema for the Employees Database.

employees

employeeid⌇	firstname	lastname	deptcode ⫿FK	salary
1	Al	Betheleader	ADMIN	70000.00
2	PI	Rsquared	ACCNT	40000.00
3	Harry	Hardware	HDWRE	50000.00
4	Sussie	Software	CNSLT	60000.00
5	Abe	Advice	CNSLT	30000.00
6	Hardly	Aware	NULL	65000.00

departments—Company departments.

Column	Type	Description
code⌇	CHAR(5)	Unique department identifier
name	VARCHAR(30)	Department name
managerid ⫿FK	NUMERIC(9)	Identifier of employee who manages the department. Foreign key referencing *employees.employeeid*
subdeptof ⫿FK	CHAR(5)	Code of department that includes this department as one of its immediate subdepartments. Foreign key referencing *departments.code*

departments

code	name	managerid FK	subdeptof FK
ADMIN	Administration	1	NULL
ACCNT	Accounting	2	ADMIN
HDWRE	Hardware	3	CNSLT
CNSLT	Consulting	4	ADMIN

projects—Projects managed by company.

Column	Type	Description
projectid	CHAR(8)	Unique project identifier
deptcode FK	CHAR(5)	Identifier of department managing this project. Foreign key referencing *departments.code*
description	VARCHAR(200)	Project description
startdate	DATE	Project start date
stopdate	DATE	Project stop date. *NULL* value indicates that the project is ongoing
revenue	NUMERIC(12, 2)	Total project revenue

projects

projectid	deptcode FK	description	startdate	enddate	revenue
EMPHAPPY	ADMIN	Employee Moral	2002-03-14	NULL	0.00
ADT4MFIA	ACCNT	Mofia Audit	2003-07-03	2003-11-30	100000.00
ROBOSPSE	CNSLT	Robotic Spouse	2002-03-14	NULL	242000.00
DNLDCLNT	CNSLT	Download Client	2005-02-03	NULL	18150.00

workson—Project employees: Join table for the many-to-many relationship between *employees* and *departments*.

Column	Type	Description
employeeid FK	NUMERIC(9)	Identifier of employee working on a project. Foreign key referencing *employees.employeeid*
projectid FK	CHAR(8)	Identifier of project that employee is working on. Foreign key referencing *projects.projectid*
assignedtime	DECIMAL(3,2)	Percentage of time employee is assigned to project

workson

employeeid 🔑 FK	projectid 🔑 FK	assignedtime
2	ADT4MFIA	0.50
3	ROBOSPSE	0.75
4	ROBOSPSE	0.75
5	ROBOSPSE	0.50
5	ADT4MFIA	0.60
3	DNLDCLNT	0.25

1. What must be true about the values of *projectid* and *deptcode* in a row of the *projects* table?

2. Can an employee who works on no projects be in this database?

3. Can an employee work on a project that is assigned to a department other than the one he or she works for?

4. Describe the various relationships in the Employees Database. For example, *employees* has a one-to-many relationship with *departments* because an employee works for one department and a department has many employees.

5. Which attributes in the *departments* table can be *NULL*?

6. Which is higher, the largest possible employee ID or the highest salary?

7. For each table, give an example of a new row that could be added.

8. Can a department be a subdepartment of itself? Explain.

9. Can an employee be assigned hours on a project that is not in the database? Explain.

10. Can the end date of a project precede the start date of the project?

11. Can the revenue of a project be negative?

chapter **2**

Retrieval: Basic SELECTion

We start our discussion of SQL with the most basic operation: retrieving information. Often, a database of interest already exists, complete with data, and we want to query that data. As we've already noted, the best way to learn SQL is by doing it. You should experiment with the example database as much as possible. Try the statements from the book. Then make up some of your own. Scripts to create and populate the example database are available from the book Web site. Chapter 9 covers creating a database using SQL. If desired, you can skip to that chapter and return here after your database is created.

In SQL the workhorse for data retrieval is the SELECT statement:

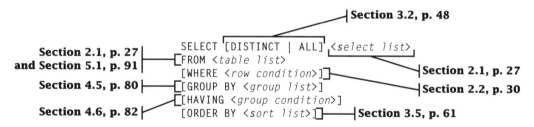

SELECT may look complex, but don't be intimidated. You can do amazing things with the simplest of queries.

2.1 Simple SELECT

At its simplest, you only need to tell SELECT two things: 1) the data attributes you want and 2) the table where it should get it. Let's start with a simple query. Suppose you wanted

27

to find the names of all individual items on your menu. In the Restaurant Database, this information is contained in the *name* column of the *items* table.

Query 2.1 Find the names of all items

```
SELECT name
FROM items;
```

name
Chicken Salad
Fruit Salad
Garden Salad
Millennium Salad
Soda
Water
Fruit Plate

[7 row(s)]

This SQL statement fetches the values from a single column, *name,* from all of the rows in the *items* table and displays the results.

To retrieve multiple columns, specify a comma-delimited list of column names.

Query 2.2 Find the name, item ID, and price of all items

```
SELECT name, itemid, price
FROM items;
```

name	itemid	price
Chicken Salad	CHKSD	2.85
Fruit Salad	FRTSD	3.45
Garden Salad	GDNSD	0.99
Millennium Salad	MILSD	NULL
Soda	SODA	0.99
Water	WATER	0.00
Fruit Plate	FRPLT	3.99

[7 row(s)]

The order in which the attributes are specified in the column name list determines the order of attributes in the result. The presentation of a *NULL* value in a result is DBMS specific.

What if we want all of the columns in a table? Typing them all is both painful and error-prone. Fortunately, SQL provides * as a shorthand for all columns.

Query 2.3 Find all items

```
SELECT *
FROM items;
```

itemid	name	price	dateadded
CHKSD	Chicken Salad	2.85	1998-11-13
FRTSD	Fruit Salad	3.45	2000-05-06
GDNSD	Garden Salad	0.99	2001-03-02
MILSD	Millennium Salad	NULL	2002-08-16
SODA	Soda	0.99	2003-02-06
WATER	Water	0.00	2002-05-19
FRPLT	Fruit Plate	3.99	2000-09-02

[7 row(s)]

SQL has two types of comments. The first type begins with two minus signs ('–') and ends with the end of the line. The second type begins with /*, ends with */, and can span multiple lines.

```
/* This is a
   multiline comment */
SELECT itemid -- This comment goes to the end of the line
FROM items;
```

Before we go on, there are several important things to note about SQL statements:

White space is not significant—For readability we break our statements into separate lines, one for each part of the SQL statement; however, SQL would be just as happy if we put the entire statement on the same line. We can also use multiple spaces, tabs, or other white space characters to separate elements in the query.

SQL statements are not case sensitive—For readability we use uppercase for SQL keywords and use lowercase for our table and column names; however, SQL is mostly case insensitive for keywords and table/column names. Even if we create our table as *vendors,* we can refer to it in SQL as *vEnDOrS.* Whereas SQL statements and table/column names are case insensitive, character data may be sensitive to case, such as when it is stored and compared. We will point out when character comparison is case sensitive.

Semicolons are optional—SQL statements may be terminated by a semicolon. This is useful for separating multiple SQL statements. Most DBMSs do not require a semicolon for the final (or, in the case of a single statement, only) statement. We include semicolons in our examples for completeness.

SELECT generates a new table—Logically, the execution of a SELECT statement generates a new table, called the *result table,* with its own columns and rows. Although your DBMS may not actually create the table, it is helpful to think about queries this way.

2.2 Selecting Rows

Using basic SELECT/FROM, we can retrieve data from any table and even specify columns. That's nice, but what if we want to limit the *rows* in the result? SQL uses the WHERE clause to specify the condition that a particular row must satisfy to be in the query result. SQL provides many different operators for condition construction. Table 2.1 provides an overview of these operators. We discuss each of these operators in detail in the following.

Operator	Evaluates	Usage
=	Equal	*repfname* = 'Bob'
>, <	Greater/less than	*unitprice* > 10
>=, <=	Greater/less than or equal to	*inventory* <= 5000
<>	Not equal	*vendorid* <> 3
[NOT] BETWEEN	Between two values (inclusive)	vendorid BETWEEN 'A' AND 'M'
IS [NOT] NULL	Value is NULL	referredby IS NULL
[NOT] LIKE	Equal strings using wildcards (e.g., '%', '_')	replname LIKE '%ith'
[NOT] IN	Equal to any element in a list	name IN ('Soda', 'Water')
NOT	Negates a condition	NOT itemid IN ('GDNSD', 'CHKSD')

Table 2.1: SQL Operators

2.3 Standard Comparison Operators

For starters, SQL provides the standard comparison operators: = (equal), <> (not equal), > (greater than), < (less than), >= (greater than or equal), and <= (less than or equal). Suppose we want to create a value menu of all items costing $0.99 or less.

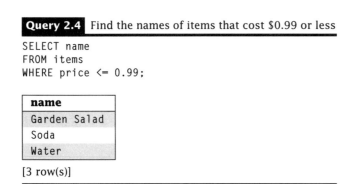

Query 2.4 Find the names of items that cost $0.99 or less

```
SELECT name
FROM items
WHERE price <= 0.99;
```

name
Garden Salad
Soda
Water

[3 row(s)]

How does Query 2.4 work? To construct the result set, SQL begins by fetching the *items* table specified in the FROM clause. Next, SQL goes through each row, evaluating the

WHERE condition. SQL eliminates any rows where price <= 0.99 does not evaluate to true. Finally, SQL eliminates any columns not in the SELECT list. Note that the column list does not necessarily need to contain the attribute(s) used in the WHERE clause.

In Query 2.4, we use a numeric literal, 0.99, for the price comparison. The specific form of a literal depends on the needed data type. We discuss literal format for the various data types in Chapter 1. Let's look at a few examples. Literal strings in SQL must be enclosed in single quotes ('). Let's verify that our Cheese ingredient is in the correct food group.

Query 2.5 Find the ID and food group of ingredients named Cheese

```
SELECT ingredientid, foodgroup
FROM ingredients
WHERE name = 'Cheese';
```

ingredientid	foodgroup
CHESE	Milk

[1 row(s)]

Dates use a literal expressed as 'YYYY-MM-DD'.

Query 2.6 Find the food items added after 1999

```
SELECT *
FROM items
WHERE dateadded > '1999-12-31';
```

itemid	name	price	dateadded
FRTSD	Fruit Salad	3.45	2000-05-06
GDNSD	Garden Salad	0.99	2001-03-02
MILSD	Millennium Salad	NULL	2002-08-16
SODA	Soda	0.99	2003-02-06
WATER	Water	0.00	2002-05-19
FRPLT	Fruit Plate	3.99	2000-09-02

[6 row(s)]

2.4 String Comparisons

How does SQL compare values to determine what is greater than, less than, or equal to? For most data types, it is just what we expect. For character data, comparison is complicated by issues such as collating sequences, case sensitivity, and padding. Unfortunately, the result of string comparison is usually DBMS specific. Most DBMSs allow administrators to configure each of these.

Collating sequence dictates how the system orders characters to allow character comparisons. '3' is obviously less than '4', but what about '5' and 'a'? ASCII (American Standard Code for Information Interchange) is a commonly used collating sequence, where '5' happens to be less than 'a'.

Case sensitivity determines whether character comparisons distinguish between uppercase and lowercase. If comparisons are case sensitive, then the collating sequence determines which case is smaller. Case sensitivity can have a significant impact on query results. To avoid confusion, many SQL users will convert all strings to uppercase or lowercase before comparison.

Padding determines how strings of different lengths are handled when compared. If padding is enabled, then the shorter string is padded with the padding character (usually space) so that both strings are the same length.

To compare two strings, SQL evaluates the strings character by character, starting at the head of each string. If it finds two corresponding characters (e.g., the third character of both strings) that are not equal, the string with the lowest character in the collating sequence is less than the other string. If SQL runs out of corresponding characters before finding two characters that do not match, then the strings are equal if they are the same length; otherwise, the shorter string is less than the longer string. For example, consider Query 2.7.

Query 2.7   Find all items with a name less than or equal to 'garden'

```
SELECT name
FROM items
WHERE name <= 'garden';
```

name
Chicken Salad
Fruit Salad
Fruit Plate

[3 row(s)]

Our result is from a database that is case insensitive. As expected, Garden Salad is not in the results because garden is shorter and the comparison is case insensitive.

Recall that if a literal string contains the quote character ('), we quote it.

Query 2.8   Find the name of the representative for Don's Dairy

```
SELECT repfname, replname
FROM vendors
WHERE companyname = 'Don''s Dairy';
```

repfname	replname
Marla	Milker

[1 row(s)]

2.5 Matching String Patterns with LIKE

What if we cannot remember if a particular customer's name is Bill, Phill, or Will? SQL provides wildcard-based, pattern-matching capabilities with the LIKE operator. SQL wildcard characters include the following:

Wildcard	Description
%	matches any substring containing 0 or more characters
_	matches any single character

Use LIKE as you would the = operator, except the comparison string may contain wildcard characters.

Query 2.9 Find the list of vendor representative first names that begin with 'S'

```
SELECT repfname
FROM vendors
WHERE repfname LIKE 'S%';
```

repfname
Sherman
Sam

[2 row(s)]

Case sensitivity and padding characters are determined by the DBMS configuration. Without any wildcard characters, LIKE works just like =.

Let's try a few examples using LIKE. Suppose you have the following list of character strings: Ball, Beggy, Bill, Billy, ill, Meg, Phill, Philly, Peg, Peggy. Following are some example LIKE expressions along with what they match:

LIKE	Matches strings	Matches
%ill	ending in 'ill'	Bill, ill, Phill
Peg%	starting with 'Peg'	Peg, Peggy
B%y	starting with B and ending with y	Beggy, Billy
_ill	starting with any single character and ending in 'ill'	Bill
B_ll	starting with B and ending with 'll' with any single character in between	Ball, Bill
%__ill_	starting with 2 or more characters and ending with 'ill' followed by any single character	Philly

Other wildcard characters may be supported by your particular DBMS, so check your documentation. In fact, some DBMSs allow regular expressions. The SQL standard includes the operator SIMILAR TO, which works similarly to LIKE except it takes regular expressions. Few DBMSs implement SIMILAR TO.

What about using LIKE to find strings containing wildcard characters? For example, what if we wanted to find all strings containing an underscore character? We could try LIKE '%_%', but this finds all strings containing 1 or more characters because SQL treats '_' as a wildcard character. We need some way to turn a wildcard into a regular character. To do this, SQL allows us to specify an escape character. *Any* character that immediately follows an escape character is interpreted as a regular character, even if it is normally a wildcard or even the escape character. We define '#' as the escape character in Query 2.10.

Query 2.10 Find all vendor names containing an '_'

```
SELECT companyname
FROM vendors
WHERE companyname LIKE '%#_%' ESCAPE '#';
```

companyname
Veggies_R_Us

[1 row(s)]

Because '#' is designated as the escape character, '_' is interpreted literally, not as a wildcard. What if you want to search for the escape character? Escape it (e.g., '##').

2.6 Getting What We Haven't Got with NOT

To fetch the rows that evaluate to false, prefix the condition with NOT.

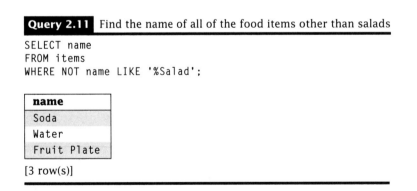

Query 2.11 Find the name of all of the food items other than salads

```
SELECT name
FROM items
WHERE NOT name LIKE '%Salad';
```

name
Soda
Water
Fruit Plate

[3 row(s)]

You can use NOT with any of the comparison operators from Table 2.1.

2.7 **Combining Conditions with AND and OR**

Sometimes the criteria for including or excluding a row is more complicated than a simple condition can express. Fortunately, we can combine two or more conditions using AND and OR. Two conditions joined by AND must both be true for the entire condition to evaluate to true.

| **Query 2.12** | Find all of the ingredients from the Fruit food group with an inventory greater than 100 |

```
SELECT ingredientid, name
FROM ingredients
WHERE foodgroup = 'Fruit' AND inventory > 100;
```

ingredientid	name
GRAPE	Grape

[1 row(s)]

For two conditions joined by OR, the entire condition is true if either or both are true.

| **Query 2.13** | Find the name of all ingredients with unit price over $0.40 or with a unit of glass |

```
SELECT name, unitprice, unit
FROM ingredients
WHERE unitprice > 0.40 OR unit = 'glass';
```

name	unitprice	unit
Chicken	0.45	strip
Water	0.06	glass
Soda	0.69	glass

[3 row(s)]

Note that Soda is true for both conditions, whereas the Chicken and Water are only true for one.

You can combine as many ANDs and ORs together as needed, but beware. SQL may not interpret the WHERE clause as you intended. Why? SQL doesn't strictly evaluate an expression from left to right. Some operators have a higher precedence than others. Operators with a higher precedence get evaluated before operators with a lower precedence, no matter where they are in the condition.

In SQL, the precedence order from highest to lowest is as follows:

Precedence	Operator
Highest	Comparison Operators
	NOT
	AND
Lowest	OR

The evaluation of a condition begins with the individual comparisons. Next, conditions prefixed with a NOT are negated. The ANDs are then applied from left to right. Finally, the ORs are applied from left to right. Consider the incorrect solution in Query 2.14.

Query 2.14	**INCORRECT!** Find the food items that have a name beginning with either F or S that cost less than $3.50

```
SELECT name, price
FROM items
WHERE name LIKE 'F%' OR name LIKE 'S%' AND price < 3.50;
```

name	price
Fruit Salad	3.45
Soda	0.99
Fruit Plate	3.99

[3 row(s)]

How did the Fruit Plate get into our result? Because AND has a higher precedence, `name LIKE 'S%' AND price > 3.50` is evaluated first. For the Fruit Plate, this returns false; however, `name LIKE 'F%'` returns true, making the condition true for the row. This query really finds the food items with a name beginning with F plus the food items with a price less than $3.50 that begin with S.

How do we write the correct query? Use parentheses.

Query 2.15	**CORRECT!** Find the food items that have a name beginning with either F or S that cost less than $3.50

```
SELECT name, price
FROM items
WHERE (name LIKE 'F%' OR name LIKE 'S%') AND price < 3.50;
```

name	price
Fruit Salad	3.45
Soda	0.99

[2 row(s)]

In Query 2.15, the condition inside the parenthesis has the highest priority so it is executed first, just as we wanted. Inside parentheses, normal precedence rules apply. It is always best to use parentheses with a WHERE clause containing more than two conditions to ensure the interpretation of the query is correct.

We can nest parentheses to get any execution order desired. The condition inside the innermost parenthesis always has the highest priority. Once a parenthetical expression has been evaluated, the normal rules of precedence apply. That means ((name LIKE 'F%' OR name LIKE 'S%') AND price < 3.50) would execute just like Query 2.15.

2.8 Selecting a Range of Values with BETWEEN

The BETWEEN operator allows us to specify a range of values (inclusive) for matching as in Query 2.16.

Query 2.16 Find the food items costing between $2.50 and $3.50

```
SELECT *
FROM items
WHERE price BETWEEN 2.50 AND 3.50;
```

itemid	name	price	dateadded
CHKSD	Chicken Salad	2.85	1998-11-13
FRTSD	Fruit Salad	3.45	2000-05-06

[2 row(s)]

To get the values that are not within a specified range, use NOT BETWEEN.

Query 2.17 Find the food items costing less than $2.50 or more than $3.50

```
SELECT *
FROM items
WHERE price NOT BETWEEN 2.50 AND 3.50;
```

itemid	name	price	dateadded
GDNSD	Garden Salad	0.99	2001-03-02
SODA	Soda	0.99	2003-02-06
WATER	Water	0.00	2002-05-19
FRPLT	Fruit Plate	3.99	2000-09-02

[4 row(s)]

The result includes any food items costing less than $2.50 or greater than $3.50. Note that WHERE x BETWEEN y AND z is equivalent to WHERE x >= y AND x <= z so it is really just another way to answer the same query. Usually, there are many ways to answer the same query in SQL. In most cases, the choice of syntax should not change the performance of the query; however, in a few cases, one variant can be much more efficient than another. This will depend on your database and your DBMS.

2.9 Selecting a Set of Values Using IN

The IN operator determines if a value is contained in a list of values.

Query 2.18 Find the vendor representatives with last names of Corn or Sherbert

```
SELECT vendorid, repfname, replname
FROM vendors
WHERE replname IN ('Corn', 'Sherbert');
```

vendorid	repfname	replname
VGRUS	Candy	Corn
FLVCR	Sherman	Sherbert

[2 row(s)]

The list of values must be comma-delimited and enclosed within parentheses. To evaluate `WHERE x IN (y1, ..., yn)`, SQL evaluates x = yi for each yi in the list. If at least one x = yi evaluates to true, the condition evaluates to true.

As you probably already suspect, you can use NOT IN to find all of the values not contained in a list.

Query 2.19 Find the ingredient ID, name, and unit of items not sold in pieces or strips

```
SELECT ingredientid, name, unit
FROM ingredients
WHERE unit NOT IN ('piece', 'strip');
```

ingredientid	name	unit
CHESE	Cheese	scoop
LETUS	Lettuce	bowl
PICKL	Pickle	slice
SCTDR	Secret Dressing	ounce
TOMTO	Tomato	slice
WATER	Water	glass
SODA	Soda	glass
ORNG	Orange	slice

[8 row(s)]

2.10 IS NULL: Exploring the Unknown

How do we find all of the vendors who were not referred by any other vendor? We need all of the rows from *vendors* with a *referredby* value of *NULL,* but beware—*NULL* is a strange animal. SQL interprets *NULL* as unknown. If we compare something that is unknown to *any* value, even unknown, the result is unknown. This makes sense if you think about it. Consider a new vendor representative with first name Bob and an unknown last name. If somebody asked you if Bob's last name was Smith, how could you most accurately answer? That's right—"I don't know." The database equivalent is unknown. Our system of evaluation now has three values: true, false, and unknown. It is not surprising that the system for evaluating conditions with three possible results is called *three-valued logic*.

How does SQL handle unknown? SQL only reports the rows for which the WHERE condition evaluates to true. Rows evaluating to false or unknown are not included in the answer. Compare Queries 2.20 and 2.21.

Query 2.20 **INCORRECT!** Find all vendors not referred by anyone

```
SELECT *
FROM vendors
WHERE referredby = NULL;
```

vendorid	companyname	repfname	replname	referredby

[0 row(s)]

This query returns no rows because each evaluation of *referredby = NULL* returns unknown, even for the rows where *referredby* is *NULL*. So how do we test for *NULL?* We use IS NULL.

Query 2.21 **CORRECT!** Find all vendors not referred by anyone

```
SELECT *
FROM vendors
WHERE referredby IS NULL;
```

vendorid	companyname	repfname	replname	referredby
VGRUS	Veggies_R_Us	Candy	Corn	NULL

[1 row(s)]

As you might expect, we can find the rows with non-*NULL* values using the IS NOT NULL.

The implications of *NULL* comparison can be subtle. The rule to remember is that comparing *NULL* to an attribute (e.g., *referredby*), a literal (e.g., 'A', 3, etc.), or even to NULL itself always returns unknown. This means that NULL = NULL evaluates to unknown. Of course, NULL IS NULL always evaluates to true. Consider the Queries 2.22 and 2.23.

Query 2.22 Find all items with price greater than $0.99

```
SELECT *
FROM items
WHERE price > 0.99;
```

itemid	name	price	dateadded
CHKSD	Chicken Salad	2.85	1998-11-13
FRTSD	Fruit Salad	3.45	2000-05-06
FRPLT	Fruit Plate	3.99	2000-09-02

[3 row(s)]

Query 2.23 Find all items with price less than or equal to $0.99

```
SELECT *
FROM items
WHERE price <= 0.99;
```

itemid	name	price	dateadded
GDNSD	Garden Salad	0.99	2001-03-02
SODA	Soda	0.99	2003-02-06
WATER	Water	0.00	2002-05-19

[3 row(s)]

Where's the Millennium Salad? Its price is *NULL,* so comparing it to $0.99 always returns unknown, which SQL excludes from both results. In effect, the *NULL* price for Millennium Salad is not less than, greater than, or equal to $0.99. To list this salad's row (and any other rows with a price of *NULL*), we need Query 2.24.

Query 2.24 Find all items with no price

```
SELECT *
FROM items
WHERE price IS NULL;
```

itemid	name	price	dateadded
MILSD	Millennium Salad	NULL	2002-08-16

[1 row(s)]

The incomparability of *NULL* has other implications. For example, neither LIKE '%' nor NOT LIKE '%' match *NULL*. *NULL* is neither BETWEEN nor NOT BETWEEN any two values, including *NULL* itself.

2.11 ANDs, ORs, NOTs with NULLs: Three-Valued Logic

What happens when we AND, OR, or NOT a value of unknown? SQL evaluates conditions using three-valued logic. Table 2.2 shows the logic tables for AND, OR, and NOT.

AND	true	false	unknown
true	true	false	unknown
false	false	false	false
unknown	unknown	false	unknown

OR	true	false	unknown
true	true	true	true
false	true	false	unknown
unknown	true	unknown	unknown

NOT	
true	false
false	true
unknown	unknown

Table 2.2: Three-valued logic tables.

Let's try our three-valued logic tables on an example.

Query 2.25	Find the ingredient ID, food group, and inventory for fruits or ingredients with inventory not less than or equal to 200

```
SELECT ingredientid, foodgroup, inventory
FROM ingredients
WHERE foodgroup = 'Fruit' OR NOT inventory <= 200;
```

ingredientid	foodgroup	inventory
CRUTN	Bread	400
GRAPE	Fruit	300
PICKL	Vegetable	800
TOMTO	Fruit	15
SODA	NULL	5000
WTRML	Fruit	NULL
ORNG	Fruit	10

[7 row(s)]

The results for rows with non-*NULL* values for both *foodgroup* and *inventory* are not surprising. Let's consider two other rows in the *ingredients* table: the ones identified by WTRML and SCTDR.

First, let's evaluate the condition for the WTRML row from *ingredients:*

$$\left.\begin{array}{lll} foodgroup = \text{'Fruit'} & = & = true \\ NOT\ inventory <= 200 & = NOT\ unknown & = unknown \end{array}\right\} OR = true$$

The first condition, `foodgroup = 'Fruit'`, evaluates to true. `inventory <= 200` evaluates to unknown, and the NOT of unknown is itself unknown. For this row, SQL evaluates true OR unknown, which is true so the WTRML row is included.

Now consider the SCTDR row.

$$\left.\begin{array}{lll} foodgroup = \text{'Fruit'} & = & = unknown \\ NOT\ inventory <= 200 & = NOT\ true & = false \end{array}\right\} OR = unknown$$

`foodgroup = 'Fruit'` evaluates to unknown, and `NOT inventory <= 200` evaluates to false. Because false OR unknown is unknown, the SCTDR row is not included in the results of Query 2.25.

2.12   Three-Valued Logic and the IN Operator

Let's consider the implications of three-valued logic for the IN operator. As we've already stated, to evaluate x IN (y1, ..., yn), SQL evaluates x = yi for each yi in the list. If at least one x = yi evaluates to true, the condition evaluates to true. If all x = yi evaluate to false or the IN list is empty, the condition evaluates to false. If neither of these cases holds, then the condition returns unknown.

The condition x NOT IN (y1, ..., yn) is equivalent to NOT x IN (y1, ..., yn), leading to the nonintuitive result of Query 2.26.

| Query 2.26 | **INCORRECT!** Find all of the vendors whose vendor ID is neither BADID or *NULL* |

```
SELECT *
FROM vendors
WHERE vendorid NOT IN ('BADID', NULL);
```

vendorid	companyname	repfname	replname	referredby

[0 row(s)]

Why is the result empty? Comparing each *vendorid* with BADID returns false and with *NULL* returns unknown; consequently, IN returns unknown for each row. Applying NOT still returns unknown. Because the condition evaluates to unknown for all rows, the result is empty. Clearly, the solution is to avoid *NULL* with the IN operator, but as we will see in later chapters, IN can be used in situations where we do not have that much control.

2.13 How WHERE Determines What's In and Out

What determines which rows are in or out? SQL evaluates the WHERE condition for each row, and a row is only included if the condition evaluates to true for that particular row. Consider Query 2.27.

Query 2.27 Find all items

```
SELECT *
FROM items
WHERE 1 = 1;
```

itemid	name	price	dateadded
CHKSD	Chicken Salad	2.85	1998-11-13
FRTSD	Fruit Salad	3.45	2000-05-06
GDNSD	Garden Salad	0.99	2001-03-02
MILSD	Millennium Salad	NULL	2002-08-16
SODA	Soda	0.99	2003-02-06
WATER	Water	0.00	2002-05-19
FRPLT	Fruit Plate	3.99	2000-09-02

[7 row(s)]

For each row, 1 = 1 is true, so this query returns all rows in the *items* table. If we change the WHERE condition to 1 = 2, our query result will contain no rows because 1 = 2 is always false. Although this particular example is trivial, it is important to understand how SQL thinks when we consider more complex queries later.

As this example shows, it is perfectly legal in SQL for the condition in the WHERE clause to have nothing to do with the values in the row. SQL does require that any column referenced in the SELECT and WHERE clauses must be an attribute in a table in the FROM clause; otherwise, SQL returns an error.

2.14 Wrap Up

In this chapter, we've learned how to extract data from a single table. We specify the attributes we want in the SELECT list. The rows in the result are determined by the WHERE condition. SQL evaluates the WHERE condition for each row, including only those rows in the result where the condition evaluates to true. SQL provides a powerful set of comparison operators for use in the WHERE clause to determine which rows are in and out. We can join individual conditionals together using AND and OR, and we can negate using NOT. Some attributes may have a value of *NULL,* which SQL interprets as unknown. To allow for unknown values, SQL evaluates a conditional using three-valued logic.

Review Questions

1. The result of a SELECT statement is a new _____.
2. SQL uses _____-valued logic. The possible values of the system are _____, _____, and _____.
3. Does 5 BETWEEN 3 AND 5 return true or false? _____
4. NOT unknown AND NOT false OR unknown evaluates to _____.
5. Circle the strings that LIKE '__s%l' matches: [baseball, football, soccer, basketball, cricket]
6. *NULL* > *NULL* evaluates to _____.
7. *NULL* > *NULL* AND true OR false evaluates to _____.
8. *NULL* > *NULL* OR true AND false evaluates to _____.
9. What string matching pattern matches all strings beginning with 'B' and ending with 'll' with exactly one character in between (e.g., 'Bill', 'Ball') _____? Same question with one *or more* characters in between _____.
10. Are string comparisons case sensitive for your database?
11. The easiest way to select all columns in a table is to use _____.
12. Does an attribute in the SELECT clause have to appear in the WHERE clause?
13. Does an attribute in the WHERE clause have to appear in the SELECT clause?
14. Which operators are equivalent to NOT >, NOT <=, and NOT <>?
15. In the Restaurant Database, how many rows does the following query return?

    ```
    SELECT *
    FROM vendors;
    ```

16. Will this query execute?

    ```
    SELECTnameFROMingredients;
    ```

17. Will this query execute?

    ```
    SELECT
    name
    FROM
    ingredients
    ;
    ```

Practice

For these exercises, use the Employees Database presented at the end of Chapter 1. For each question, give the single SQL statement to answer it. Your query must work for any set of data in the Employees Database, not just the set of data we provide.

1. List the first and last names of all employees.

2. List all attributes of the projects with revenue greater than $40,000.

3. List the department codes of the projects with revenue between $100,000 and $150,000.

4. List the project IDs for the projects that started on or before July 1, 2004.

5. List the names of the departments that are top level (i.e., not a subdepartment).

6. List the ID and descriptions of the projects under the departments with code ACCNT, CNSLT, or HDWRE.

7. List all of the information about employees with last names that have exactly 8 characters and end in 'ware'.

8. List the ID and last name of all employees who work for department ACTNG and make less than $30,000.

9. List the "magical" projects that have not started (indicated by a start date in the future or *NULL)* but are generating revenue.

10. List the IDs of the project either from the ACTNG department or that are ongoing (i.e., *NULL* end date). Exclude any projects that have a revenue of $50,000 or less.

11. Consider the table *T* with columns *C1* VARCHAR(10), *C2* INTEGER and *C3* INTEGER and the query

```
SELECT *
FROM T
WHERE C1 LIKE '%ar_' OR NOT C2 BETWEEN 3 AND 7 AND C3 < 5;
```

Fill in the missing results for the example rows.

C1	C2	C3	Row Value	In result?
No	4	9	false	No
Share	*NULL*	5		
Car	2	*NULL*		
Sarah	8	1		
NULL			true	Yes

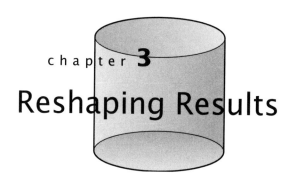

chapter **3**

Reshaping Results

Remember that we can think of the execution of a SELECT statement as generating a completely new table, called the result table, which usually only exists long enough to output the query results. The result table's columns are determined by the column list of the SELECT statement, and the WHERE expression determines the result table rows. Often, simply selecting a subset of the rows and columns is not sufficient to answer our question. We may need to perform some operations on the raw data to generate the desired results. We might also want to control the form of the result table itself. In this chapter, we explore the various SQL capabilities for manipulating result tables.

3.1 AS: Naming Result Table Columns

If a SELECT statement generates a new table, what are the names of the columns of that table? By default, result table columns have the same name as attributes in the original table; however, you can change the result table column name using a column alias. We assign a column alias in the column list of the SELECT statement using AS.

Query 3.1 Alias example

```
SELECT companyname AS company, repfname AS "First Name"
FROM vendors;
```

company	First Name
Veggies_R_Us	Candy
Don's Dairy	Marla
Flavorful Creams	Sherman
"Fruit Eating" Friends	Gilbert
Ed's Dressings	Sam
Spring Water Supply	Gus

[6 row(s)]

The AS keyword is optional. To specify a column alias with a space or other special character, enclose the alias name in quotes; otherwise the quotes are optional. Consult your DBMS documentation on specific restrictions.

3.2 DISTINCT and ALL: Dealing with Duplicates

Duplicate rows are okay in SQL; however, you may not be so happy with all of that repeatedly repeating repetition. Let's generate a list of food groups.

Query 3.2 Find the food groups served by your restaurant

```
SELECT foodgroup
FROM ingredients;
```

foodgroup
Milk
Meat
Bread
Fruit
Vegetable
Vegetable
NULL
Fruit
NULL
NULL
Fruit
Fruit

[12 row(s)]

We can eliminate duplicate rows by prefixing the SELECT column list with the DISTINCT keyword, as in Query 3.3.

Query 3.3 Find the food groups served by your restaurant without duplication

```
SELECT DISTINCT foodgroup
FROM ingredients;
```

foodgroup
Bread
Fruit
Meat
Milk
Vegetable
NULL

[6 row(s)]

Note that *NULL* is treated as a distinct value, and duplicate *NULL*s are eliminated.

DISTINCT may only appear once in the SELECT statement at the head of the attribute list, and it applies to *all* attributes in the attribute list.

Query 3.4 Find the distinct list of food groups provided by each vendor

```
SELECT DISTINCT foodgroup, vendorid
FROM ingredients;
```

foodgroup	vendorid
Bread	EDDRS
Fruit	FRTFR
Fruit	VGRUS
Meat	DNDRY
Milk	DNDRY
Vegetable	VGRUS
NULL	SPWTR
NULL	NULL

[8 row(s)]

In this example, SQL uses the values for *both* attributes to determine if each row value is unique. The Fruit food group shows up twice because two different vendors provide ingredients from that food group. Again, note that *NULL* is treated as a distinct value. You can use ALL instead of DISTINCT to indicate that you do not want to eliminate duplicates. Because keeping duplicates is the default, ALL is unnecessary.

3.3 Derived Attributes

Data can be somewhat raw. SQL provides the ability to create attributes in our result table that are derived using operations and functions over existing attributes and literals. The default column name of a derived attribute is system dependent; however, a name can be assigned using a column alias.

3.3.1 Numeric

SQL can evaluate simple arithmetic expressions containing numeric columns and literals. Table 3.1 shows the SQL arithmetic operators in precedence order from highest to lowest. Unary +/- have the highest precedence. Multiplication and division have the next highest precedence. Addition and subtraction have the lowest precedence. Operators with the same precedence are executed left to right. We can control the order of evaluation using parentheses. SQL evaluates an expression for each row in the table specified in the FROM clause that satisfies the condition in the WHERE clause. Let's look at an example.

Query 3.5 Find the value of your pickle inventory if you double your stock of pickles

```
SELECT ingredientid, inventory * 2 * unitprice AS "Inventory Value"
FROM ingredients
WHERE name = 'Pickle';
```

ingredientid	Inventory Value
PICKL	64.00

[1 row(s)]

Operator	Returns	Example	Precedence
+*numexp* −*numexp*	*numexp* with sign unchanged *numexp* with negated sign	+inventory −3	Highest
lnumexp * *rnumexp* *lnumexp* / *rnumexp*	Product of *lnumexp* and *rnumexp* Division of *lnumexp* by *rnumexp*	inventory * unitprice quantity / 3	Middle
lnumexp + *rnumexp* *lnumexp* − *rnumexp*	Sum of *lnumexp* and *rnumexp* Difference of *lnumexp* and *rnumexp*	inventory + 10 discount − 0.1	Lowest

Table 3.1: SQL Arithmetic Operators

How does this work? For each row in the *ingredients* table that satisfies the WHERE condition, SQL computes the value of the expression(s) in the attribute list. Let's try another example.

Query 3.6 Arithmetic literal example

```
SELECT 5 - 4 + 8 / 4 * 2 AS "Example Equation"
FROM vendors
WHERE referredby IS NOT NULL;
```

Example Equation
5
5
5
5
5

[5 row(s)]

Why does the same value show up so many times in Query 3.6? There are 5 rows in the *vendors* table that satisfy the predicate referredby IS NOT NULL. SQL evaluates the expression for *each* of these rows and reports the results. Note that the expression itself is evaluated according to operator precedence, not simply from left to right.

SQL also includes many standard mathematic functions. Table 3.2 contains some of the more common functions. The exact set of available functions is DBMS dependent. In fact, your DBMS will likely have additional functions.

Function	Returns	Example
ABS(N)	Absolute value of N	ABS(inventory − 100)
CEIL[ING](N)	Ceiling of N	CEILING(inventory/10)
EXP(N)	e^N	EXP(5)
FLOOR(N)	Floor of N	FLOOR(inventory/10)
LN(N)	Natural log of N	LN(5)
MOD(N, D)	Remainder of N divided by D	MOD(11, 3)
POWER(B, E)	B to the power of E (B^E)	POWER(2, 3)
SQRT(N)	$\sqrt{N}$	SQRT(4)

Table 3.2: SQL Arithmetic Functions

What about the infamous *NULL?* An arithmetic expression evaluated with *NULL* for any value returns *NULL.* Arithmetic functions given a *NULL* parameter value return *NULL,* as in Query 3.7.

Query 3.7 Find the inventory value of each ingredient in both dollars and euros

```
SELECT name, inventory * unitprice AS Dollars,
    CEIL(inventory * unitprice * 1.2552) AS euros, 1.2552 AS "Exchange Rate"
FROM ingredients;
```

name	dollars	euros	Exchange Rate
Cheese	4.50	6	1.2552
Chicken	54.00	68	1.2552
Crouton	4.00	6	1.2552
Grape	3.00	4	1.2552
Lettuce	2.00	3	1.2552
Pickle	32.00	41	1.2552
Secret Dressing	3.60	5	1.2552
Tomato	0.45	1	1.2552
Water	NULL	NULL	1.2552
Soda	3450.00	4331	1.2552
Watermelon	NULL	NULL	1.2552
Orange	0.50	1	1.2552

[12 row(s)]

We compute our inventory value in both U.S. dollars and euros. To hedge our bets against fluctuations in the exchange rate, we take the ceiling of the European currency value. As you can see in the example query results, if either *inventory* or *unitprice* is *NULL*, their product is *NULL*. In the case of a *NULL* product of *inventory* and *unitprice*, the ceiling function also returns *NULL*. We name our computed columns using column aliases.

3.3.2 Character String

The typical database is full of character strings, such as names, addresses, and ingredients. The string you really want may be a combination of data strings, substrings, string literals, and so on. Perhaps you want to generate address labels or salutations (e.g., "Dear *first name last name*,"). SQL provides a wide range of mechanisms for combining and manipulating character strings.

Concatenating Strings With ||

We begin with the || (concatenation) operator to construct a new string from a combination of string expressions.

Query 3.8 Create a mailing label for each store

```
SELECT manager, address || ' ' || city || ' ' || state || ' ' || zip
    || ' USA' as mail
FROM stores;
```

manager	mail
Greg Speegle	2222 2nd Ave. Waco TX 76798-7356 USA
Greg Donahoo	4444 4th Blvd San Francsico CA 94101-4150 USA
Jeff Donahoo	1111 Main St. Waco TX 76798 USA
Jeff Speegle	3333 3rd St. Fargo ND 58106 USA
Man Ager	NULL

[5 row(s)]

There are several things worth noting from Query 3.8:

1. You may use string literals in the SELECT list either by themselves or in concatenations.

2. The concatenation operator can take both literals and columns. In fact, it takes any expression that returns (or can be coerced to) a string.

3. Concatenation with *NULL* is always *NULL*.

4. String concatenation does not add a space. Any spacing must be explicitly added.

5. Because strings of type CHAR are padded with trailing blanks, concatenation with such strings includes these extra blanks. See the spaces between the zip code and USA in some of the rows.

6. VARCHARs are not padded with trailing spaces; they only include the explicitly specified characters.

SUBSTRING: Getting the String Within the String

```
SUBSTRING(<source> FROM <start> [FOR <length>])
```

SUBSTRING returns the substring from *<source>* string, starting from the character at position *<start>* (numbering from 1) and containing up to *<length>* characters. The *<source>* may be any string expression. *<start>* and *<length>* may be any integer expression. If *<length>* is not specified, SUBSTRING returns all characters from *<start>* to the end of *<source>*. If the *<source>* string is empty or if the *<start>* position is beyond the end of the *<source>* string, SUBSTRING returns an empty string (length of 0). If any of the parameters are *NULL*, SUBSTRING returns *NULL*.

Query 3.9 SUBSTRING example

```
SELECT SUBSTRING(repfname FROM 1 FOR 1) || '. ' || replname AS name
FROM vendors;
```

name
C. Corn
M. Milker
S. Sherbert
G. Grape
S. Sauce
G. Hing

[6 row(s)]

TRIM: Removing Unwanted Leading and Trailing Characters

```
TRIM([[LEADING | TRAILING | BOTH] [<trim characters>] FROM] <source>)
```

TRIM returns the *<source>* after removing the longest substring of leading and/or trailing sequences of *<trim characters>*. The *<source>* and *<trim characters>* can be any string expression. If LEADING, TRAILING, or BOTH is not specified, the default is BOTH. If *<trim characters>* is not specified, the default is a single space. If any of the parameters are *NULL,* TRIM returns *NULL.*

Query 3.10 TRIM example

```
SELECT DISTINCT ingredientid, foodgroup || '.' AS "with trailing",
TRIM(TRAILING ' ' FROM foodgroup) || '.' AS "without trailing"
FROM ingredients
WHERE inventory > 500;
```

ingredientid	with trailing	without trailing
PICKL	Vegetable	Vegetable
SODA	NULL	NULL

[2 row(s)]

UPPER and LOWER: Controlling Character Case

```
LOWER(<source>)
UPPER(<source>)
```

LOWER returns the *<source>* string with all alphabetic characters changed to lowercase. UPPER returns the *<source>* string with all alphabetic characters changed to uppercase. The *<source>* can be any string expression. LOWER and UPPER do not change nonalphabetic characters. If *<source>* is *NULL,* UPPER and LOWER return *NULL.*

| Query 3.11 | UPPER and LOWER example |

```
SELECT UPPER(repfname || ' ' || replname) AS rep, LOWER(companyname) AS company
FROM vendors WHERE referredby = 'VGRUS';
```

rep	company
MARLA MILKER	Don's Dairy
SHERMAN SHERBERT	Flavorful Creams

[2 row(s)]

POSITION: Finding Where a Substring Begins

```
POSITION(<substring> IN <source>)
```

POSITION returns a number representing the character position (numbering from 1) of the first character of the first occurrence of *<substring>* in *<source>*. The *<source>* and the *<substring>* can be any string expression. If *<substring>* does not appear in *<source>*, POSITION returns 0. If *<substring>* or *<source>* are *NULL*, POSITION returns *NULL*.

| Query 3.12 | POSITION example |

```
SELECT name, POSITION('Salad' IN name)
FROM items;
```

name	position
Chicken Salad	9
Fruit Salad	7
Garden Salad	8
Millennium Salad	12
Soda	0
Water	0
Fruit Plate	0

[7 row(s)]

CHAR[ACTER]_LENGTH: Counting Characters in a String

```
CHARACTER_LENGTH(<source>)
```

CHARACTER_LENGTH returns the number of characters in *<source>*. *<source>* can be any string expression. If *<source>* is *NULL*, CHARACTER_LENGTH returns *NULL*. CHARACTER_LENGTH may be abbreviated as CHAR_LENGTH.

Query 3.13   CHARACTER_LENGTH example

```
SELECT name, CHAR_LENGTH(name) AS namelen, CHAR_LENGTH(foodgroup) AS fglen
FROM ingredients;
```

name	namelen	fglen
Cheese	6	15
Chicken	7	15
Crouton	7	15
Grape	5	15
Lettuce	7	15
Pickle	6	15
Secret Dressing	15	NULL
Tomato	6	15
Water	5	NULL
Soda	4	NULL
Watermelon	10	15
Orange	6	15

[12 row(s)]

Combining String Functions

The parameters to the various string functions can be any expression returning the correct data type. Such expressions can even include other string functions. Query 3.14 is a complex example to show how to combine string functions. This query returns the first word in uppercase of a multiword company name with any trailing 's (apostrophe s) removed. The results are in all uppercase.

Query 3.14   Combining string functions

```
SELECT vendorid, companyname,
    TRIM(TRAILING '''S' FROM
        TRIM(SUBSTRING(UPPER(companyname) FROM 1 FOR
            POSITION(' ' IN companyname)))) AS "CoName"
FROM vendors;
```

vendorid	companyname	CoName
VGRUS	Veggies_R_Us	
DNDRY	Don's Dairy	DON
FLVCR	Flavorful Creams	FLAVORFUL
FRTFR	"Fruit Eating" Friends	"FRUIT
EDDRS	Ed's Dressings	ED
SPWTR	Spring Water Supply	SPRING

[6 row(s)]

Let's take this step-by-step:

- POSITION(' ' IN companyname) finds the character position of the first occurrence of a space. Let's call this value P. For Ed's Dressing, P is 5.

- UPPER(companyname) returns the company name with all alphabetic characters converted to uppercase. Let's call this string C. For Ed's Dressing, C is ED'S DRESSING.

- SUBSTRING then finds the substring in C starting at character position 1 and ending at position P, inclusive. Let's call this substring S. For Ed's Dressing, S is "ED'S ". Note the trailing space.

- The inner TRIM then eliminates any leading and trailing spaces. If the company name has a space, then S has a space because S includes the character in position C, which must be a space. If the company name does not have a space, then P is 0 and S is the empty string. Let's call this substring T. For Ed's Dressing, T is ED'S. Note that the trailing space has been removed.

- Finally, the outer TRIM eliminates any trailing occurrences of the string 'S. Note that we had to quote the single quote ('). For Ed's Dressing, this final value is ED.

What happened to Veggies_R_Us? Recall that POSITION returns 0 if it cannot find the substring. Given a *<length>* of 0, SUBSTRING returns an empty string.

Your DBMS will likely have other string manipulation functions. The SQL standard describes a few other string manipulation functions, which are not widely implemented. Such functions include OVERLAY (substituting substrings), CONVERT (changing character encoding), and TRANSLATE (mapping between character sets).

3.3.3 Temporal

Time is no simple concept. To deal with this complexity, SQL provides a wide range of techniques for operating on temporal data types. Unfortunately, temporal types and arithmetic are not supported by all DBMSs. Consult your documentation for the exact limitations and syntax of your system.

Finding the Current Date or Time

Let's start with the basic question: "What time is it?" SQL provides several functions to help you find out.

Temporal Function	Description	Return Type
CURRENT_TIME[(precision)]	Current time with time zone displacement	TIME WITH TIMEZONE
CURRENT_DATE	Current date	DATE
CURRENT_TIMESTAMP[(precision)]	Current date and time with timezone displacement	TIMESTAMP WITH TIMEZONE
LOCALTIME[(precision)]	Current time	TIME WITHOUT TIMEZONE
LOCALTIMESTAMP[(precision)]	Current date	TIMESTAMP WITHOUT TIMEZONE

The optional precision argument specifies the fractional seconds precision. `LOCALTIME` and `LOCALTIMESTAMP` are not widely implemented.

Using Arithmetic Operators with Temporal Types

SQL allows the use of basic arithmetic operators with temporal data types. For example, you may want to know the date 3 days from now. To get that, you can add the current date to an interval of 3 days. Of course, not all arithmetic operations make sense with temporal data. For example, dividing a date by an interval makes no sense so it is not allowed by SQL. Here are the allowable operations and the resulting data types:

Expression	Result Type	Precedence
Interval * / Numeric	Interval	Highest
Numeric * Interval	Interval	
Datetime + – Interval	Datetime	
Interval + Datetime	Datetime	
Datetime – Datetime	Interval	Lowest
Interval + – Interval	Interval	

The table doesn't cover all restrictions. The operation must make sense. Subtracting a DATE value from a TIME value has no meaning so it is not allowed by SQL. Let's look at an example.

Query 3.15 Find how long each item has been on the menu as of midnight January 2, 2005

```
SELECT name, dateadded, DATE '2005-01-02' - dateadded AS "Days on Menu"
FROM items;
```

name	dateadded	Days on Menu
Chicken Salad	1998-11-13	2242
Fruit Salad	2000-05-06	1702
Garden Salad	2001-03-02	1402
Millennium Salad	2002-08-16	870
Soda	2003-02-06	696
Water	2002-05-19	959
Fruit Plate	2000-09-02	1583

[7 row(s)]

According to the 2003 SQL specification, subtracting two dates should result in an interval. Naturally, this must be a DAY–TIME interval, or precision would be lost. Because there is no time data, our DBMS chose to represent the results as a number of days. Your DBMS may be different.

EXTRACT: Getting Fields from Temporal Data

Datetime and interval data are made up of fields such as year, month, and so on. EXTRACT gets a specified field from temporal data.

```
EXTRACT(<field label> FROM <source>)
```

EXTRACT returns a numeric value representing the field specified by *<field label>* from *<source>*. The *<source>* is any expression returning a datetime or interval, and *<field label>* must be YEAR, MONTH, DAY, HOUR, MINUTE, SECOND, TIMEZONE_HOUR, or TIMEZONE_MINUTE. If *<source>* or *<field label>* is *NULL,* EXTRACT returns *NULL.*

Query 3.16 EXTRACT example

```
SELECT name, EXTRACT(YEAR FROM dateadded) AS year,
    EXTRACT(MONTH FROM dateadded + INTERVAL '30' DAY) AS
month
FROM items;
```

name	year	month
Chicken Salad	1998	12
Fruit Salad	2000	6
Garden Salad	2001	4
Millennium Salad	2002	9
Soda	2003	3
Water	2002	6
Fruit Plate	2000	10

[7 row(s)]

Your DBMS will likely specify other temporal functions. Other SQL standard temporal functions include OVERLAPS (test if two time periods intersect) and ABS (returns the absolute value of an interval); however, these functions are not widely implemented.

3.3.4 Binary

The binary data types are called *binary strings* because SQL treats them like a strings of 0s and 1s. Most (but not all) things that you can do with a character string, you can do with a binary string using the same operators and functions, including concatenation, trimming (using the hexadecimal value X'00' as the default trim character), using substrings, and using LIKE. Query 3.17 is a simple binary string example.

Query 3.17 Binary string example

```
SELECT SUBSTRING(X'F0' FROM 3) || B'11' AS bits
FROM stores
WHERE storeid LIKE '#%';
```

bits
11000011

[1 row(s)]

One of the differences between character strings and binary strings is that binary strings can only be compared using = and <>; comparisons with > and < are not allowed. Binary strings also cannot follow DISTINCT or appear in the ORDER BY clause (see Section 3.5) or in many other parts of SQL that we discuss later. If you need to use binary strings, consult your DBMS documentation.

3.4   Computation in the WHERE Clause

The usefulness of SQL's powerful repertoire of operators and functions doesn't stop at derived column values. You can use these capabilities within predicates in the WHERE clause.

Query 3.18   Find the name and inventory value of the ingredients with an inventory value of $10 or more

```
SELECT name, inventory * unitprice AS "invalue"
FROM ingredients
WHERE inventory * unitprice > 10;
```

name	invalue
Chicken	54.00
Pickle	32.00
Soda	3450.00

[3 row(s)]

How does SQL handle this statement? It first gets the specified table, *ingredients.* Next it evaluates the predicate for each row. Finally, it evaluates the expressions in the SELECT list. One subtle consequence of this order of execution is that you cannot use column aliases in the WHERE clause. Why? The WHERE clause is evaluated *before* the SELECT list so the column aliases don't exist when the WHERE executes. Replacing the WHERE class in Query 3.18 with WHERE invalue > 10 may return an error.

Consider Query 3.19. Here we are searching for a particular vendor, S. Sauce. You might be given such a string by some application program. The problem is that we don't know the case of the names in the database or the case sensitivity of string matching. To fix this, we simply change all of the names to uppercase and format them correctly (first initial and last name).

Query 3.19 Find the vendors with the name S. Sauce

```
SELECT repfname || ' ' || replname AS name, companyname
FROM vendors
WHERE UPPER(SUBSTRING(repfname FROM 1 FOR 1) || '. ' || replname) =
        UPPER('S. Sauce');
```

name	companyname
Sam Sauce	Ed's Dressings

[1 row(s)]

3.5 ORDER BY: Ordering Result Table Traversal

The rows in a table in the relational model have no order. Because the result of a SELECT is itself a table, query results also have no order. Never rely on the DBMS to produce results in any particular order, even if it appears to work. Although a table has no order, SQL will allow us to control the order in which we access the rows of a table using ORDER BY. To use ORDER BY, we specify the sort key(s) that SQL should use to order the result output.

```
ORDER BY <sort specification> [{, <sort specification>}...]
<sort specification> = <key expression> [ASC | DESC] [NULLS FIRST | NULLS LAST]
```

Let's try a simple example.

Query 3.20 Find all items from least to most expensive

```
SELECT name, price
FROM items
ORDER BY price ASC;
```

name	price
Water	0.00
Garden Salad	0.99
Soda	0.99
Chicken Salad	2.85
Fruit Salad	3.45
Fruit Plate	3.99
Millennium Salad	NULL

[7 row(s)]

This query fetches the name and price of each item and then presents the results in sorted order by price. The ordering depends on the data type. For numeric types, ordering is straightforward. Character string ordering follows the same rules as character string comparison (see Chapter 2). The default ordering is ascending. You control the order direction using either ASC (ascending) or DESC (descending).

Note where the infamous *NULL* goes in the sort order. Because *NULL* is not comparable to any other value, even itself, the default ordering of *NULL* values is DBMS-specific. You may specify the placement of *NULL* in the sort order using either NULLS FIRST or NULLS LAST. Unfortunately, this feature is not widely implemented.

Query 3.21 Find items added in 2001 or later in decreasing order of price

```
SELECT itemid, price
FROM items
WHERE EXTRACT(YEAR FROM dateadded) >= 2001
ORDER BY price DESC;
```

itemid	price
MILSD	NULL
GDNSD	0.99
SODA	0.99
WATER	0.00

[4 row(s)]

In Query 3.21, SQL evaluates the query by fetching the *items* table, applying the WHERE predicate, extracting the item ID, and finally sorting by price. SQL does not require the sort key to be in the select list.

ORDER BY takes any expression. For example, we can sort our ingredients by a computed inventory value. We can even use column aliases in the ORDER BY.

Query 3.22 Find the name and inventory value of all ingredients ordered by value

```
SELECT name, inventory * unitprice AS value
FROM ingredients
ORDER BY value DESC;
```

name	value
Water	NULL
Watermelon	NULL
Soda	3450.00
Chicken	54.00
Pickle	32.00
Cheese	4.50
Crouton	4.00
Secret Dressing	3.60
Grape	3.00
Lettuce	2.00
Orange	0.50
Tomato	0.45

[12 row(s)]

You may specify multiple sort keys. SQL sorts primarily by the first key in the ORDER BY list. The second key is only used to break ties for rows where the first key values match and so on. Of course, if all values of the first sort key are distinct, then specifying additional sort keys does nothing.

Query 3.23 Find the order number, line number, and item ID ordered at #2STR, last order first

```
SELECT ordernumber, linenumber, menuitemid
FROM orders
WHERE storeid = '#2STR'
ORDER BY ordernumber DESC, linenumber ASC;
```

ordernumber	linenumber	menuitemid
3	1	CHKSD
3	2	FRPLT
3	3	GDNSD
2	1	CHKSD
2	2	SODA
1	1	CKSDS
1	2	CHKSD
1	3	SODA
1	4	GDNSD

[9 row(s)]

We really didn't need to specify ASC after *linenumber* because ascending order is the default.

Many DBMS also allow specification of the sort key by the positional number of the attribute in the select list. The attributes in the select list are numbered starting with 1. We can refer to these positional numbers in the ORDER BY clause. Consider Query 3.24.

Query 3.24 Positional ORDER BY example

```
SELECT foodgroup, name, unitprice * inventory AS value
FROM ingredients
ORDER BY 1 ASC, 3 DESC;
```

foodgroup	name	value
Bread	Crouton	4.00
Fruit	Watermelon	NULL
Fruit	Grape	3.00
Fruit	Orange	0.50
Fruit	Tomato	0.45
Meat	Chicken	54.00

Continued on next page

Query 3.24 (cont'd)

Milk	Cheese	4.50
Vegetable	Pickle	32.00
Vegetable	Lettuce	2.00
NULL	Water	NULL
NULL	Soda	3450.00
NULL	Secret Dressing	3.60

[12 row(s)]

The results are sorted primarily by food group in ascending order and secondarily by inventory value (i.e., *unitprice * inventory*) in descending order. You may mix sort key expressions and positional numbers. Positional column numbers are convenient for graphical user interface (GUI) based SQL tools that need to sort on arbitrary result columns, but in other cases, positional attribute numbers are almost always a bad idea. Adding an attribute to the select list may change the relative position of the attributes, and the developer may forget to update the ORDER BY clause. As a result, positional attribute numbers were deprecated in SQL-92 so they shouldn't be used.

3.6   CAST: Data Type Conversion

In SQL, all data have a type, whether it is data in a table or data returned by some expression. Sometimes the data type needs to change. Consider Query 3.25.

Query 3.25 Type cast example

```
SELECT name || ' was added on ' || dateadded || ' and is ' || price AS message
FROM items;
```

message
Chicken Salad was added on 1998-11-13 and is 2.85
Fruit Salad was added on 2000-05-06 and is 3.45
Garden Salad was added on 2001-03-02 and is 0.99
NULL
Soda was added on 2003-02-06 and is 0.99
Water was added on 2002-05-19 and is 0.00
Fruit Plate was added on 2000-09-02 and is 3.99

[7 row(s)]

Here the *dateadded* and *price* fields must be converted to character strings for concatenation. In many cases, the DBMS silently converts data types. Such conversions are called *implicit type conversions*. SQL uses the context to determine the needed type. In the previous example, the string concatenation implies that *dateadded* and *price* must be converted to character strings.

In some cases, the DBMS needs help in determining the correct data type. To handle this, SQL provides the CAST operator, which allows the specification of the resulting data type.

```
CAST(<source expression> AS <result type>)
```

CAST converts the type of the data specified by *<source expression>* to *<result type>*. A conversion using the CAST operator is called an *explicit type conversion*. Be aware that data type conversion may result in data loss. This happens when the result type represents *less* information than the source data. For example, conversion from a floating-point to an integer results in either truncation or rounding, depending on your DBMS. However, if the conversion would result in the loss of leading significant digits, then an exception is raised. Similarly, converting from a TIMESTAMP to a DATE will lose the time information.

What happens when the result type has *more* precision than the source data? For numeric types, it's straightforward. In some cases, SQL actually makes up data. For example, when converting from a DATE to a TIMESTAMP, the time is set to 00:00:00.0. Some type conversions are not allowed, even with the CAST operator. For example, SQL will give you an error if you try to cast a boolean to a numeric type. Query 3.26 generates a neatly formatted menu and uses CAST in the WHERE clause.

Query 3.26 Formatted menu

```
SELECT CAST(name AS CHAR(20)) || '$' || CAST(price AS NUMERIC(5,2)) AS "Menu"
FROM menuitems
WHERE CAST(menuitemid AS CHAR(1)) IN ('S', 'C', 'V');
```

Menu	
Chicken Salad	$2.85
Chicken N Suds	$3.68
Soda	$0.99
Vegan Eatin'	$4.38

[4 row(s)]

The cast of *name* to CHAR(20) makes a fixed-width character string. Character strings longer than 20 characters are truncated, and character strings shorter than 20 characters are padded with spaces. You can use CAST in the ORDER BY clause as well. Just don't forget that sort order depends on data type.

Query 3.27 Numbers as characters example

```
SELECT name, price * 10 AS "high price"
FROM menuitems
ORDER BY CAST (price * 10 AS CHAR(7));
```

name	high price
Water	0.00
Chicken Salad	28.50
Fruit Salad	34.50
Chicken N Suds	36.80
Fruit Plate	39.90
Vegan Eatin'	43.80
Garden Salad	9.90
Soda	9.90
Millennium Salad	NULL

[9 row(s)]

3.7   CASE, COALESCE, and NULLIF: Conditional Expressions

SQL also provides basic conditional constructs to determine the correct result. CASE provides a general mechanism for specifying conditional results. SQL also provides the COALESCE and NULLIF statements to deal with *NULL* values, but these have equivalent CASE statements.

3.7.1   CASE: Value List

The simplest form of the CASE statement determines if a value matches any values from a list and returns the corresponding result.

```
CASE <target expression>
WHEN <candidate expression> THEN <result expression>
WHEN <candidate expression> THEN <result expression>
...
WHEN <candidate expression> THEN <result expression>
[ELSE <result expression>]
END
```

CASE finds the *first* WHEN clause where *<candidate expression>* = *<target expression>* and returns the value of the corresponding *<result expression>*. If no matches are found, the value of the *<result expression>* for the ELSE clause is returned. If the ELSE clause is not specified, an implicit ELSE NULL is added to the CASE statement.

Consider the case where you want to list ingredients and their corresponding goodness as determined by the food group. The goodness assignments are as follows: Vegetable and Fruit are Good, Milk and Bread are Acceptable, Meat is Bad, and any other value is *NULL,* representing an unknown value.

Query 3.28 CASE value list example

```
SELECT name,
    CASE foodgroup
        WHEN 'Vegetable' THEN 'Good'
        WHEN 'Fruit' THEN 'Good'
        WHEN 'Milk' THEN 'Acceptable'
        WHEN 'Bread' THEN 'Acceptable'
        WHEN 'Meat' THEN 'Bad'
    END AS quality
FROM ingredients;
```

name	quality
Cheese	Acceptable
Chicken	Bad
Crouton	Acceptable
Grape	Good
Lettuce	Good
Pickle	Good
Secret Dressing	NULL
Tomato	Good
Water	NULL
Soda	NULL
Watermelon	Good
Orange	Good

[12 row(s)]

3.7.2 CASE: Conditional List

Matching values from a list is a good start, but we may need more powerful matching capabilities. SQL provides a more general version of the CASE statement that allows conditionals in the WHEN clause.

```
CASE
WHEN <match conditional> THEN <result expression>
WHEN <match conditional> THEN <result expression>
...
WHEN <match conditional> THEN <result expression>
[ELSE <result expression>]
END
```

In this conditional form, CASE finds the first WHEN clause where the *<match conditional>* evaluates to true and returns the value of the corresponding *<result expression>*. The

<match conditional> can be any conditional expression using expressions, functions, boolean connectives, and so on. Note that the value-list CASE is just a special case of the conditional CASE where each *<match conditional>* is of the form *<target expression>* = *<candidate expression>*.

To show the power of the CASE statement, let's put together an order for ingredients. The amount that we want to order is based on the current inventory. If that inventory is below a threshold, then we want to place an order to raise it to the threshold; otherwise, we want to order a percentage of our inventory. The exact amount is based on the type of the food item because some will spoil more quickly than others. A query to create the order is Query 3.29.

Query 3.29 CASE conditional list example

```
SELECT name,
    FLOOR(
        CASE
            WHEN inventory < 20 THEN 20 - inventory
            WHEN foodgroup = 'Milk' THEN inventory * 0.05
            WHEN foodgroup IN ('Meat', 'Bread') THEN inventory * 0.10
            WHEN foodgroup = 'Vegetable' AND unitprice <= 0.03 THEN inventory * 0.10
            WHEN foodgroup = 'Vegetable' THEN inventory * 0.03
            WHEN foodgroup = 'Fruit' THEN inventory * 0.04
            WHEN foodgroup IS NULL THEN inventory * 0.07
            ELSE 0
        END) AS size, vendorid
FROM ingredients
WHERE inventory < 1000 AND vendorid IS NOT NULL
ORDER BY vendorid, size;
```

name	size	vendorid
Cheese	7	DNDRY
Chicken	12	DNDRY
Crouton	40	EDDRS
Orange	10	FRTFR
Grape	12	FRTFR
Tomato	5	VGRUS
Lettuce	20	VGRUS
Pickle	24	VGRUS

[8 row(s)]

There are a couple of things to note about this query.

■ The CASE statement stops executing when the first condition is matched. This makes the order of the *<match conditionals>* very important.

- The constants used for inventory and percentages should be stored in the database. This would allow the user to update the database and automatically update this order query.

- Items with a *NULL* inventory are filtered out by the WHERE clause. Including an item with a *NULL* inventory would result in a *NULL* size.

- CASE returns data that can be used in expressions, conditionals, function arguments, and even database modification statements. Thus, if we had an appropriate table, we could store the result of this query directly in the database.

3.7.3 NULLIF

NULLIF takes two values and returns *NULL* if they are equal or the first value if the two values are not equal. You can think of it as "*NULL* IF equal."

```
NULLIF(<value1>,<value2>)
```

The NULLIF is actually a special case of the CASE statement. It is equivalent to the CASE statement:

```
CASE WHEN value1=value2 THEN NULL ELSE value1 END
```

Let's try an example. The World Health Organization (WHO) has declared that Meat is no longer a food group. Query 3.30 shows the *ingredients* table with the food group of all meats as *NULL*.

Query 3.30 NULLIF example

```
SELECT ingredientid, name, unit, unitprice,
    NULLIF(foodgroup, 'Meat') AS foodgroup, inventory, vendorid
FROM ingredients;
```

ingredientid	name	unit	unitprice	foodgroup	inventory	vendorid
CHESE	Cheese	scoop	0.03	Milk	150	DNDRY
CHIKN	Chicken	strip	0.45	NULL	120	DNDRY
CRUTN	Crouton	piece	0.01	Bread	400	EDDRS
GRAPE	Grape	piece	0.01	Fruit	300	FRTFR
LETUS	Lettuce	bowl	0.01	Vegetable	200	VGRUS
PICKL	Pickle	slice	0.04	Vegetable	800	VGRUS
SCTDR	Secret Dressing	ounce	0.03	NULL	120	NULL
TOMTO	Tomato	slice	0.03	Fruit	15	VGRUS
WATER	Water	glass	0.06	NULL	NULL	SPWTR
SODA	Soda	glass	0.69	NULL	5000	SPWTR
WTRML	Watermelon	piece	0.02	Fruit	NULL	FRTFR
ORNG	Orange	slice	0.05	Fruit	10	FRTFR

[12 row(s)]

3.7.4 COALESCE

COALESCE takes a list of values and returns the first non-*NULL* value.

```
COALESCE(<value1>, <value2>, ..., <valueN>)
```

COALESCE is also shorthand for a complicated CASE statement. When the number of values is 2, it is exactly equivalent to the following:

```
CASE WHEN value1 IS NOT NULL THEN value1 ELSE value2 END
```

and when the number of values is greater than 2, it is equivalent to the following:

```
CASE WHEN value1 IS NOT NULL THEN value1
ELSE COALESCE (value2, . . ., valueN) END
```

One practical use for COALESCE is providing a substitute for *NULL* values in the results. For example, if we want to display all of our items with a price, we would have to handle the ones with a *NULL* price. Query 3.31 does this.

Query 3.31 COALESCE example

```
SELECT name, price, COALESCE(price, 0.00) AS "no nulls"
FROM items;
```

name	price	no nulls
Chicken Salad	2.85	2.85
Fruit Salad	3.45	3.45
Garden Salad	0.99	0.99
Millennium Salad	NULL	0.00
Soda	0.99	0.99
Water	0.00	0.00
Fruit Plate	3.99	3.99

[7 row(s)]

3.8 Wrap Up

The basic SELECT statement allows control over result table rows and columns. In some cases, this is not sufficient to get our final answer. SQL provides several mechanisms for manipulating the result table and its data. We can select result table column names and eliminate duplicates. Because data can be somewhat raw, SQL provides us with the ability to derive data using expressions of basic operators and functions. We can even control result table column data types with explicit type conversion. Finally, we can determine the order in which the rows of our result table are traversed by specifying sort key(s) to ORDER BY. With all of these capabilities, SQL gives us great control over the final form of our result table.

Review Questions

1. **True/False** NULLs always appear first when using the ORDER BY clause.

2. What's the difference between the output of the following two queries? Explain.

   ```
   SELECT vendorid FROM vendors;
   SELECT DISTINCT vendorid FROM vendors;
   ```

3. How many rows does the following query return? _____
   SELECT 'apples' FROM vendors;

4. Fully parenthesize the following WHERE clause to indicate the order of execution:
   WHERE NOT - x + 2 * y >= 3 AND z + 9 < 12;
   x, y, and z are all integers.

5. What happens when you CAST a *NULL* value?

6. Consider the blood donor table that follows. Place an × in the rows that would *not* be in the result of a query with the select clause.

   donor

id	gender	type	SELECT DISTINCT gender	SELECT DISTINCT type	SELECT DISTINCT gender, type
1	M	A			
2	F	B			
3	NULL	A			
4	NULL	NULL			
5	M	NULL			
6	M	A			

7. What is the result of the following expression?
   5 * 8 + 2 / ABS(NULL)

8. Modify Query 3.14 so that single word company names are also returned.

9. AS is optional in SQL. In the Restaurant Database, what is the difference between the SELECT clause aliasing repfname as vendorid (without AS) and the SELECT clause returning both repfname and vendorid?

10. $e^{\ln x} = x$. Write a query to test these SQL functions.

11. In the Restaurant Database, how would you combine substring and position to return the first word in a VARCHAR field? You can assume words are separated by spaces.

12. Write a query to return tomorrow's date.

13. Explain the difference between Query 3.32 and Query 3.33.

Query 3.32

```
SELECT ingredientid, price
FROM ingredients
ORDER BY CAST(price * 10 AS
VARCHAR(10))
```

Query 3.33

```
SELECT ingredientid, price
FROM ingredients
ORDER BY price * 10
```

14. The conditional list (see Section 3.7.2) is similar to if-then-elseif constructs in programming languages. Construct a conditional list equivalent to the following pseudo code:

```
if (A<>B) then {
    if (C>0) then output A*C;
    if (C==0) then output A*B;
    if (C<0) then output B*C;
}
```

15. What is the result of NULLIF(X,NULL)? NULLIF(NULL,X)? NULLIF(NULL, NULL)?

16. What is the result of COALESCE(NULLIF(X,X),X)?

Practice

For these exercises, we use the Employees Database presented at the end of Chapter 1. Answer each question with a single SQL statement. Your query must work for any set of data in the Employees Database, not just the set of data we provide.

1. List all employee names as one field called name.

2. List all of the department codes assigned to a project. Remove all duplicates.

3. Find the project ID and duration of each project.

4. Find the project ID and duration of each project. If the project has not finished, report its execution time as of now.

5. For each completed project, find the project ID and average revenue per day.

6. Find the years a project started. Remove duplicates.

7. Find the IDs of employees assigned to a project that is more than 20 hours per week. Write three queries using 20, 40, and 60 hour work weeks.

8. For each employee assigned to a task, output the employee ID with the following:

   - 'part time' if assigned time is < 0.33

   - 'split time' if assigned time is >= 0.33 and < 0.67

   - 'full time' if assigned time is >= 0.67

9. We need to create a list of abbreviated project names. Each abbreviated name concatenates the first three characters of the project description, a hyphen, and the department code. All characters must be uppercase (e.g., EMP-ADMIN).

10. For each project, list the ID and year the project started. Order the results in ascending order by year.

11. If every employee is given a 5% raise, find the last name and new salary of the employees who will make more than $50,000.

12. For all the employees in the HDWRE department, list their ID, first name, last name, and salary after a 10% raise. The salary column in the result should be named Next Year.

13. Create a neatly formatted directory of all employees, including their department code and name. The list should be sorted first by department code, then by last name, then by first name.

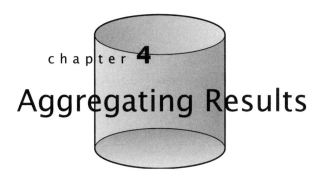

chapter **4**

Aggregating Results

Databases are designed to hold data—lots of it. Often, to answer a question, we don't want the raw data; we just need some aggregate of the data. For example, when somebody asks about your car's fuel efficiency, they don't want to know minute-by-minute fuel consumption details. Instead they want to know the average distance that your car can go on a gallon or liter of gas. To answer these types of queries, SQL computes common data aggregates.

4.1 Aggregation Functions

Given a set of data, SQL can provide us with a single, aggregate value over that data. For example, we can find the average cost of our items or sum of the values of each item in our inventory.

SQL provides several basic aggregation functions. These functions take an expression and return an aggregate value over all rows in the specified table. Table 4.1 includes information about each function, including what it computes, the acceptable data types, and how *NULL*s and repeated values are handled. There are five basic aggregate functions in SQL: AVG, SUM, MIN, MAX, and COUNT.

4.1.1 AVG and SUM

AVG computes the average of an expression over all rows in the result table. Similarly, SUM computes the sum. The expression parameter can be as simple as a single column name. In Section 4.9, we will see that more complex expressions are possible. Rows for which

Function	Returns	Data Type	*NULLs* Ignored?	DISTINCT Meaningful
AVG	Average expression value	Numeric	Yes	Yes
MAX	Largest expression value	Any	Yes	No
MIN	Smallest expression value	Any	Yes	No
SUM	Sum of expression values	Numeric	Yes	Yes
COUNT	Number of non-null values	Any	Yes	Yes
COUNT(*)	Number of rows	Any	No	Illegal

Table 4.1: SQL Aggregate Functions

the expression evaluates to *NULL* are ignored. Naturally, the parameter for AVG and SUM must be a numeric data type.

Query 4.1   Find the average and total price for all items

```
SELECT AVG(price), SUM(price)
FROM items;
```

avg	sum
2.0450000000000000	12.27

[1 row(s)]

Query 4.1 computes the average and total price of all rows in the *items* table. Both results ignore rows where the price is *NULL*.

As with any SELECT statement, the result of Query 4.1 is a table. This table contains two columns and one row containing the results of the aggregate functions. The name of each column is DBMS specific; however, we can specify the name using an attribute alias.

Query 4.2   Find the total number of ingredient units in inventory

```
SELECT SUM(inventory) AS totalinventory
FROM ingredients;
```

totalinventory
7115

[1 row(s)]

4.1.2   MIN and MAX

MIN and *MAX* find the minimum and maximum value, respectively, of the given expression over all rows in the given table. Because *NULL* is not comparable, it can be neither the minimum nor maximum value; consequently, MIN and MAX ignore *NULL* values, just like AVG and SUM.

Query 4.3 Find the smallest price of all items

```
SELECT MIN(price) AS minprice
FROM items;
```

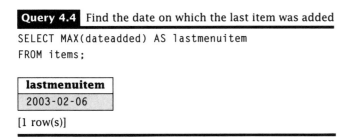

minprice
0.00

[1 row(s)]

Unlike AVG and SUM, MIN and MAX are not limited to numeric values. We can use any data type that allows for comparisons. Query 4.4 provides an example using dates.

Query 4.4 Find the date on which the last item was added

```
SELECT MAX(dateadded) AS lastmenuitem
FROM items;
```

lastmenuitem
2003-02-06

[1 row(s)]

4.1.3 COUNT

COUNT returns the number of rows. It comes in two flavors. COUNT(*) computes the number of rows in a table, including *NULL*s.

Query 4.5 Find the number of slogans

```
SELECT COUNT(*) AS numads
FROM ads;
```

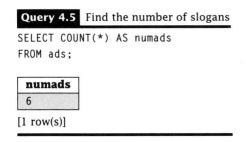

numads
6

[1 row(s)]

The second form of COUNT takes an expression as its parameter and only counts the rows where the expression does not evaluate to *NULL*.

Query 4.6 Find the number of ingredients with non-*NULL* inventories

```
SELECT COUNT(inventory) AS invct
FROM ingredients;
```

invct
10

[1 row(s)]

4.2   Removing Rows before Aggregation with WHERE

We can limit the rows used by the aggregate function with a WHERE condition.

Query 4.7 Find the total sales at FIRST store

```
SELECT SUM(price) AS sales
FROM orders
WHERE storeid = 'FIRST';
```

sales
15.66

[1 row(s)]

The WHERE condition is always applied before any aggregate function is computed. Note that AVG, SUM, MIN, and MAX over an empty set of values returns *NULL*. Because these functions ignore *NULL* values, computing one of these functions over a set of *NULL* values returns *NULL*. COUNT over an empty set of values returns 0. Query 4.8 shows an example.

Query 4.8 Aggregates and *NULL* example

```
SELECT AVG(inventory) AS ainv, SUM(inventory) AS sinv, MIN(inventory) AS mininv,
    MAX(inventory) AS maxinv, COUNT(*) AS cntall, COUNT(inventory) AS cntinv
FROM ingredients
WHERE ingredientid = 'WATER';
```

ainv	sinv	mininv	maxinv	cntall	cntinv
NULL	NULL	NULL	NULL	1	0

[1 row(s)]

In Query 4.8 AVG, SUM, MIN, and MAX returned *NULL* because the inventory for water is *NULL*, which is ignored for computing them. Because COUNT(inventory) ignores *NULL*, it computes the number of rows in an empty set, and COUNT(*) returns the number of rows, even with the *NULL* value.

4.3 Removing Repeating Data with DISTINCT before Aggregation

How do aggregate functions handle repeated values? By default, an aggregate function includes all rows, even repeats, with the noted exceptions of *NULL.* We can add the DISTINCT qualifier to remove duplicates prior to computing the aggregate function.

| **Query 4.9** | Find the number of ingredients with a non-*NULL* food group and the number of distinct non-*NULL* food groups |

```
SELECT COUNT(foodgroup) AS "FGIngreds", COUNT(DISTINCT foodgroup) AS "NoFGs"
FROM ingredients;
```

FGIngreds	**NoFGs**
9	5

[1 row(s)]

Recall that, when given an expression, COUNT ignores *NULL* values. After eliminating the *NULL foodgroup* values, we have only 5 distinct food groups.

DISTINCTions to keep in mind:

1. It is legal to use DISTINCT with MIN and MAX; however, it will not alter the results.

2. COUNT(DISTINCT *) is illegal.

3. We can explicitly request the inclusion of repeats by using the ALL qualifier instead of DISTINCT; however, this does not change the behavior because ALL is the default qualifier.

4.4 Mixing Attributes, Aggregates, and Literals

Aggregate functions return a single value, so we usually cannot mix attributes and aggregate functions in the attribute list of a SELECT statement. The following query produces an error.

```
SELECT itemid, AVG(price)
FROM items;
```

Because there are many item IDs and only one average price, SQL doesn't know how to pair them. In Section 4.5 we will see how SQL partially removes this restriction with GROUP BY.

We can mix literals and aggregate functions as shown in Query 4.10.

Query 4.10 Mixing literals with aggregates

```
SELECT 'Results: ' AS " ", COUNT(*) AS noingredients,
    COUNT(inventory) AS countedingredients,
    SUM(DISTINCT inventory) AS totalingredients
FROM ingredients;
```

	noingredients	countedingredients	totalingredients
Results:	12	10	6995

[1 row(s)]

Note that each aggregate function operates independently. COUNT(*) counts all rows, COUNT(quantity) counts all rows with non-*NULL* inventory quantities, and SUM(DISTINCT inventory) sums all rows with non-*NULL* and ignores repeated values.

4.5   Group Aggregation Using GROUP BY

Aggregate functions return a single piece of summary information about an entire set of rows. What if we wanted the aggregate over different groups of data? For example, we might want to find the total sales in all of our stores. We could repeat Query 4.7 for every store ID, but this would be impractical for large chains. Fortunately, SQL provides a simple mechanism for applying aggregates to all groups in one query. SQL uses the GROUP BY clause to specify the attribute(s) that determine the grouping. Let's look at an example.

Query 4.11 Find the storeid and total sales from all stores

```
SELECT storeid, SUM(price)
FROM orders
GROUP BY storeid;
```

storeid	sum
CASTR	28.32
#2STR	20.18
NDSTR	17.79
FIRST	15.66

[4 row(s)]

The GROUP BY is executed before the SELECT. Thus, the *orders* table is divided into groups based on the *storeid* values. For each of these groups, we then apply the SELECT, including the aggregate function, which in this case is SUM. This means the result of Query 4.11 will include one row for each store ID and the total sales at that store. This solves the problem of combining attributes and aggregates we had in Section 4.4. If we had stores with *NULL* IDs, they would form their own single group.

Groups can be defined by multiple attributes, as shown in Query 4.12.

Query 4.12 Find the total for each order

```
SELECT storeid, ordernumber, SUM(price)
FROM orders
GROUP BY storeid, ordernumber;
```

storeid	ordernumber	sum
FIRST	2	2.85
FIRST	3	9.36
FIRST	1	3.45
NDSTR	2	0.99
NDSTR	3	12.81
NDSTR	1	3.99
#2STR	2	3.84
#2STR	3	7.83
#2STR	1	8.51
CASTR	2	9.81
CASTR	3	14.67
CASTR	1	3.84

[12 row(s)]

In this example, a group is formed for each *storeid/ordernumber* pair, and the aggregate is applied just as before.

It is important to note that when we use a GROUP BY clause, we restrict the attributes that can appear in the SELECT clause. If a GROUP BY clause is present, the SELECT clause may only contain attributes appearing in the GROUP BY clause, aggregate functions (on any attribute), or literals.

GROUP BY does not require the use of aggregation functions in the attribute list. Without aggregation functions, GROUP BY acts like DISTINCT, forming the set of unique groups over the given attributes. For example, compare Query 3.4 to Query 4.13.

Query 4.13 Find the distinct list of food groups provided by each vendor

```
SELECT vendorid, foodgroup
FROM ingredients
GROUP BY vendorid, foodgroup;
```

vendorid	foodgroup
NULL	NULL
FRTFR	Fruit

Continued on next page

Query 4.13 (cont'd)

SPWTR	NULL
VGRUS	Vegetable
VGRUS	Fruit
DNDRY	Milk
DNDRY	Meat
EDDRS	Bread

[8 row(s)]

Now consider Query 4.14. In this query, we want the name of the ingredient, not the ingredient ID. However, it is possible that different ingredients have the same name. (Our example database does not, but it is not prevented.) We can still get the groups we want by using BOTH the ingredient ID and the name in the GROUP BY clause.

Query 4.14 GROUP BY example

```
SELECT name, AVG(unitprice)
FROM ingredients
WHERE unit = 'piece'
GROUP BY ingredientid, name;
```

name	avg
Grape	0.0100000000000000000
Watermelon	0.0200000000000000000
Crouton	0.0100000000000000000

[3 row(s)]

4.6 Removing Rows before Grouping with WHERE

We may want to eliminate some rows from the table before we form groups. We can eliminate rows from groups using the WHERE clause as shown in Query 4.15.

Query 4.15 Find the number of nonbeverages sold at each store

```
SELECT storeid, COUNT(*)
FROM orders
WHERE menuitemid NOT IN ('SODA','WATER')
GROUP BY storeid;
```

Query 4.15 (cont'd)

storeid	count
CASTR	8
#2STR	7
NDSTR	5
FIRST	4

[4 row(s)]

Rows not satisfying the WHERE predicate are removed before the groups are formed. The aggregate function values are computed after the groups are formed.

4.7 Sorting Groups with ORDER BY

We can order our groups using ORDER BY. It works the same as ORDER BY without grouping except that we can now also sort by group aggregates. The aggregate we use in our sort criteria need not be an aggregate from the SELECT list.

Query 4.16 Find stores and store sales sorted by number items sold

```
SELECT storeid, SUM(price)
FROM orders
GROUP BY storeid
ORDER BY COUNT(*);
```

storeid	sum
NDSTR	17.79
FIRST	15.66
#2STR	20.18
CASTR	28.32

[4 row(s)]

Just like the SELECT clause, any attributes in the ORDER BY clause must either be contained within an aggregation function or appear in the GROUP BY clause. This means that in Query 4.16 we can only sort by *storeid* or an aggregate function.

4.8 Removing Groups with HAVING

Use the HAVING clause to specify a condition for *groups* in the final result. This is different from WHERE, which removes rows *before* grouping. Groups for which the HAVING condition does not evaluate to true are eliminated. Because we're working with groups of rows, it makes sense to allow aggregate functions in a HAVING predicate.

Query 4.17	Find the number of vendors each vendor referred, and only report the vendors referring more than 1

```
SELECT referredby, COUNT(*)
FROM vendors
WHERE referredby IS NOT NULL
GROUP BY referredby
HAVING COUNT(*) > 1;
```

referredby	count
VGRUS	2

[1 row(s)]

SQL begins Query 4.17 by evaluating the WHERE clause to remove the vendors who have not been referred by anyone. Remember that *NULL* would become a group, but we do not want that in the result. Next, SQL divides the remaining rows into groups according to *referredby* values. For each referring vendor, SQL computes the number of referrals. The HAVING clause only keeps the groups with more than 1 referral. Could we have used WHERE instead of HAVING? No. WHERE conditionals apply to rows, and no single row in the *vendors* table tells us how many other vendors a vendor has referred. We can only find that after we have grouped the rows and applied the aggregate function. Because WHERE works on rows, it does not even allow aggregate functions.

The condition in the HAVING clause may be over any group attribute or group data aggregation. This means that our HAVING clause is not restricted to aggregation functions in the SELECT list or even aggregation functions over attributes in the GROUP BY.

Query 4.18	Find the maximum number of items in an order for each store with total sales of more than $20

```
SELECT storeid, MAX(linenumber) AS "Items Sold"
FROM orders
GROUP BY storeid
HAVING SUM(price) > 20;
```

storeid	Items Sold
CASTR	5
#2STR	4

[2 row(s)]

In Query 4.18, SQL first forms the groups of rows for each store ID. Next, it computes the SUM of the *price* attribute for each row in the group. If this total is higher than $20, SQL returns the store ID and greatest line number in the group.

Sometimes, we can get the same results by applying a predicate in either the WHERE clause or the HAVING clause. Compare Query 4.19 with Query 4.7.

Query 4.19 Find the total sales at FIRST store

```
SELECT SUM(price) AS sales
FROM orders
GROUP BY storeid
HAVING storeid = 'FIRST';
```

sales
15.66

[1 row(s)]

Query 4.19 will almost certainly be slower than Query 4.7 because the DBMS will have to go through the effort of creating groups that are not needed.

The HAVING clause can use AND, OR, and NOT just like the WHERE clause to form more complicated predicates on groups. The following query finds the minimum and maximum unit price of all ingredients in each non-*NULL* food group. The results are only reported for food groups with either two or more items or a total inventory of more than 500 items.

Query 4.20 Complex HAVING example

```
SELECT foodgroup, MIN(unitprice) AS minprice, MAX(unitprice) AS maxprice
FROM ingredients
WHERE foodgroup IS NOT NULL
GROUP BY foodgroup
HAVING COUNT(*) >= 2 OR SUM(inventory) > 500;
```

foodgroup	minprice	maxprice
Vegetable	0.01	0.04
Fruit	0.01	0.05

[2 row(s)]

It is legal to have a HAVING clause without a GROUP BY. In this case, the entire table is treated as a single group. Note that without the GROUP BY clause, only aggregate functions and literals can appear in the SELECT clause, so the result of a query with a HAVING clause and no GROUP BY clause will either be a single row or no rows, depending on whether the selected rows satisfy the HAVING predicate. Finally, in a query with both a HAVING clause and an ORDER BY clause, the HAVING clause comes first.

4.9 Aggregates over Expressions

Aggregate functions accept expression parameters. This allows us to aggregate complex values.

Query 4.21 Find the total value of our inventory for the vendor with ID VGRUS

```
SELECT SUM(unitprice*inventory) AS invalue
FROM ingredients
WHERE vendorid = 'VGRUS';
```

invalue
34.45

[1 row(s)]

The computation of these expressions follow the rules for handling *NULL*s as described in Section 3.3. Expressions also work with GROUP BY. We can even use aggregate functions *within* expressions. Suppose your restaurant chain has a sales goal of $25. You want to know the percentage of the sales goal that has been met by each store that has sold at least 8 items.

Query 4.22 Find the percentage of sales goals met for each store with at least 8 items sold

```
SELECT storeid, CAST(SUM(price)/25.0*100.0 AS NUMERIC(5,2)) || '%' AS "Goal"
FROM orders
GROUP BY storeid
HAVING COUNT(*) >= 8
ORDER BY SUM(price)/25.0*100.0 DESC;
```

storeid	Goal
CASTR	113.28%
#2STR	80.72%

[2 row(s)]

Query 4.22 combines much of what we have learned so far. First, it groups the orders by the *storeid.* Each group with at least 8 rows is then sorted by the percentage of the goal ($25 for our small *orders* table) met. The output is then formatted.

Let's try one more example of an aggregate over an expression.

Query 4.23 COUNT without COUNT

```
SELECT SUM(1) AS "no count", COUNT(*) AS count
FROM vendors;
```

no count	count
6	6

[1 row(s)]

How does Query 4.23 work? Because we do not have a GROUP BY clause, the entire table is considered one group. For each row in the group, SUM totals its expression. In this case, that simply adds one to the total. The end result is that both SUM(1) and COUNT(*) return the same value.

4.10 Wrap Up

Databases contain raw data, and aggregate functions allow us to derive useful summarizations. We present the use of the five basic aggregation functions: SUM, AVG, MIN, MAX, and COUNT. The SQL standard includes several more, such as boolean set operations EVERY, ANY, and SOME and statistical operations STDDEV_POP, STDDEV_SAMP, VAR_SAMP, and VAR_POP. Support for these operations is limited.

Instead of computing a single aggregate value, we can group data for aggregation using the GROUP BY clause. We can control the inclusion of rows in aggregation computation using the WHERE clause and the inclusion of groups using the HAVING clause.

Review Questions

1. If we have a column, X, with values 1, 2, 3, and *NULL,* what is AVG(X)? _____

2. Does AVG(price) = SUM(price)/COUNT(*)? Explain. If they are not equal, how can you fix it?

3. If we have a column X, when can MIN(X) = MAX(X)?

4. If X is a primary key, what is COUNT(X)? How does that value compare to COUNT(*) over the same table?

5. For each aggregate function, what is the result if the SQL statement includes WHERE 1 = 2?

6. If the result of the query is the same, which is better, eliminating rows with a WHERE clause or eliminating groups with a HAVING clause? Why?

7. Is there any relationship between the number of rows in a table and the number of rows generated by a GROUP BY?

8. What is the difference between using DISTINCT in the SELECT clause and a GROUP BY clause with the same attributes?

9. What can the HAVING clause contain that the WHERE clause cannot?

10. How many rows are returned if the GROUP BY clause contains the primary key of a table?

11. WHERE is to rows as HAVING is to _____.

12. Using the Restaurant Database, assume the FROM clause contains the *vendors* table. If the GROUP BY clause contains the *vendorid* and *replname* attributes, list all attributes that can appear by themselves in the SELECT, WHERE, HAVING, and ORDER BY clauses.

13. If a HAVING clause appears without a GROUP BY clause, what is the maximum number of rows that can be in the result? What is the minimum number of rows?

14. In statistics, the "sum-of-squares error" is used to determine the goodness of fit for an approximation. The formula is as follows:

$$\sum_i (X_i - Y_i)^2.$$

If *X* and *Y* are columns in table *test,* write an SQL statement to find the "sum-of-squares error" for the data in *test.*

Practice

For these exercises, we use the Employees Database presented at the end of Chapter 1. Answer each question with a single SQL statement. Your query must work for any set of data in the Employees Database, not just the set of data we provide.

1. Find the average salary for all employees.

2. Find the minimum and maximum project revenue for all active projects that make money.

3. Find the number of projects that are completed. You may not use a WHERE clause.

4. Find the number of projects that have been worked on or currently are being worked on by an employee.

5. Find the last name of the employee whose last name is last in dictionary order.

6. Compute the employee salary standard deviation. As a reminder, the formula for the population standard deviation is as follows:

$$\sqrt{\frac{1}{N}\sum_{i=1}^{N}(x_i - \bar{x})^2}$$

7. Find the number of employees who are assigned to some department. You may not use a WHERE clause.

8. For each department, list the department code and the number of employees in the department.

9. For each department that has a project, list the department code and report the average revenue and count of all of its projects.

10. Modify the query from Problem 9 to only include departments with 2 or more projects.

11. Modify the query from Problem 10 to only count active projects. Sort the results in descending order by count.

12. Find the employee ID of all employees where their assigned time to work on projects is 100% or more.

13. Calculate the salary cost for each department with employees that don't have a last name ending in "re" after giving everyone a 10% raise.

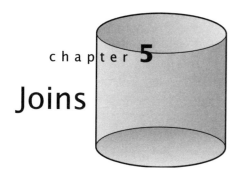

c h a p t e r **5**

Joins

Until now, all of our queries have used a single table. It is not surprising that many queries require information from more than one table. Suppose that you want a list of ingredients and their vendor (ID and company name). The names of the companies are in the *vendors* table, but the names of the ingredients are in the *ingredients* table. To answer this yourself, you could go through each row of the *ingredients* table and use the *vendorid* value to search for the company name in the *vendors* table. What a painful process!

To deal with this problem, SQL allows us to derive a single table that contains *all* of the desired data. We can then query that table using the techniques we already know. Combining tables to derive a new table is called a *join*.

5.1 Two Table Joins with WHERE

The best way to understand joins is to look at an example. Let's try our ingredients/vendor list again. Using a join, we derive a new, virtual table that includes the information we need from both the *ingredients* and *vendors* table.

Query 5.1 For each ingredient, find its name and the name and ID of the vendor that supplies it

```
SELECT vendors.vendorid, name, companyname
FROM ingredients, vendors
WHERE ingredients.vendorid = vendors.vendorid;
```

vendorid	name	companyname
DNDRY	Cheese	Don's Dairy
DNDRY	Chicken	Don's Dairy

Continued on next page

Query 5.1 (cont'd)

EDDRS	Crouton	Ed's Dressings
FRTFR	Grape	"Fruit Eating" Friends
VGRUS	Lettuce	Veggies_R_Us
VGRUS	Pickle	Veggies_R_Us
VGRUS	Tomato	Veggies_R_Us
SPWTR	Water	Spring Water Supply
SPWTR	Soda	Spring Water Supply
FRTFR	Watermelon	"Fruit Eating" Friends
FRTFR	Orange	"Fruit Eating" Friends

[11 row(s)]

Let's dissect this query. First, the FROM clause creates the new table that has the combined attributes of *all* tables in the list. In the previous example, the new table has a total of 12 attributes (5 from *vendors* + 7 from *ingredients*). Note that we now have two attributes in the new table with the name *vendorid:* one from the *ingredients* table and one from the *vendors* table. If we reference *vendorid* in the new table, do we mean the *vendorid* from *ingredients* or *vendors?* It is impossible to know which, so SQL requires us to prefix these attributes with their original table names. For example, the *vendorid* from *vendors* is called *vendors.vendorid.* The table name prefix is not required if the attribute name is unambiguous, as with *name* in the SELECT clause.

Next, the WHERE clause describes how to connect the tables. For this query, we want to match the rows in *ingredients* with the rows in *vendors* that supply them. We know that the *vendorid* in *ingredients* references the *vendorid* in *vendors.* The foreign key constraint between the two tables tells us these attributes have an association. We want to match rows from the two tables where this common attribute contains the same value. To do this, we add a condition (called the *join predicate)* to the WHERE clause that describes this relationship. To combine our two tables, we use `WHERE ingredients.vendorid = vendors.vendorid.`

We can think of executing this query by taking every row in *ingredients* and searching the *vendors* table for matching rows. Once a match is found, all of the attributes in both tables are processed by the rest of the SQL query. This allows us to display the name of the ingredient and the name and ID of the vendor that supplies it. After executing the FROM and WHERE clauses, we have a table with the attributes of both *ingredients* and *vendors* and the rows with matched vendor IDs. Finally SQL executes the SELECT clause, keeping only the attributes in the SELECT list.

Once we create our new table, we can use it just like any other table. We can apply conditions in the WHERE clause to the matched rows. Query 5.2 uses the same join predicate as Query 5.1, but it also applies the additional constraint that the company name is Veggies_R_Us.

Query 5.2 Find the names of the ingredients supplied to us by Veggies_R_Us

```
SELECT name
FROM ingredients, vendors
WHERE ingredients.vendorid = vendors.vendorid AND companyname = 'Veggies_R_Us';
```

name
Lettuce
Pickle
Tomato

[3 row(s)]

Designing a join is a two-step process:

1. Find the tables with the information that we need to answer the query.

2. Determine how to connect the tables.

Let's try an example: Find the orders made at our California store in Query 5.3. In Step 1, we list all of the tables that we need to answer the query. In this example, we need the *orders* table for the order information and the *stores* table to find out the state of each store. We list these tables in the FROM clause of our query. For Step 2, we need to give the criteria for connecting these two tables. We know that the *storeid* in *orders* references the *storeid* in *stores* from the foreign key constraint. We want to match rows from the two tables where this common attribute contains the same value. We add the join predicate WHERE orders.storeid = stores.storeid. At this point, we have the orders made in all stores. To finish we add the condition state = 'CA' and select the desired attributes.

Query 5.3 Find the store ID and price of all orders made in our California stores

```
SELECT stores.storeid, price
FROM orders, stores
WHERE orders.storeid = stores.storeid AND state = 'CA';
```

storeid	price
CASTR	2.85
CASTR	0.99
CASTR	0.99
CASTR	3.45
CASTR	0.99
CASTR	4.38
CASTR	4.38
CASTR	3.99
CASTR	3.45
CASTR	0.00
CASTR	2.85

[11 row(s)]

Here we join the two tables from Step 1 using the join predicate from Step 2 to derive a new table. We can then treat this like any other table, applying additional conditions and selecting specific attributes.

We can even apply aggregation and grouping to a derived table. Suppose you want to know the total sales in each state. Step 1 tells us we need the *stores* (to find the states) and the *orders* tables. We connect our tables using the *storeid* column in Step 2. Now that we have the derived table, we perform aggregation and grouping.

Query 5.4 Find the total sales by state

```
SELECT state, SUM(price)
FROM stores, orders
WHERE stores.storeid = orders.storeid
GROUP BY state;
```

state	sum
TX	35.84
ND	17.79
CA	28.32

[3 row(s)]

5.2   Table Aliases

It becomes tiresome and error prone to prefix attributes with the full table name every time. Fortunately, SQL allows aliases for the table names.

Query 5.5 Find the name of all ingredients supplied by Veggies_R_Us or Spring Water Supply

```
SELECT v.vendorid AS "Vendor ID", name
FROM ingredients AS i, vendors AS v
WHERE i.vendorid = v.vendorid AND
      v.companyname IN ('Veggies_R_Us', 'Spring Water Supply')
ORDER BY v.vendorid;
```

Vendor ID	name
SPWTR	Water
SPWTR	Soda
VGRUS	Lettuce
VGRUS	Pickle
VGRUS	Tomato

[5 row(s)]

The keyword AS is optional for table aliases. In our example query, we use i for *ingredients* and v for *vendors*. We can use the table alias in all other clauses. We SELECT and ORDER BY *v.vendorid*. We would get the same results using *i.vendorid* because the WHERE clause ensures that the vendor IDs are equal.

5.3 Joins Needing More Than Two Tables

Sometimes when we're answering a query the tables containing the information we need aren't directly related so they don't share a common attribute. For example, suppose we ask the query to find the names and prices of items that are made from ingredients supplied by Veggies_R_Us. Step 1 tells us we need information in the *items* and *vendors* tables. However, we cannot complete Step 2 because *items* and *vendors* have no common attributes. The solution is to use additional tables to connect *items* with *vendors*. The *madewith* table pairs items and vendors. The foreign key constraints tell us how they are connected.

Our FROM clause now contains four tables: *items, madewith, ingredients,* and *vendors.* As in Section 5.1, we apply join predicates over the common attributes to find rows where the items are made with ingredients supplied by the vendor. In other words, we want all of the rows to meet three criteria:

1. *items.itemid* matches *madewith.itemid*

2. *madewith.ingredientid* matches *ingredients.ingredientid*

3. *ingredients.vendorid* matches *vendors.vendorid*

All of these constraints can be part of a single WHERE clause. Once we have the table constructed, all that remains is the selection of the name attribute of the *items* table and the additional selection criteria of the company named Veggies_R_Us.

Query 5.6 Find the name and price of all items using an ingredient supplied by Veggies_R_Us

```
SELECT DISTINCT mi.name, price
FROM ingredients i, vendors v, items mi, madewith mw
WHERE i.vendorid = v.vendorid AND i.ingredientid = mw.ingredientid AND
      mw.itemid = mi.itemid AND companyname = 'Veggies_R_Us';
```

name	price
Chicken Salad	2.85
Fruit Plate	3.99
Garden Salad	0.99

[3 row(s)]

Note that we know the attributes *itemid* and *vendorid* refer to the same real-world objects because of the foreign key constraints. Without these constraints, or similar additional information, no assumptions should be made about attribute compatibility. For example, the *name* attribute in *items* and the *name* attribute in *ingredients* do not have anything to do with each other and will rarely be used as join predicates.

In general, whenever we join N tables to answer a query, we will need N−1 join predicates in the WHERE clause. In our two-table query examples, we use one join predicate. In Query 5.6, we join four tables, requiring three join predicates. Leaving out a join predicate is a common error. The result of leaving out a join predicate is almost always an incorrect result. One sign of join predicate omission is too many rows in the answer. We explain why this happens in Section 5.6.

As with our previous queries, once we have figured out how to construct the needed table, we can then process this new table with any of our single table techniques. Let's look at a few examples.

Query 5.7   Find the cost of the most expensive item that uses an ingredient supplied by each vendor

```
SELECT companyname, MAX(price) AS price
FROM ingredients i, vendors v, items mi, madewith mw
WHERE i.vendorid = v.vendorid AND i.ingredientid = mw.ingredientid AND
      mw.itemid = mi.itemid
GROUP BY v.vendorid, companyname;
```

companyname	price
Spring Water Supply	0.99
"Fruit Eating" Friends	3.99
Veggies_R_Us	3.99
Don's Dairy	3.99
Ed's Dressings	3.99

[5 row(s)]

Query 5.8   Find all of the vendors who supply an ingredient used to make a fruit plate

```
SELECT DISTINCT(companyname)
FROM ingredients i, vendors v, items mi, madewith mw
WHERE i.vendorid = v.vendorid AND i.ingredientid = mw.ingredientid AND
      mw.itemid = mi.itemid AND mi.name = 'Fruit Plate';
```

companyname
Don's Dairy
Ed's Dressings
"Fruit Eating" Friends
Veggies_R_Us

[4 row(s)]

5.4 Self-Join: Joining a Table with Itself

In some situations, we need to connect a table to itself. Suppose we want to find all of the vendors that were referred to us by Veggies_R_Us. To answer this, we must first find the vendor ID of Veggies_R_Us. Next we must find all of the vendors with a *referredby* value matching that ID. To answer both of these questions at the same time, we need two copies of the *vendors* table—one to find the *vendorid* of Veggies_R_Us and the other to find all vendors referred by that vendor ID.

     SQL handles this situation by allowing two copies of the same table to appear in the FROM clause. The only requirement is that each copy of the table must be given a distinct alias to distinguish between the copies of the table. Therefore, our FROM clause has vendors v1, vendors v2. Now the query table–building process proceeds exactly as if we had two distinct copies of the *vendors* table. We want only rows in which the *referredby* value of v2 matches the *vendorid* from v1. Joining a table to itself is called a *self-join*.

Query 5.9 Find all of the vendors referred by Veggies_R_Us

```
SELECT v2.companyname
FROM vendors v1, vendors v2
WHERE v1.vendorid = v2.referredby AND v1.companyname = 'Veggies_R_Us';
```

companyname
Don's Dairy
Flavorful Creams

[2 row(s)]

In this query, we use a join over attributes with different names. This is correct because the attributes refer to the same domain—vendor IDs.

5.5 Example Joins

We now give some examples to show the two-step process for creating joins.

Query 5.10 List all the items for each meal

```
SELECT i.name, m.name
FROM items i, meals m, partof p
WHERE i.itemid = p.itemid and p.mealid = m.mealid;
```

name	name
Chicken Salad	Chicken N Suds
Soda	Chicken N Suds

Continued on next page

Query 5.10 (cont'd)

Garden Salad	Vegan Eatin'
Fruit Salad	Vegan Eatin'
Water	Vegan Eatin'

[5 row(s)]

The names of items appear in the answer, so Step 1 requires the *items* table to be in our query. Likewise, meals appears in the answer, so the *meals* table must be in the query. For Step 2, because *meals* and *items* share no common attributes, we need a join table, specifically *partof,* to complete the join.

As far as SQL is concerned, the join attributes are not special. We can compare any two attributes. However, join attributes should refer to the same real-world objects or the query must require the comparison.

Query 5.11 Find all ingredients with an inventory equal to the quantity required to make some item

```
SELECT i.name
FROM ingredients i, madewith mw
WHERE i.ingredientid = mw.ingredientid AND inventory = quantity;
```

name
Orange

[1 row(s)]

Step 1 requires the ingredients (for the result) and madewith (to filter the results) tables. For Step 2, we can use the common *ingredientid* column to find which ingredients are used in an item, but that is not enough. We also need the fact that the inventory of the item is equal to the quantity required. This is an example of a compound join predicate, because we are using multiple attributes to join the tables together.

Query 5.12 might sound like an unusual query, but a data entry error—entering the vendor company name for the ingredient name—could require a query like this to find. Fortunately, no such errors are present in our database, so the results are empty.

Query 5.12 Find all ingredients with the same name as a vendor

```
SELECT ingredientid
FROM ingredients, vendors
WHERE name = companyname;
```

ingredientid

[0 row(s)]

Query 5.12 also has a different join predicate. From Step 1, we know we need the *vendors* table and the *ingredients* table. In our other queries (such as Query 5.1) over these two tables we used the common *vendorid* column to connect the two tables together. However, in this case, that might miss some errors in the data. Therefore, we use the join predicate suggested by the query of matching the name of the ingredient and the vendor's company name. If any match, we have our error.

5.6 How Does a Join Really Work?

As Query 5.12 indicates, Step 2 in our process is the difficult part. In this section, we look at the details of performing joins. This is not always obvious, but it is important in order to understand how to connect tables together.

SQL begins in the FROM clause. When more than one table is listed in the FROM clause, the first step of query processing is to create one table from the multiple tables listed. To do this, SQL pairs every row in the first table with every row in the second table. SQL then pairs every row in this new table with every row in the third table, and so on. This combination is called a *Cartesian product* or a *cross product*. Let's look at an example.

Query 5.13 Cartesian product

```
SELECT *
FROM meals, partof;
```

mealid	name	mealid	itemid	quantity	discount
CKSDS	Chicken N Suds	CKSDS	CHKSD	1	0.02
CKSDS	Chicken N Suds	CKSDS	SODA	1	0.10
CKSDS	Chicken N Suds	VGNET	GDNSD	1	0.03
CKSDS	Chicken N Suds	VGNET	FRTSD	1	0.01
CKSDS	Chicken N Suds	VGNET	WATER	1	0.00
VGNET	Vegan Eatin'	CKSDS	CHKSD	1	0.02
VGNET	Vegan Eatin'	CKSDS	SODA	1	0.10
VGNET	Vegan Eatin'	VGNET	GDNSD	1	0.03
VGNET	Vegan Eatin'	VGNET	FRTSD	1	0.01
VGNET	Vegan Eatin'	VGNET	WATER	1	0.00

[10 row(s)]

Here each row from *meals* is paired with each row from *partof.* Note that the result table has all of the attributes from both tables in the FROM clause.

The result of a cross product is a set of rows and columns, just like a table, so all of the previous WHERE conditions and SELECT clauses can be applied. We can apply the join predicate *meals.mealid = partof.mealid*. We can use an aggregate function such as COUNT(*), *with* or *without* a join predicate. Similarly, we can use ORDER BY, GROUP BY,

HAVING, or anything else that can be applied to a table with this schema. As an example, consider Query 5.14.

Query 5.14 Find the IDs of the items in each meal

```
SELECT m.name AS meal, i.name AS item
FROM meals m, partof p, items i
WHERE m.mealid = p.mealid AND i.itemid = p.itemid;
```

meal	item
Chicken N Suds	Chicken Salad
Chicken N Suds	Soda
Vegan Eatin'	Garden Salad
Vegan Eatin'	Fruit Salad
Vegan Eatin'	Water

[5 row(s)]

We apply our same two-step process to answer the query. Step 1 tells us we need the *meals* and *items* tables. Placing them in the FROM clause creates the Cartesian product. Step 2 tells us we need the *partof* table to connect them, so we add it to the FROM clause, creating the cross product of all three tables. Query 5.14 finds the names of the items in each meal by reporting the rows where *meals.mealid = partof.mealid* and *partof.itemid = items.itemid*. Our new table now has all of the attributes from all three tables, including duplicate meal and item IDs, so the last step is to limit the attributes in the final result with the SELECT list.

What happens with a self-join? It's really not a special case. As before, SQL computes the cross product of the two copies of the table. Query 5.15 is a small example of a table crossed with itself.

Query 5.15 Self-Cartesian product

```
SELECT *
FROM meals m1, meals m2;
```

mealid	name	mealid	name
CKSDS	Chicken N Suds	CKSDS	Chicken N Suds
CKSDS	Chicken N Suds	VGNET	Vegan Eatin'
VGNET	Vegan Eatin'	CKSDS	Chicken N Suds
VGNET	Vegan Eatin'	VGNET	Vegan Eatin'

[4 row(s)]

The Cartesian product of even small tables can be very large. In fact, the total number of rows is equal to the product of the number of rows in each of the tables. Making the results even larger, every attribute of every table is present in every row. Fortunately for us, although the Cartesian product is large, the DBMS uses query optimization to avoid having to create all of it at once. If the Cartesian product cannot be avoided, your performance may be very poor. If you are executing a query with a potentially large join and the performance is poor, make sure that your query is not forcing the DBMS to perform a Cartesian product.

Earlier we said that a join of N tables needs N−1 join predicates. What would happen in Query 5.14 if we missed one of the join predicates?

Query 5.16 Missing join predicate

```
SELECT m.name AS meal, i.name AS item
FROM meals m, partof p, items i
WHERE i.itemid = p.itemid;
```

meal	item
Chicken N Suds	Chicken Salad
Vegan Eatin'	Chicken Salad
Chicken N Suds	Soda
Vegan Eatin'	Soda
Chicken N Suds	Garden Salad
Vegan Eatin'	Garden Salad
Chicken N Suds	Fruit Salad
Vegan Eatin'	Fruit Salad
Chicken N Suds	Water
Vegan Eatin'	Water

[10 row(s)]

Here every item used in any meal is paired with *every* meal, not just the meals the item is used in. Of course, this isn't the answer we wanted.

5.7 Theta Joins: Generalizing Join Predicates

The tables built so far have been based on the notions of equality in the join predicates. This is the most common type of join, often used when there is a referential integrity constraint between tables. This type of join is called an *equijoin*. However, we are not limited to using only the = operator in join predicates. A join where the join predicate uses any of the comparison operators is called a *theta join*. Note that an equijoin is a special case of a theta join.

Let's make a slight change to Query 5.11 to generate Query 5.17.

Query 5.17 Find all of the items and ingredients where we do not have enough of the ingredient to make three items

```
SELECT items.name, ing.name
FROM items, madewith mw, ingredients ing
WHERE items.itemid = mw.itemid AND mw.ingredientid = ing.ingredientid AND
        3 * mw.quantity > ing.inventory;
```

name	name
Garden Salad	Tomato
Fruit Plate	Tomato
Fruit Plate	Orange

[3 row(s)]

We follow the same two-step process to answer theta joins as with equijoins. Step 1 for Query 5.17 requires the tables *items, madewith,* and *ingredients.* Step 2 has the foreign key connections of matching *itemid* and *ingredientid,* but it also contains the inequality between the amount needed to make three of the items and the current inventory. This requires the last join predicate.

Query 5.18 is another example of a theta join.

Query 5.18 Find the name of all items that cost more than the garden salad

```
SELECT a.name
FROM items a, items q
WHERE a.price > q.price AND q.name = 'Garden Salad';
```

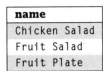

name
Chicken Salad
Fruit Salad
Fruit Plate

[3 row(s)]

To answer Query 5.18, Step 1 tells us we need two copies of the *items* table. However, instead of matching items with the same *itemid* values, we want to compare those items that have a price greater than the price of the garden salad. Within the WHERE clause, we use a join predicate that compares the price of the garden salad item and the price of all other items. To help with the query construction, we use the alias 'a' to represent the answer copy of the *items* table, and the alias 'q' to represent the question or Garden Salad part.

We can likewise extend Query 5.18 to Query 5.19. This simply combines the table we built in Query 5.6 with Query 5.18.

Query 5.19 Find all of the ingredients that are in items and cost more than the garden salad

```
SELECT DISTINCT(i.name)
FROM items a, items q, madewith m, ingredients i
WHERE a.price > q.price AND q.name = 'Garden Salad' AND
      i.ingredientid = m.ingredientid AND m.itemid = a.itemid;
```

name
Cheese
Chicken
Crouton
Grape
Lettuce
Orange
Secret Dressing
Tomato
Watermelon

[9 row(s)]

Finally, the theta join allows us to provide a "ranking" for values without ties. We can do a theta self-join to compare a value in a table with all of the other values. If we use >= as the join predicate for any given value, we can count the number of times another value is less. This is the number of values ahead of the given value in the ranking. Query 5.20 is an example.

Query 5.20 Alphabetic ranking of ingredients

```
SELECT i1.name, COUNT(*) AS rank
FROM ingredients i1, ingredients i2
WHERE i1.name >= i2.name
GROUP BY i1.ingredientid, i1.name
ORDER BY rank;
```

name	rank
Cheese	1
Chicken	2
Crouton	3
Grape	4
Lettuce	5
Orange	6
Pickle	7
Secret Dressing	8

Continued on next page

Query 5.20	(cont'd)
Soda	9
Tomato	10
Water	11
Watermelon	12

[12 row(s)]

Note that this does not work with ties, but your DBMS may provide a better function for ranking.

5.8   JOIN Operator

Joining tables together is so common that SQL provides a JOIN operator for use in the FROM clause. There are several variants of the JOIN, which we explore here.

5.8.1   INNER JOIN

INNER JOIN is identical to the joins we have discussed so far. INNER JOIN takes two tables and a join specification describing how the two tables should be joined. The join specification may be specified as a condition. The condition follows the keyword ON. Compare Query 5.21 with the Query 5.2.

Query 5.21 Find the names of the ingredients supplied to us by Veggies_R_Us

```
SELECT name
FROM ingredients i INNER JOIN vendors v ON i.vendorid = v.vendorid
WHERE v.companyname = 'Veggies_R_Us';
```

name
Lettuce
Pickle
Tomato

[3 row(s)]

We follow the exact same two-step process with the INNER JOIN syntax as with the join predicates in the WHERE clause. The only difference is the syntax. Compare the theta self-join in Query 5.22 with Query 5.18.

Query 5.22 Find the name of all items that cost more than the garden salad

```
SELECT i1.name
FROM items i1 INNER JOIN items i2 ON i1.price > i2.price
WHERE i2.name = 'Garden Salad';
```

name
Chicken Salad
Fruit Salad
Fruit Plate

[3 row(s)]

It is common to join tables over attributes with the same name. Thus, SQL provides a shorthand for this type of join. The USING clause lists those attributes common to both tables that must have the same value to be in the result. Here USING is identical to the equijoin. Note that INNER may be omitted because it is the default type of JOIN. Query 5.23 is a modified version (different SELECT clause to demonstrate a subtlety) of Queries 5.21 and 5.2.

Query 5.23 Find the names of the ingredients supplied to us by Veggies_R_Us

```
SELECT companyname, name, vendorid
FROM ingredients JOIN vendors v USING (vendorid)
WHERE v.companyname = 'Veggies_R_Us';
```

companyname	name	vendorid
Veggies_R_Us	Lettuce	VGRUS
Veggies_R_Us	Pickle	VGRUS
Veggies_R_Us	Tomato	VGRUS

[3 row(s)]

The one subtle difference between Query 5.21 and Query 5.23 is that after performing the Cartesian product, Query 5.21 includes all attributes from both tables, *including both copies of the attributes used for matching.* Because USING requires equal values for the specified attributes, Query 5.23 only needs to include one copy of the attribute. This is why *vendorid* must be table qualified in Query 5.21 but not in Query 5.23.

JOIN returns a new table that can be used by another JOIN, as in Query 5.24.

Query 5.24 Find the names of items that are made from ingredients supplied by the company Veggies_R_Us

```
SELECT DISTINCT(i.name)
FROM vendors JOIN ingredients USING (vendorid) JOIN
    madewith USING(ingredientid) JOIN items i USING (itemid)
WHERE companyname = 'Veggies_R_Us';
```

Continued on next page

Query 5.24 (cont'd)

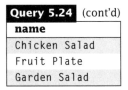

name
Chicken Salad
Fruit Plate
Garden Salad

[3 row(s)]

The new table created in the FROM clause may be used with any other SQL clauses, as in Query 5.25.

Query 5.25 Find the number of items in each meal that were added to the menu in 2000 or 2001

```
SELECT m.mealid, COUNT(i.itemid) AS ct
FROM meals m JOIN partof p USING (mealid) JOIN
    items i ON p.itemid = i.itemid
WHERE EXTRACT(YEAR FROM dateadded) BETWEEN 2000 AND 2001
GROUP BY m.mealid
ORDER BY ct;
```

mealid	ct
VGNET	2

[1 row(s)]

Note that the WHERE clause is not needed because the EXTRACT predicate could be part of the ON. However, because the date is not part of the join predicate (it is a filter on the table resulting from the join), we place it in the WHERE clause. Of course, your standard practices should dictate your choice of locations. One problem is that this query does not return meals containing no items added in 2000 or 2001. We'll see how to fix this in Section 5.8.2.

5.8.2 OUTER JOIN

In Query 5.25, we found the meals that added at least one item in 2000 and 2001. However, we might also want the meals that did not add an item. This is an example where we want not only the rows that satisfy the join predicate, but also the rows that do not satisfy it. Chapter 6 provides one technique for finding those results, but SQL also includes a join variant that does so. This variant is called the OUTER JOIN.

There are three types of OUTER JOIN: FULL, LEFT, and RIGHT. We begin with FULL OUTER JOIN. FULL OUTER JOIN includes three kinds of rows:

1. All rows that satisfy the join predicate (same as INNER JOIN)

2. All rows from the first table that don't satisfy the join predicate for any row in the second table

3. All rows from the second table that don't satisfy the join predicate for any row in the first table

Just like an INNER JOIN, an OUTER JOIN returns all of the columns in both tables. Because a row that satisfies Condition 2 has no values for attributes from the second table, the OUTER JOIN uses *NULL* for those values. Similarly, a row satisfying Condition 3 has *NULL* values for all attributes from the first table.

Like the INNER JOIN, the join predicate can be specified using either ON or USING. Similar to INNER, the keyword OUTER is not required, but one of FULL, LEFT, or RIGHT must be included. Query 5.26 is a simple example. Compare its results with Query 5.1.

| **Query 5.26** | For each ingredient, find its name and the name and ID of the vendor that supplies them. Include vendors who supply no ingredients and ingredients supplied by no vendors |

```
SELECT companyname, i.vendorid, i.name
FROM vendors v FULL JOIN ingredients i ON v.vendorid = i.vendorid;
```

companyname	vendorid	name
Don's Dairy	DNDRY	Cheese
Don's Dairy	DNDRY	Chicken
Ed's Dressings	EDDRS	Crouton
Flavorful Creams	NULL	NULL
"Fruit Eating" Friends	FRTFR	Grape
"Fruit Eating" Friends	FRTFR	Watermelon
"Fruit Eating" Friends	FRTFR	Orange
Spring Water Supply	SPWTR	Water
Spring Water Supply	SPWTR	Soda
Veggies_R_Us	VGRUS	Lettuce
Veggies_R_Us	VGRUS	Pickle
Veggies_R_Us	VGRUS	Tomato
NULL	NULL	Secret Dressing

[13 row(s)]

Query 5.26 includes the vendors with the ingredients they provide, the vendors who do not provide an ingredient, and the ingredients not supplied by a vendor. Notice the row containing Flavorful Creams as a vendor. This row is not in Query 5.1 because Flavorful Creams does not supply any ingredients. All of the attributes that are derived from the *ingredients* table are *NULL*. Likewise, the Secret Dressing ingredient row is not in Query 5.1, and it contains *NULL* for all columns coming from the *vendors* table.

Because the *vendorid* is the primary key of the *vendors* table, any rows retrieved from the *vendors* table cannot contain a *NULL* value for that field. We can use this information to discover which rows in *ingredients* do not match a row in *vendors*. If *vendorid* is *NULL,* then there is no match. Similarly, we can determine which vendors do not supply us with any ingredients. If the primary key of the *ingredients* table has a *NULL* value, then we have found a *vendors* row with no matching ingredients row.

Query 5.27 Find the vendors who do not provide us with any ingredients

```
SELECT companyname
FROM vendors v LEFT JOIN ingredients i USING(vendorid)
WHERE ingredientid IS NULL;
```

companyname
Flavorful Creams

[1 row(s)]

In Query 5.27, we use a LEFT JOIN. This means the table on the left side (*vendors*) would have all rows included in the results even if it did not satisfy the join predicate. However, rows from *ingredients* would only be included if they satisfied the join predicate (just like an INNER JOIN). In other words, vendors who do not provide us any ingredients are included, and the *ingredientid* column for such rows is *NULL*. As with INNER JOIN, if the name of the join attributes match, we can use the USING clause with OUTER JOIN.

Now we are ready to use OUTER JOIN to improve Query 5.25. This time, we want all meals included, even those containing no items added in 2000 or 2001.

Query 5.28 Find the number of items in each meal that were added to the menu in 2000 or 2001

```
SELECT m.mealid, COUNT(i.itemid) AS ct
FROM partof p JOIN items i ON p.itemid = i.itemid AND
    EXTRACT(YEAR FROM dateadded) BETWEEN 2000 AND 2001 RIGHT JOIN meals m USING (mealid)
GROUP BY m.mealid
ORDER BY ct;
```

mealid	ct
CKSDS	0
VGNET	2

[2 row(s)]

Let's look at Query 5.28 closely. First, it performs the INNER JOIN between *partof* and *items* with the join predicate `p.itemid=i.itemid AND EXTRACT(YEAR FROM dateadded) BETWEEN 2000 AND 2001`. The result of that (with only the important columns retained) is in Query 5.29.

Query 5.29 Partial result of Query 5.28

```
SELECT p.mealid, i.itemid
FROM partof p JOIN items i ON p.itemid = i.itemid AND
    EXTRACT(YEAR FROM dateadded) BETWEEN 2000 AND 2001;
```

Query 5.29 (cont'd)

mealid	itemid
VGNET	GDNSD
VGNET	FRTSD

[2 row(s)]

Next, the result of Query 5.29 is combined in a RIGHT OUTER JOIN with the *meals* table. Because the ID of "Chicken N Suds" is not in the results of Query 5.29, it is included with *NULL* for the missing values, as seen in Query 5.30.

Query 5.30 More partial results of Query 5.28

```
SELECT m.mealid, i.itemid
FROM partof p JOIN items i ON p.itemid = i.itemid AND
     EXTRACT(YEAR FROM dateadded) BETWEEN 2000 AND 2001 RIGHT JOIN meals m USING (mealid);
```

mealid	itemid
CKSDS	NULL
VGNET	FRTSD
VGNET	GDNSD

[3 row(s)]

The final results are obtained by applying the GROUP BY and ORDER BY clauses and the COUNT aggregate function, as discussed in Chapter 4.

There is one thing to note about Query 5.28 as opposed to Query 5.25. In Query 5.25 we put

```
EXTRACT(YEAR FROM dateadded) BETWEEN 2000 AND 2001
```

in the WHERE clause, but in Query 5.28 it *must* go in the FROM clause, although it isn't really a join predicate. The reason for the change is that INNER JOIN returns the same results no matter which order we execute join predicates and predicates that apply to only one table. OUTER JOIN does not, as evidenced by Query 5.28.

5.8.3 NATURAL JOIN

By now we've done enough join queries that you may have noticed we often use equality predicates where both tables contain attribute(s) using the same name. This is a common join query. In fact, it is so common that it is often called the *natural join*. Again, to simplify the syntax, SQL has a NATURAL modifier for both the inner and outer joins. With this modifier present, we don't need a join specification, so the ON or USING clauses are not needed. Once more, we present the answer to Query 5.2, this time using NATURAL JOIN.

Query 5.31 Find the names of the ingredients supplied to us by Veggies_R_Us

```
SELECT name
FROM ingredients NATURAL JOIN vendors
WHERE companyname = 'Veggies_R_Us';
```

name
Lettuce
Pickle
Tomato

[3 row(s)]

As with USING, the NATURAL JOIN eliminates the duplicate copy of the join attribute. The NATURAL modifier applies to outer joins as well. Compare Query 5.32 with Query 5.27.

Query 5.32 Find the vendors who do not provide us with any ingredients

```
SELECT companyname
FROM vendors v NATURAL LEFT JOIN ingredients i
WHERE ingredientid IS NULL;
```

companyname
Flavorful Creams

[1 row(s)]

Beware! NATURAL JOIN requires equality of *all* attributes with the same name. Compare Query 5.33 with Query 5.6.

Query 5.33 **INCORRECT!** Find the names of items that are made from ingredients supplied by Veggies_R_Us

```
SELECT name
FROM vendors NATURAL JOIN ingredients NATURAL JOIN madewith NATURAL JOIN items
WHERE companyname = 'Veggies_R_Us';
```

name

[0 row(s)]

Why doesn't this work? The *items* and *ingredients* table both contain an attribute *name*. Thus, NATURAL JOIN requires that the name of the ingredient also match the name of the item. Note that if the tables contain no matching attribute names, the NATURAL JOIN performs a Cartesian product.

5.8.4 CROSS JOIN

SQL also provides a CROSS JOIN. It computes the cross product of two tables. We cannot use OUTER, NATURAL, USING, or ON with CROSS JOINS. Note that this is the same behavior as using a comma-delimited list of tables in the FROM clause. Compare Query 5.34 to Query 5.13.

Query 5.34 Cartesian product

```
SELECT *
FROM meals CROSS JOIN partof;
```

mealid	name	mealid	itemid	quantity	discount
CKSDS	Chicken N Suds	CKSDS	CHKSD	1	0.02
CKSDS	Chicken N Suds	CKSDS	SODA	1	0.10
CKSDS	Chicken N Suds	VGNET	GDNSD	1	0.03
CKSDS	Chicken N Suds	VGNET	FRTSD	1	0.01
CKSDS	Chicken N Suds	VGNET	WATER	1	0.00
VGNET	Vegan Eatin'	CKSDS	CHKSD	1	0.02
VGNET	Vegan Eatin'	CKSDS	SODA	1	0.10
VGNET	Vegan Eatin'	VGNET	GDNSD	1	0.03
VGNET	Vegan Eatin'	VGNET	FRTSD	1	0.01
VGNET	Vegan Eatin'	VGNET	WATER	1	0.00

[10 row(s)]

5.9 Join Strategies

The different join strategies presented here are fairly interchangeable. This means that (in general) you may use whichever technique you want. We present a few guidelines to help you make the right choice.

Rule 1: Use OUTER JOIN *only* if you need to include nonmatching rows. OUTER JOIN will never produce a smaller result than INNER JOIN and therefore will never be faster.

Rule 2: *NEVER* use NATURAL JOIN when tables contain common attributes that you do not want to join. This will lead to incorrect results.

Rule 3: The USING clause and NATURAL JOIN will not match rows where the corresponding attributes contain *NULL* values. Either the WHERE clause or the ON clause must be used instead.

Rule 4: When the same attribute name is in multiple tables, SQL requires that you use the table qualifier to distinguish them.

The following are some general guidelines for your other choices:

Policy: If you are working in a group and the group has a policy about the style of join to use, follow it. If the group does not have a policy, try to create one. Maintaining SQL queries is significantly easier than maintaining code (primarily because SQL queries are shorter), but common practice is important in maintenance of all programming projects.

Performance: The execution differences between the various join techniques in this chapter should be small. However, your DBMS may do better on a particular query with one type of join as opposed to another. If your performance is not what you want, changing the type of join might help.

Preference: If there is no policy and there are no performance differences, then the choice is primarily personal preference. The join technique that most appeals to you is probably the one you understand the best and, therefore, the one you are most likely to use correctly.

5.10   Wrap Up

Joins are common in data processing applications. They allow us to combine different tables together and perform complex queries on the results. We will see in later chapters additional techniques for answering these queries, but joins are commonly used.

There are two different syntaxes for performing joins. The first uses a comma-delimited list of tables in the FROM clause and join predicates in the WHERE clause. This syntax has the advantage of relieving us from worrying about commutativity and associativity, but it is not as intuitive to all users. The second syntax uses the JOIN keyword in the FROM clause. An INNER JOIN is similar to the first JOIN syntax, but we can also use OUTER JOIN, which includes not only the matching rows but also the nonmatching rows.

It is important to understand not only the syntax, but also the semantics of what is happening during join processing. Poorly constructed joins can waste large amounts of computing resources.

Review Questions

1. Table *A(A1, A2, A3)* has 5 rows, and table *B(B1, B2)* has 10 rows. Consider the following query:

   ```
   SELECT *
   FROM A, B;
   ```

   The number of rows in the result table is _____, and the number of attributes is _____.

2. To join three tables, we need _____ join predicates.

3. What does the first step in designing a join query determine?

4. What is the second step in designing a join query?

5. **True/False** A foreign key constraint is a good clue for a join predicate.

6. **True/False** All attributes with the same name should always be in a join predicate.

7. **True/False** In a join query, only the join predicates can appear in the WHERE clause.

8. **True/False** In a join query with a GROUP BY clause, the GROUP BY must include an attribute in a join predicate.

9. Provide the FROM clause of a self-join of table *T*.

10. **True/False** Self-joins do not require a join predicate.

11. In the Restaurant Database, what would be the result of the following?

    ```
    SELECT *
    FROM vendors v1 NATURAL JOIN vendors v2;
    ```

12. In the Restaurant Database, provide a theta self-join to rank all items by price, with most expensive first. What happens with ties?

13. In the Restaurant Database, what would be some other examples of "error finding" queries like Query 5.12?

14. Consider Queries 5.35 and 5.36. Query 5.36 can never return a smaller result set, but it can return the same size. Under what conditions is that true?

Query 5.35 INNER JOIN
```
SELECT *
FROM r JOIN r1 USING(pk);
```

Query 5.36 OUTER JOIN
```
SELECT *
FROM r FULL JOIN r1 USING(pk);
```

15. Technically, the requirement of using a primary key in Query 5.27 to find rows that don't satisfy the join predicate is too strong. What is required?

16. INNER JOIN is commutative and associative. That means we can arrange the tables in any order and get the same results. Is this true for FULL OUTER JOIN? LEFT OUTER JOIN?

17. Modify Query 5.28 to put `EXTRACT(YEAR FROM dateadded) BETWEEN 2000 AND 2001 RIGHT JOIN` in the WHERE clause. Explain the results.

18. For the following queries, leave out one of the predicates marked with "***." Repeat for each of the other predicates. What happens? Leave out two or more such predicates. What happens? Obviously, the "***" must be removed from each line for the query to execute.

```
SELECT M.name
FROM ingredients i, madewith w, partof p, meals m
WHERE i.name = 'Lettuce' AND
***    i.ingredientid = w.ingredientid AND
***    m.itemid = p.itemid AND
***    p.mealid = m.mealid;
```

19. What is the result of the following query:

```
SELECT *
FROM ingredients INNER JOIN vendors ON 1=1;
```

Practice

For these exercises, we use the Employees Database presented at the end of Chapter 1. Answer each question with a single SQL statement. Your query must work for any set of data in the Employees Database, not just the set of data we provide.

1. Find the names of all people who work in the Consulting department. Solve it two ways: 1) using only WHERE-based join (i.e., no INNER/OUTER/CROSS JOIN) and 2) with CROSS JOIN.

2. Find the names of all people who work in the Consulting department and who spend more than 20% of their time on the project with ID ADT4MFIA. Solve three ways: 1) using only WHERE-based join (i.e., no INNER/OUTER/CROSS JOIN), 2) using JOIN ON, and 3) using NATURAL JOIN whenever possible and JOIN ON otherwise.

3. Find the total percentage of time assigned to employee Abe Advice. Solve it two ways: 1) using only WHERE-based join (i.e., no INNER/OUTER/CROSS JOIN) and 2) using some form of JOIN.

4. Find the descriptions of all projects that require more than 70% of an employee's time. Solve it two ways: 1) using only WHERE-based join (i.e., no INNER/OUTER/CROSS JOIN) and 2) using some form of JOIN.

5. For each employee, list the employee ID, number of projects, and the total percentage of time for the current projects to which she is assigned. Include employees not assigned to any project.

6. Find the description of all projects with no employees assigned to them.

7. For each project, find the greatest percentage of time assigned to one employee. Solve it two ways: 1) using only WHERE-based join (i.e., no INNER/OUTER/CROSS JOIN) and 2) using some form of JOIN.

8. For each employee ID, find the last name of all employees making more money than that employee. Solve it two ways: 1) using only WHERE-based join (i.e., no INNER/OUTER/CROSS JOIN) and 2) using some form of JOIN.

9. Rank the projects by revenue. Solve it two ways: 1) using only WHERE-based join (i.e., no INNER/OUTER/CROSS JOIN) and 2) using some form of JOIN.

c h a p t e r **6**

Set Queries: UNION, INTERSECT, and EXCEPT

A result table can be thought of as a set[1] of rows. In mathematics, you have probably seen set operators like union ($\cup$) and intersection ($\cap$). SQL has operators that perform similar operations. In SQL, these operators are UNION, INTERSECT, and EXCEPT. Unlike the previous operators that create results from tables, the SQL set operators combine query results to create new results.

6.1 UNION

The UNION operator corresponds to $\cup$ in sets. Where $\cup$ combines two sets, UNION combines two query results. The syntax for UNION is as follows:

```
<left SELECT> UNION [{ALL | DISTINCT}] <right SELECT>
```

The *<left SELECT>* and *<right SELECT>* can be almost any SQL query, provided that the result sets from the left and right SELECT are compatible. Two result sets are compatible if they have the same number of attributes and each corresponding attribute is compatible. Two attributes are compatible if SQL can implicitly cast them to the same type. Let's look at an example.

---

[1]Mathematically, result tables are really bags, not sets, because they allow duplicates.

Query 6.1 Find the first and last names of all store managers and vendor representatives

```
    SELECT repfname AS "First Name", replname AS "Last Name"
    FROM vendors
UNION
    SELECT SUBSTRING(manager FROM 1 FOR POSITION (' ' IN manager)),
        SUBSTRING(manager FROM POSITION (' ' IN manager)+1)
    FROM stores;
```

First Name	Last Name
Candy	Corn
Gilbert	Grape
Greg	Donahoo
Greg	Speegle
Gus	Hing
Jeff	Donahoo
Jeff	Speegle
Man	Ager
Marla	Milker
Sam	Sauce
Sherman	Sherbert

[11 row(s)]

The left SELECT returns the first and last names of the vendors. The right SELECT breaks the store manager's name into two parts at the first space. These two result sets are compatible because they have the same number of attributes (2) and both attributes are character strings. Note that the names of the attributes in the final result table are determined by the left SELECT.

By default, UNION eliminates duplicate values. For duplicate elimination, NULL values are considered a single value.

Query 6.2 Find the list of item prices and ingredient unit prices

```
    SELECT price
    FROM items
UNION
    SELECT unitprice
    FROM ingredients;
```

price
0.00
0.01
0.02
0.03

Query 6.2 (cont'd)

0.04
0.05
0.06
0.45
0.69
0.99
2.85
3.45
3.99
NULL

[14 row(s)]

Note that all duplicate prices are eliminated. To keep duplicates, use UNION ALL. We can use DISTINCT instead of ALL to eliminate duplicate values; however, duplicate elimination is the default behavior so specifying DISTINCT is optional.

UNION combines results in a totally different way from joins. Some queries cannot be answered using joins, but they can be answered with UNION. Query 6.3 is a perfect example. We cannot generate this result with a join.

Query 6.3 Find the names and prices of meals and items

```
    SELECT name, price
    FROM items
UNION
    SELECT m.name, SUM(quantity * price * (1.0 - discount))
    FROM meals m, partof p, items i
    WHERE m.mealid = p.mealid AND p.itemid = i.itemid
    GROUP BY m.mealid, m.name;
```

name	price
Chicken N Suds	3.6840
Chicken Salad	2.85
Fruit Plate	3.99
Fruit Salad	3.45
Garden Salad	0.99
Millennium Salad	NULL
Soda	0.99
Vegan Eatin'	4.3758
Water	0.00

[9 row(s)]

6.2   INTERSECT

The intersection of two sets are all elements that are common to both sets. In SQL, the INTERSECT operator returns all rows that are the same in both results. The syntax for INTERSECT is as follows:

    <left SELECT> INTERSECT [{ALL |DISTINCT}] <right SELECT>

The *<left SELECT>* and *<right SELECT>* must be compatible, as with UNION (see Section 6.1). By default, INTERSECT eliminates duplicates.

| **Query 6.4** | Find all item IDs with ingredients in both the Fruit and Vegetable food groups |

```
SELECT itemid
FROM madewith mw, ingredients ing
WHERE mw.ingredientid = ing.ingredientid and foodgroup = 'Vegetable'
INTERSECT
SELECT itemid
FROM madewith mw, ingredients ing
WHERE mw.ingredientid = ing.ingredientid and foodgroup = 'Fruit';
```

itemid
GDNSD

[1 row(s)]

The ALL modifier can be added to INTERSECT to require SQL to keep duplicates. If the left and right tables have l and r duplicates of a value, v, the number of duplicate values resulting from an INTERSECT ALL is the minimum of l and r. Query 6.5 provides an example.

| **Query 6.5** | Find all food groups in both fruit plates and fruit salads |

```
SELECT foodgroup
FROM madewith m, ingredients i
WHERE m.ingredientid = i.ingredientid AND m.itemid = 'FRTSD'
INTERSECT ALL
SELECT foodgroup
FROM madewith m, ingredients i
WHERE m.ingredientid = i.ingredientid AND m.itemid = 'FRPLT';
```

foodgroup
Fruit
Fruit

[2 row(s)]

Queries 6.6 and 6.7 show the results of both parts of Query 6.5.

Query 6.6 Left SELECT of Query 6.5

```
SELECT foodgroup
FROM madewith m, ingredients i
WHERE m.ingredientid = i.ingredientid AND m.itemid = 'FRTSD';
```

foodgroup
Fruit
Fruit

[2 row(s)]

Query 6.7 Right SELECT of Query 6.5

```
SELECT foodgroup
FROM madewith m, ingredients i
WHERE m.ingredientid = i.ingredientid AND m.itemid = 'FRPLT';
```

foodgroup
Milk
Bread
Fruit
Fruit
Fruit
Fruit

[6 row(s)]

6.3 EXCEPT

Another common set operation is set difference. If R and S are sets, then $R - S$ contains all of the elements in R that are not in S. The EXCEPT operator in SQL is similar, in that it returns the rows in the first result that are not in the second one. The syntax for EXCEPT is as follows:

```
<left SELECT> EXCEPT [ALL | DISTINCT] <right SELECT>
```

The *<left SELECT>* and *<right SELECT>* must be compatible, as with UNION and INTERSECT (see Section 6.1). As with UNION, there are queries that can be answered with EXCEPT that cannot be answered with a join or a union. Usually, these queries are "negative information" queries—that is, queries that are trying to find out information that is not found in the database. Query 6.8 provides an example.

Query 6.8 Find all item IDs of items not made with Cheese

```
    SELECT itemid
    FROM items
EXCEPT
    SELECT itemid
    FROM madewith mw, ingredients ing
    WHERE mw.ingredientid = ing.ingredientid AND ing.name = 'Cheese';
```

itemid
FRTSD
GDNSD
MILSD
SODA
WATER

[5 row(s)]

In some respects, these queries are like Sherlock Holmes' famous maxim, "When you have excluded the impossible, whatever remains, however improbable, must be the truth." The right SELECT produces the item IDs of all items having Cheese as an ingredient. Query 6.9 demonstrates this.

Query 6.9 Right SELECT of Query 6.8

```
SELECT itemid
FROM madewith mw, ingredients ing
WHERE mw.ingredientid = ing.ingredientid and ing.name = 'Cheese';
```

itemid
CHKSD
FRPLT

[2 row(s)]

Because we want the items without cheese, these are the impossible answers. EXCEPT allows us to eliminate them from the set of all possible answers, so what remains is the truth.

Some might be tempted to use Query 6.10 to answer this query, but that would be an error.

Query 6.10 INCORRECT! Find all item IDs of items not made with Cheese

```
SELECT DISTINCT(itemid)
FROM madewith mw, ingredients ing
WHERE mw.ingredientid = ing.ingredientid AND ing.name != 'Cheese';
```

Query 6.10 (cont'd)

itemid
CHKSD
FRPLT
FRTSD
GDNSD
SODA
WATER

[6 row(s)]

Note that this answer is incorrect in two ways:

1. The Millennium Salad is not included. The Millennium Salad is not made with any ingredients, so it clearly does not include cheese. However, because it is not made with any ingredients, it is not in the *madewith* table, so it cannot be in the results of Query 6.10.

2. More importantly, note that the Chicken Salad (itemid CHKSD) is in the results for Query 6.10 and in Query 6.9. How can it have both cheese and no cheese? Obviously, it can't. In fact, the Chicken Salad is made with cheese, but it is also made with chicken, lettuce, and our secret dressing. Those last three rows all satisfy the predicate ing.name != 'Cheese', so the Chicken Salad is in the results. Query 6.10 is actually finding all items made with something besides cheese.

Like UNION and INTERSECT, EXCEPT eliminates duplicates. To keep duplicates, use EXCEPT ALL. If the left and right tables have l and r duplicates of a value, v, the number of duplicate values resulting from an EXCEPT ALL is the minimum of $l - r$ and 0.

Query 6.11 List all the food groups provided by some ingredient that is in the Fruit Plate but not the Fruit Salad

```
SELECT foodgroup
FROM madewith m, ingredients i
WHERE m.ingredientid = i.ingredientid AND m.itemid = 'FRPLT'
EXCEPT ALL
    SELECT foodgroup
    FROM madewith m, ingredients i
    WHERE m.ingredientid = i.ingredientid AND m.itemid = 'FRTSD';
```

foodgroup
Bread
Fruit
Fruit
Milk

[4 row(s)]

As with UNION and INTERSECT, *NULL* values are not considered distinct by EXCEPT when eliminating duplicates.

6.4 Wrap Up

Sets are powerful representations of the way we look at data. UNION operations cannot be performed by any other SQL function. For example, consider a query that finds the first names of customers and company representatives in one column. As such, it is supported by almost all database management systems. Likewise, the EXCEPT operator, used to perform set difference, cannot be performed by JOIN or UNION operations. Thus, it is important for SQL programmers to understand these operators and know how to use them. Note that the INTERSECT operator can be implemented by the EXCEPT operator (see the exercises).

Review Questions

1. Rewrite Query 5.27 to use EXCEPT instead of an OUTER JOIN.

2. From set theory, $R \cap S = R - (R - S)$. Rewrite the following query using EXCEPT instead of INTERSECT.

   ```
   SELECT itemid
   FROM madewith m, ingredients i
   WHERE m.ingredientid = i.ingredientid AND foodgroup='Milk'
   INTERSECT
   SELECT itemid
   FROM madewith m, ingredients i
   WHERE m.ingredientid = i.ingredientid AND foodgroup='Fruit';
   ```

3. If you wanted to use UNION over a NUMERIC(5,2) type and a CHAR(5) type, what could you do to make it work?

4. How many rows are in the result of Query 6.12? What if you used UNION ALL?

   Query 6.12 UNION Review Question

   ```
   SELECT *
   FROM vendors
   UNION
   SELECT *
   FROM vendors;
   ```

5. How many rows are in the result of Query 6.13? What if you used INTERSECT ALL?

   Query 6.13 INTERSECT Review Question

   ```
   SELECT *
   FROM vendors
   INTERSECT
   SELECT *
   FROM vendors;
   ```

6. How many rows are in the result of Query 6.14? What if you used EXCEPT ALL?

   Query 6.14 EXCEPT Review Question

   ```
   SELECT *
   FROM vendors
   EXCEPT
   SELECT *
   FROM vendors;
   ```

7. The OUTER JOIN contains rows that do not satisfy a join predicate. Use EXCEPT to find the rows in vendors that are not in the NATURAL JOIN of *vendors* and *ingredients.*

8. Can you use UNION to combine your answer from the previous question to generate `vendors LEFT OUTER JOIN ingredients`? Explain.

Practice

For these exercises, we use the Employees Database presented at the end of Chapter 1. Answer each question with a single SQL statement. Your query must work for any set of data in the Employees Database, not just the set of data we provide.

1. Find all dates on which projects either started or ended. Eliminate any duplicate or *NULL* dates. Sort your results in descending order.

2. Use INTERSECT to find the first and last name of all employees who both work on the Robotic Spouse and for the Hardware department.

3. Use EXCEPT to find the first and last name of all employees who work on the Robotic Spouse but not for the Hardware department.

4. Find the first and last name of all employees who work on the Download Client project but not the Robotic Spouse project.

5. Find the first and last name of all employees who work on the Download Client project and the Robotic Spouse project.

6. Find the first and last name of all employees who work on either the Download Client project or the Robotic Spouse project.

7. Find the first and last name of all employees who work on either the Download Client project or the Robotic Spouse project but not both.

8. Using EXCEPT, find all of the departments without any projects.

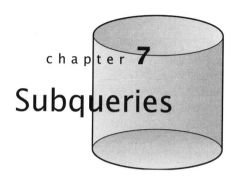

chapter **7**

Subqueries

So far, we've seen joins (Chapter 5) and set operators (Chapter 6) for combining tables together. SQL provides another way to combine tables. You can nest queries within queries. Such an embedded query is called a *subquery.* A subquery computes results that are then used by an outer query. Basically, a subquery acts like any other expression we've seen so far. A subquery can be nested inside the SELECT, FROM, WHERE, and HAVING clauses. You can even nest subqueries inside another subquery.

7.1 What Are Subqueries?

Let's find the names of the ingredients supplied by Veggies_R_Us. In the subquery approach, we think of this query as two operations. The first query (Query 7.1) finds the *vendorid* of Veggies_R_Us:

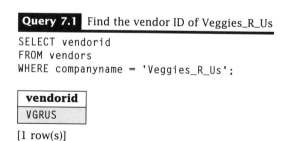

Query 7.1 Find the vendor ID of Veggies_R_Us

```
SELECT vendorid
FROM vendors
WHERE companyname = 'Veggies_R_Us';
```

vendorid
VGRUS

[1 row(s)]

The second query (Query 7.2) uses that *vendorid* in its WHERE clause.

Query 7.2 Find the names of ingredients provided by VGRUS

```
SELECT name
FROM ingredients
WHERE vendorid = 'VGRUS';
```

name
Lettuce
Pickle
Tomato

[3 row(s)]

We combine the two queries by replacing the literal string in Query 7.2 with Query 7.1.

Query 7.3 Find the names of the ingredients supplied by Veggies_R_Us

```
SELECT name
FROM ingredients
WHERE vendorid =
        (SELECT vendorid
         FROM vendors
         WHERE companyname = 'Veggies_R_Us');
```

name
Lettuce
Pickle
Tomato

[3 row(s)]

So what's going on in Query 7.3? SQL starts by executing the inner query. The results are simply plugged into the outer query. Next SQL executes the outer query and creates the result table. In this example, Query 7.1 becomes the *subquery* or the *inner query,* and Query 7.2 becomes the *outer query.* SQL marks the boundaries of a subquery with parentheses. Here are some points to remember when using subqueries:

1. Only the columns of the outermost query can appear in the result table. When creating a new query, the outermost query must contain all of the attributes needed in the answer.

2. There must be some way of connecting the outer query to the inner query. All SQL comparison operators (see Table 2.1) work with subqueries.

3. Subqueries are restricted in what they can return. First, the row and column count must match the comparison operator. Second, the data types must be compatible. Of course, SQL may implicitly convert types.

Let's look again at Query 7.3. The names of the ingredients have to appear in the answer; therefore, the *ingredients* table must be in the outer query. The = operator makes the connection between the queries. Because = expects a single value, the inner query may only return a result with a single attribute and row. In this query, only the *vendorid* attribute is returned, and there is only one vendor named Veggies_R_Us, satisfying the requirements of the = operator. If there happened to be multiple vendors named Veggies_R_Us, SQL would report an error during query execution.

If our subquery returns multiple rows, we must use a different operator. In Query 7.4, we use the IN operator, which expects a subquery result with zero or more rows.

Query 7.4 Find the name of all ingredients supplied by Veggies_R_Us or Spring Water Supply

```
SELECT name
FROM ingredients
WHERE vendorid IN
        (SELECT vendorid
         FROM vendors
         WHERE companyname = 'Veggies_R_Us' OR
               companyname = 'Spring Water Supply');
```

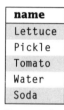

name
Lettuce
Pickle
Tomato
Water
Soda

[5 row(s)]

In Query 7.4, several vendor IDs are returned from the subquery. The outer query then returns all ingredients with vendor IDs in the subquery list.

Suppose you want a list of vendor companies that provide ingredients with a depleted inventory.

Query 7.5 Find the company name of all vendors who provide an ingredient with an inventory of fewer than 50

```
SELECT companyname
FROM vendors
WHERE vendorid IN
        (SELECT vendorid
         FROM ingredients
         WHERE inventory < 50);
```

companyname
Veggies_R_Us
"Fruit Eating" Friends

[2 row(s)]

We begin by finding the ingredients with an inventory less than 50 in the *ingredients* table. Each row in the *ingredients* table contains the ID of the vendor supplying the ingredient. Now we need the company name for each vendor ID returned by the inner query. To do this, we create an outer query that finds the company names of the vendors with a *vendorid* returned from the inner query. Again, we use the IN operator because there may be multiple vendor IDs returned from the subquery.

The outer query works just like any other single table query. For example, it can use aggregation functions as in Query 7.6.

Query 7.6 Find the average unit price for all items provided by Veggies_R_Us

```
SELECT AVG(unitprice) AS avgprice
FROM ingredients
WHERE vendorid IN
        (SELECT vendorid
         FROM vendors
         WHERE companyname = 'Veggies_R_Us');
```

avgprice
0.02666666666666666667

[1 row(s)]

In Query 7.6, the outer query must contain the average price, while the inner query must contain the company name. Note that we may use IN to connect the queries although we know that there's only one Veggies_R_Us.

The inner and outer query may even use the same table. As far as SQL is concerned, there is nothing special about this case—every row in the outer query is compared with the result of the inner query. In Query 7.7, the outer query uses the *vendors* table to obtain the name of the vendor, and the inner query uses the *vendors* table to obtain the *vendorid* of Veggies_R_Us.

Query 7.7 Find the names of all vendors referred to us by Veggies_R_Us

```
SELECT companyname
FROM vendors
WHERE referredby IN
        (SELECT vendorid
         FROM vendors
         WHERE companyname = 'Veggies_R_Us');
```

companyname
Don's Dairy
Flavorful Creams

[2 row(s)]

All of the other comparison operators work with subqueries. Let's try a subquery with BETWEEN in Query 7.8.

Query 7.8	Find all of the ingredients with an inventory within 25% of the average inventory of ingredients

```
SELECT name
FROM ingredients
WHERE inventory BETWEEN
        (SELECT AVG(inventory) * 0.75
          FROM ingredients)
     AND
        (SELECT AVG(inventory) * 1.25
          FROM ingredients);
```

name
Pickle

[1 row(s)]

Query 7.8 also demonstrates the use of a subquery result in an expression.

Subqueries can even be combined with other predicates in the WHERE clause, including other subqueries as demonstrated in Query 7.9.

Query 7.9	Find the companies who were referred by Veggies_R_Us and provide an ingredient in the milk food group

```
SELECT companyname
FROM vendors
WHERE (referredby IN
           (SELECT vendorid
            FROM vendors
            WHERE companyname = 'Veggies_R_Us')) AND
        (vendorid IN
           (SELECT vendorid
            FROM ingredients
            WHERE foodgroup = 'Milk'));
```

companyname
Don's Dairy

[1 row(s)]

The type of the results of a subquery is determined by the context of the query. The standard comparison operators, BETWEEN, IS NULL, and LIKE assume scalar values. When these operators are used, SQL assumes a scalar context, and the result of the subquery is converted into a scalar value. Of course, multiple values returned by query in a scalar context generate an error. Operators such as IN assume a table subquery. The result of a table subquery is always a table. If the result contains only a single value, it is treated as a table with a single row and a single column.

7.2 Multilevel Subquery Nesting

SQL allows many levels of subquery nesting, as in Query 7.10.

Query 7.10 Find the name and price for all items using an ingredient supplied by Veggies_R_Us

```
SELECT name, price
FROM items
WHERE itemid IN
        (SELECT itemid -- Subquery 3
        FROM madewith
        WHERE ingredientid IN
                (SELECT ingredientid -- Subquery 2
                FROM ingredients
                WHERE vendorid =
                        (SELECT vendorid -- Subquery 1
                        FROM vendors
                        WHERE companyname = 'Veggies_R_Us')));
```

name	price
Chicken Salad	2.85
Garden Salad	0.99
Fruit Plate	3.99

[3 row(s)]

The query must return the name and price of the item so the outer query must contain the *items* table. We use the common attribute *itemid* between the *items* and *madewith* tables as the basis for the first subquery. The *madewith* table also has a common attribute with the *ingredients* table, specifically, *ingredientid*. We use that to build the next subquery. The innermost subquery is similar to others we have seen in this chapter.

Let's trace the execution of this SELECT statement:

1. SQL first executes the innermost subquery, Subquery 1. This returns a table containing one column, *vendorid*, with one row (for Veggies_R_Us).

2. Subquery 2 executes next and returns a table containing one column, *ingredientid*, with a row for each ingredient supplied by the vendor ID returned from Subquery 1. Because we know Subquery 1 produces a single row, we can use the = operator to connect Subquery 1 and Subquery 2.

3. Next Subquery 3 executes and returns a table containing one column, *itemid*, with a row for each ingredient returned by Subquery 2.

4. Finally, the outer query executes and returns a table containing two columns, *name* and *price*, with a row for each item returned by Subquery 3.

Finally, it is instructive to compare Query 7.10 to Query 5.6, which both answer a similar query. Query 5.6 contains DISTINCT in the SELECT, but Query 7.10 does not. Why? Query 7.10 executes the outer query *once* for each row, so each name can only appear one time. In Query 5.6, the query is applied to a Cartesian product, so the name may appear multiple times. In fact, without DISTINCT, the name would appear once for each ingredient supplied by Veggies_R_Us used by the item.

There are few restrictions on subqueries. Query 7.11 uses aggregation over a numeric expression in the subquery.

Query 7.11	Find the names and inventory value for all ingredients with an inventory value greater than the total inventory value of all ingredients provided by Veggies_R_Us

```
SELECT name, unitprice * inventory AS stock
FROM ingredients
WHERE (unitprice * inventory) >
        (SELECT SUM(unitprice * inventory) -- Subquery 2
         FROM ingredients
         WHERE vendorid =
                (SELECT vendorid -- Subquery 1
                 FROM vendors
                 WHERE companyname = 'Veggies_R_Us'));
```

name	stock
Chicken	54.00
Soda	3450.00

[2 row(s)]

The innermost query, Subquery 1, finds the vendor ID for Veggies_R_Us. Subquery 2 finds the total value of the inventory from Veggies_R_Us. As before, we can use the = operator because we know that there is only one vendor. Finally, the outer query finds the names and inventory values for all ingredients with an inventory value greater than the total inventory value of all ingredients provided by Veggies_R_Us. Note that all DBMSs have a limit to the depth of nested subqueries, but in commercial-grade databases, that number is usually high enough to perform any query (32 or more).

We can use GROUP BY, HAVING, and ORDER BY with subqueries.

Query 7.12	For each store, find the total sales of items made with ingredients supplied by Veggies_R_Us. Ignore meals and only consider stores with at least two such items sold

```
SELECT storeid, SUM(price) AS sales
FROM orders
WHERE menuitemid IN
        (SELECT itemid -- Subquery 3
         FROM madewith
         WHERE ingredientid IN
                (SELECT ingredientid -- Subquery 2
                 FROM ingredients
                 WHERE vendorid =
                        (SELECT vendorid -- Subquery 1
                         FROM vendors
                         WHERE companyname = 'Veggies_R_Us')))
GROUP BY storeid
HAVING COUNT(*) > 2
ORDER BY sales DESC;
```

Continued on next page

Query 7.12 (cont'd)

storeid	sales
#2STR	14.52
CASTR	10.68
NDSTR	8.97

[3 row(s)]

It is possible to use GROUP BY and HAVING in an inner query as well.

Query 7.13 Find the managers of stores with more than $20 in sales

```
SELECT manager
FROM stores
WHERE storeid IN
        (SELECT storeid
         FROM orders
         GROUP BY storeid
         HAVING SUM(price) > 20);
```

manager
Greg Speegle
Greg Donahoo

[2 row(s)]

Using ORDER BY in a subquery makes little sense because the order of the results is determined by the execution of the outer query.

7.3 Subqueries Using NOT IN

We can also find the outer query rows that do not match anything in the inner query by using NOT IN.

Query 7.14 Find all of the ingredients supplied by someone other than Veggies_R_Us

```
SELECT name
FROM ingredients
WHERE vendorid NOT IN
        (SELECT vendorid
         FROM vendors
         WHERE companyname = 'Veggies_R_Us');
```

Query 7.14 (cont'd)

name
Cheese
Chicken
Crouton
Grape
Water
Soda
Watermelon
Orange

[8 row(s)]

Care is required when using NOT IN to answer this type of question. Every row in the outer query is compared with the results of the inner query. In this case, there is only one vendor for each ingredient. Compare Query 7.15 to Queries 6.8 and 6.10.

Query 7.15 **INCORRECT!** Find all of the items not made with cheese

```
SELECT DISTINCT itemid
FROM madewith
WHERE ingredientid NOT IN
        (SELECT ingredientid
         FROM ingredients
         WHERE name = 'Cheese');
```

itemid
CHKSD
FRPLT
FRTSD
GDNSD
SODA
WATER

[6 row(s)]

Notice that Chicken Salad and Fruit Plate appear in the output, although they both have Cheese. Again, that is because every row in the outer query is compared to the inner query. If one ingredient in the outer row is not Cheese, NOT IN returns true. Also note that Millennium Salad is not in the results of Query 7.15.

Recall from Chapter 2 that we warned you about *NULL* values and NOT IN. Basically, if any element in the NOT IN list is *NULL,* then no rows evaluate to true, and the final result table is empty.

Query 7.16	**INCORRECT!** Find the company name of the small vendors who don't provide any ingredients with large (>100) inventories

```
SELECT companyname
FROM vendors
WHERE vendorid NOT IN
        (SELECT vendorid
         FROM ingredients
         WHERE inventory > 100);
```

companyname

[0 row(s)]

By examining the *ingredients* table, we can see that Flavorful Creams ought to be the answer. What happened? The ingredient Secret Dressing does not have a vendor, so the list of values contains a *NULL*. How do we fix this? Eliminate *NULL* values from the subquery result.

Query 7.17	Find the company name of the small vendors who don't provide any ingredients with large (>100) inventories

```
SELECT companyname
FROM vendors
WHERE vendorid NOT IN
        (SELECT vendorid
         FROM ingredients
         WHERE inventory > 100 AND vendorid IS NOT NULL);
```

companyname
Flavorful Creams

[1 row(s)]

7.4 Subqueries with Empty Results

What happens when a subquery result is empty? The answer depends on what SQL is expecting from the subquery. Let's look at a couple of examples. Remember that the standard comparison operators expect a scalar value; therefore, SQL expects that any sub-queries used with these operators always return a single value. If the subquery result is empty, SQL returns *NULL*.

Query 7.18	Empty subquery returning scalar

```
SELECT companyname
FROM vendors
WHERE referredby =
        (SELECT vendorid
         FROM vendors
         WHERE companyname = 'No Such Company');
```

Query 7.18 (cont'd)

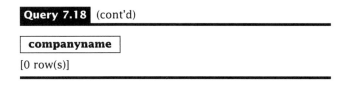

companyname

[0 row(s)]

Here the subquery results are empty so the subquery returns *NULL.* Evaluating the outer query, `referredby = NULL` returns unknown for each row in *vendors.* Consequently, the outer query returns an empty result table.

Let's look at another example. When using the IN operator, SQL expects the subquery to return a table. When SQL expects a table from a subquery and the subquery result is empty, the subquery returns an empty table. IN over an empty table always returns false, therefore NOT IN always returns true.

Query 7.19 Empty subquery returning table

```
SELECT companyname
FROM vendors
WHERE referredby NOT IN
          (SELECT vendorid
           FROM vendors
           WHERE companyname = 'No Such Company');
```

companyname
Veggies_R_Us
Don's Dairy
Flavorful Creams
"Fruit Eating" Friends
Ed's Dressings
Spring Water Supply

[6 row(s)]

In Query 7.19, the subquery returns a table with zero rows (and one column). For every row in the *vendors* table, NOT IN returns true over the subquery, so every row is returned.

7.5 Combining JOIN and Subqueries

Nested queries are not restricted to a single table. Consider Queries 7.10 and 5.6. They return the same results, although they are constructed very differently. Query 7.20 combines the two strategies.

| **Query 7.20** | Find the name and price of all items using an ingredient supplied by Veggies_R_Us |

```
SELECT itemid, price
FROM items
WHERE itemid IN
        (SELECT itemid
         FROM madewith mw, ingredients i, vendors v
         WHERE mw.ingredientid = i.ingredientid AND i.vendorid = v.vendorid
               AND companyname = 'Veggies_R_Us');
```

itemid	price
CHKSD	2.85
GDNSD	0.99
FRPLT	3.99

[3 row(s)]

Remember, all desired attributes must appear in the outermost query, but other combinations of JOIN and subquery are dependent on the practices of your organization and the performance of your DBMS. It is a common tactic for a DBMS to change subqueries like these into joins anyway, so despite the different appearance, there may be no difference in the underlying execution at all.

Similarly, Query 7.21 is another way to answer the same question. It uses a join in the outer query and a subquery.

| **Query 7.21** | Find the name and price of all items using an ingredient supplied by Veggies_R_Us |

```
SELECT DISTINCT itemid, price
FROM items NATURAL JOIN madewith
WHERE ingredientid IN
        (SELECT ingredientid
         FROM ingredients NATURAL JOIN vendors
         WHERE companyname = 'Veggies_R_Us');
```

itemid	price
CHKSD	2.85
FRPLT	3.99
GDNSD	0.99

[3 row(s)]

Notice that DISTINCT is again required to eliminate duplicate results, because each row in the *items* table appears multiple times in the outer query.

7.6 Standard Comparison Operators with Lists Using ANY, SOME, or ALL

We can modify the meaning of the SQL standard comparison operators with ANY, SOME, and ALL so that the operator applies to a list of values instead of a single value. As with

IN, SQL expects the subquery to return a table. The basic syntax is as follows:

<expr> <op> {SOME | ANY | ALL} *<subquery>*

7.6.1 ANY or SOME

The ANY or SOME modifiers determine if the expression evaluates to true for at least one row in the subquery result. Here's how SQL determines the result for ANY or SOME:

Result	Condition
true	if at least one row in *<subquery>* evaluates to true
false	if all rows in *<subquery>* evaluate to false or the subquery returns no rows
unknown	otherwise

Query 7.22 uses > ANY to connect the subquery. The outer query simply returns the name of the item. The inner subquery returns all of the prices of all the items that have salad in their names.

Query 7.22 Find all items that have a price that is greater than any salad item

```
SELECT name
FROM items
WHERE price > ANY
        (SELECT price
         FROM items
         WHERE name LIKE '%Salad');
```

name
Chicken Salad
Fruit Salad
Fruit Plate

[3 row(s)]

Note that without the ANY modifier, SQL would reject this query if we have more than one salad item.

The IN operator is defined to be the same as = ANY. Compare Query 7.4 to Query 7.23.

Query 7.23 Find the name of all ingredients supplied by Veggies_R_Us or Spring Water Supply

```
SELECT name
FROM ingredients
WHERE vendorid = ANY
        (SELECT vendorid
         FROM vendors
         WHERE companyname = 'Veggies_R_Us' OR
               companyname = 'Spring Water Supply');
```

name
Lettuce
Pickle
Tomato
Water
Soda

[5 row(s)]

Be aware of the difference between <> ANY and NOT IN. x <> ANY y returns true if *any* of the values in y are not equal to x. x NOT IN y returns true only if *none* of the values in y are equal to x or if the list y is empty. Compare Queries 7.24 and 7.25.

Query 7.24 Find the name of all ingredients supplied by someone other than Veggies_R_Us or Spring Water Supply

```
SELECT name
FROM ingredients
WHERE vendorid NOT IN
        (SELECT vendorid
         FROM vendors
         WHERE companyname = 'Veggies_R_Us' OR
               companyname = 'Spring Water Supply');
```

name
Cheese
Chicken
Crouton
Grape
Watermelon
Orange

[6 row(s)]

| Query 7.25 | **INCORRECT!** Find the name of all ingredients supplied by someone other than Veggies_R_Us or Spring Water Supply |

```
SELECT name
FROM ingredients
WHERE vendorid <> ANY
        (SELECT vendorid
         FROM vendors
         WHERE companyname = 'Veggies_R_Us' OR
               companyname = 'Spring Water Supply');
```

name
Cheese
Chicken
Crouton
Grape
Lettuce
Pickle
Tomato
Water
Soda
Watermelon
Orange

[11 row(s)]

Note that we were careful in the wording of Query 7.24. The results of Query 7.24 do not include Secret Dressing, so this query does not find all ingredients not supplied by Veggies_R_Us or Spring Water Supply. To answer that query, we have to use a more complicated subquery or an EXCEPT query as shown in Query 7.26.

| Query 7.26 | Find all ingredients not supplied by Veggies_R_Us or Spring Water Supply |

```
SELECT name
FROM ingredients
WHERE ingredientid NOT IN
        (SELECT ingredientid
         FROM ingredients
         WHERE vendorid = ANY
                (SELECT vendorid
                 FROM vendors
                 WHERE companyname = 'Veggies_R_Us' OR
                       companyname = 'Spring Water Supply'));
```

name
Cheese
Chicken

Continued on next page

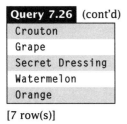

Query 7.26 (cont'd)

Crouton
Grape
Secret Dressing
Watermelon
Orange

[7 row(s)]

7.6.2   ALL

The ALL modifier determines if the expression evaluates to true for *all* rows in the subquery result. Here's how SQL determines the result for ALL:

Result	Condition
true	if every row in *<subquery>* evaluates to true or the subquery returns no rows
false	if at least one row in *<subquery>* evaluates to false
unknown	otherwise

Query 7.27   Find all ingredients that cost at least as much as every ingredient in a salad

```
SELECT name
FROM ingredients
WHERE unitprice >= ALL
        (SELECT unitprice
        FROM ingredients ing NATURAL JOIN madewith mw JOIN
            items i USING(itemid)
        WHERE i.name LIKE '%Salad');
```

name
Chicken
Soda

[2 row(s)]

A common mistake is to assume that the = ALL operator returns true if all of the rows in the outer query match all of the rows in the inner query. This is not the case. A row in the outer query will satisfy the = ALL operator only if it is equal to *all* of the values in the subquery. If the inner query returns multiple rows, each outer query row will only satisfy the = ALL predicate if all rows in the inner query have the same value and that value equals the outer query row value. Notice that the exact same result is achieved by using = alone and ensuring that only a distinct value is returned by the inner query.

In Query 7.23 we saw that = ANY works exactly the same as IN. It should not be surprising that <> ALL works the same as NOT IN. Compare Query 7.24 with Query 7.28.

Query 7.28	Find the name of all ingredients supplied by someone other than Veggies_R_Us or Spring Water Supply

```
SELECT name
FROM ingredients
WHERE vendorid <> ALL
        (SELECT vendorid
         FROM vendors
         WHERE companyname = 'Veggies_R_Us' OR
             companyname = 'Spring Water Supply');
```

name
Cheese
Chicken
Crouton
Grape
Watermelon
Orange

[6 row(s)]

You might be tempted to believe that >= ALL is equivalent to >= (SELECT MAX()), but this is not correct. Let's say we wanted to find the items that cost as much as the most expensive item. Consider Queries 7.29 and 7.30.

Query 7.29	**INCORRECT!** Find the most expensive items

```
SELECT *
FROM items
WHERE price >= ALL
        (SELECT price
         FROM items);
```

itemid	name	price	dateadded

[0 row(s)]

Query 7.30	Find the most expensive items

```
SELECT *
FROM items
WHERE price >=
        (SELECT MAX(price)
         FROM items);
```

itemid	name	price	dateadded
FRPLT	Fruit Plate	3.99	2000-09-02

[1 row(s)]

What's going on here? Recall that for ALL to return true, the condition must be true for *all* rows in the subquery. *NULL* prices evaluate to unknown; therefore, >= ALL evaluates to unknown so the result is empty. Of course, we can solve this problem by eliminating *NULL* prices. However, *NULL* isn't the only problem. What happens when the subquery result is empty? Again, we get different results, as seen in Queries 7.31 and 7.32.

Query 7.31 Empty results with MAX

```
SELECT *
FROM items
WHERE price >=
        (SELECT MAX(price)
         FROM items
         WHERE itemid = 'BADID');
```

itemid	name	price	dateadded

[0 row(s)]

Query 7.32 Empty results with >= ALL

```
SELECT *
FROM items
WHERE price >= ALL
        (SELECT price
         FROM items
         WHERE itemid = 'BADID');
```

itemid	name	price	dateadded
CHKSD	Chicken Salad	2.85	1998-11-13
FRTSD	Fruit Salad	3.45	2000-05-06
GDNSD	Garden Salad	0.99	2001-03-02
MILSD	Millennium Salad	NULL	2002-08-16
SODA	Soda	0.99	2003-02-06
WATER	Water	0.00	2002-05-19
FRPLT	Fruit Plate	3.99	2000-09-02

[7 row(s)]

For ALL, an empty subquery *always* returns true; however, MAX() over an empty result returns *NULL*. It is crucial that you understand the semantics of your query and the capabilities of the operations to make sure the correct result is returned.

7.7 Correlated Subqueries

All of our subquery examples thus far contain simple subqueries. A *simple* subquery can be executed by itself, independent of the outer query. Simple subqueries work by first executing the inner query, filling the resulting values into the outer query, and finally executing the outer query.

Correlated subqueries are not independent of the outer query. Correlated subqueries work by first executing the outer query and then executing the inner query for each row from the outer query. Query 7.33 is a typical example.

Query 7.33 Find the items that contain 3 or more ingredients

```
SELECT itemid, name
FROM items
WHERE (SELECT COUNT(*)
       FROM madewith
       WHERE madewith.itemid = items.itemid) >= 3;
```

itemid	name
CHKSD	Chicken Salad
FRPLT	Fruit Plate

[2 row(s)]

Look closely at the inner query. It cannot be executed independently from the outer query because the WHERE clause references the *items* table from the outer query. Note that in the inner query we must use the table name from the outer query to qualify *itemid*.

How does this execute? Because it's a correlated subquery, the outer query fetches all the rows from the *items* table. For each row from the outer query, the inner query is executed to determine the number of ingredients for the particular *itemid*. For example, the outer query fetches the row for Chicken Salad and then executes Query 7.34.

Query 7.34 Find the number of ingredients in a Chicken Salad

```
SELECT COUNT(*)
FROM madewith
WHERE itemid = 'CHKSD';
```

count
4

[1 row(s)]

The WHERE clause in Query 7.33 is evaluated for the Chicken Salad row in the outer query using the value returned by Query 7.34. Because the WHERE clause evaluates to true, Chicken Salad is added to the final result set.

For you programmer types, think of the implementation as a nested loop. For every row returned by the outer query, the inner query is executed, much like a nested loop structure. We can continue this analogy further. In nested loops, variables declared in the outer loop can be accessed in the inner loop. We can do the same thing with subqueries— values in the row returned by the outer query can be used by the inner query.

Let's try some examples. Query 7.35 is similar to Query 4.17.

Query 7.35   Find all of the vendors who referred two or more vendors

```
SELECT vendorid, companyname
FROM vendors v1
WHERE (SELECT COUNT(*)
       FROM vendors v2
       WHERE v2.referredby = v1.vendorid) >= 2;
```

vendorid	companyname
VGRUS	Veggies_R_Us

[1 row(s)]

Here we use the *vendors* table in both the inner and outer query so we need table aliases.

Let's look at another example. Compare Query 7.36 with Query 7.13.

Query 7.36   Find the managers of stores with more than $20 in sales

```
SELECT manager
FROM stores s
WHERE (SELECT SUM(price)
       FROM orders o
       WHERE o.storeid = s.storeid) > 20;
```

manager
Greg Speegle
Greg Donahoo

[2 row(s)]

Query 7.36 uses a correlated subquery to answer the same question as Query 7.13, which uses a simple query.

7.8   EXISTS

Sometimes we only want to know if there are any rows that satisfy a query. This is especially useful if we want to automatically check a condition, such as the error condition we saw in Query 5.12. In these cases, we can use the EXISTS operator.

```
EXISTS <subquery>
```

EXISTS is a conditional that determines if any rows exist in the result of a subquery. EXISTS returns true if *<subquery>* returns at least one row and false otherwise. The subquery can be simple or correlated; however, most meaningful examples use correlated subqueries.

Query 7.37 Find the meals containing an ingredient from the Milk food group

```
SELECT *
FROM meals m
WHERE EXISTS
    (SELECT *
     FROM partof p JOIN items USING (itemid)
                   JOIN madewith USING (itemid)
                   JOIN ingredients USING (ingredientid)
     WHERE foodgroup = 'Milk' AND m.mealid = p.mealid);
```

mealid	name
CKSDS	Chicken N Suds

[1 row(s)]

For every meal, SQL executes the subquery to find the items with ingredients from the Milk food group. If it finds any such ingredients, then EXISTS returns true, and the meal will be in the results. If not, EXISTS returns false, and the meal will not be in the results.

We can use NOT with EXISTS to determine if something does not exist, as in Query 7.38.

Query 7.38 Find all of the vendors that did not recommend any other vendor

```
SELECT vendorid, companyname
FROM vendors v1
WHERE NOT EXISTS (SELECT *
                 FROM vendors v2
                 WHERE v2.referredby = v1.vendorid);
```

vendorid	companyname
DNDRY	Don's Dairy
SPWTR	Spring Water Supply

[2 row(s)]

7.9   Derived Relations—Subqueries in the FROM Clause

Subqueries can also appear in the FROM clause. Such subqueries create *derived tables* because the subquery forms a table that does not exist in the database. These derived tables may be used like any other table.

Query 7.39	List the name and inventory value of each ingredient in the Fruit or Vegetable food group and its supplier

```
SELECT food, companyname, val
FROM vendors v, (SELECT name, vendorid, unitprice * inventory
                 FROM ingredients i
                 WHERE foodgroup IN ('Fruit', 'Vegetable')) AS d(food, vdrno, val)
WHERE v.vendorid = d.vdrno;
```

food	companyname	val
Tomato	Veggies_R_Us	0.45
Pickle	Veggies_R_Us	32.00
Lettuce	Veggies_R_Us	2.00
Orange	"Fruit Eating" Friends	0.50
Watermelon	"Fruit Eating" Friends	NULL
Grape	"Fruit Eating" Friends	3.00

[6 row(s)]

The subquery generates a derived table containing the name, vendor ID, and inventory value of each ingredient in the specified food groups. Using an expanded form of table aliases, we name the derived table and its attributes. Next, SQL performs the Cartesian product of the *vendors* table and the derived table and applies the join predicate. Recall that the FROM clause is executed first by the DBMS. When the subquery is executed, no rows from the other tables have been retrieved. Thus, the DBMS cannot reference another table inside a subquery in the FROM clause. All derived relations are uncorrelated subqueries.

There are two advantages of derived relations. First, it allows us to break down complex queries into easier to understand parts. For example, Query 7.40 can be answered easily by creating two derived relations. The first subquery contains the number of items provided by Spring Water Supply, and the second subquery contains the number of items provided by all the other vendors.

Query 7.40 Find all vendors who provide more ingredients than Spring Water Supply

```
SELECT p.companyname
FROM (SELECT COUNT(*)
        FROM ingredients i, vendors v
        WHERE i.vendorid = v.vendorid AND
              companyname = 'Spring Water Supply') AS q(items),
     (SELECT companyname, COUNT(*)
        FROM ingredients i, vendors v
        WHERE i.vendorid = v.vendorid
        GROUP BY v.vendorid, companyname) AS p(companyname, items)
WHERE p.items > q.items;
```

companyname
"Fruit Eating" Friends
Veggies_R_Us

[2 row(s)]

As another example, look at Query 7.41. We first find the cost of each item in a derived relation named *itemcost.* It is then straightforward to combine *itemcost* with the *items* table to determine the profit.

Query 7.41 Find the profit margin on each item

```
SELECT name, price-cost AS profit
FROM items theitm, (SELECT itm.itemid, SUM(quantity * unitprice)
                    FROM items itm, madewith mw, ingredients ing
                    WHERE itm.itemid = mw.itemid AND
                          mw.ingredientid = ing.ingredientid
                    GROUP BY itm.itemid) AS itemcost(itemid, cost)
WHERE theitm.itemid = itemcost.itemid;
```

name	profit
Soda	0.30
Garden Salad	0.71
Fruit Plate	2.55
Fruit Salad	3.25
Water	-0.06
Chicken Salad	0.95

[6 row(s)]

The second advantage of derived relations is that we can improve the performance of some queries. If a derived relation is much smaller than the original relation, then the query may execute much faster. CAUTION: The query speed might not improve as a result of several factors that are beyond the scope of this guide. It is a good idea to thoroughly test optimizations before implementing them in a production system.

7.10 Subqueries in the HAVING Clause

We can embed both simple and correlated subqueries in the HAVING clause. This works much like the WHERE clause subqueries, except we are defining predicates on groups rather than rows.

Query 7.42 Find all vendors who provide more ingredients than Spring Water Supply

```
SELECT companyname
FROM vendors v, ingredients i
WHERE i.vendorid = v.vendorid
GROUP BY v.vendorid, companyname
HAVING COUNT(*) > (SELECT COUNT(*)
                   FROM ingredients i, vendors v
                   WHERE i.vendorid = v.vendorid AND
                   companyname = 'Spring Water Supply');
```

companyname
"Fruit Eating" Friends
Veggies_R_Us

[2 row(s)]

This query works by first joining all vendors with their ingredients and grouping by vendor. Next, the simple subquery computes the number of ingredients from the Spring Water Supply and the predicate in the HAVING clause is evaluated for each group. Compare Query 7.42 with Query 7.40.

Correlated subqueries in the HAVING clause allow us to evaluate per-group conditionals.

Query 7.43 Find the average inventory values for each vendor who recommends at least one other vendor

```
SELECT v1.vendorid, AVG(unitprice * inventory)
FROM ingredients JOIN vendors v1 USING (vendorid)
GROUP BY v1.vendorid
HAVING EXISTS (SELECT *
              FROM vendors v2
              WHERE v1.vendorid = v2.referredby);
```

vendorid	avg
EDDRS	4.0000000000000000
FRTFR	1.7500000000000000
VGRUS	11.4833333333333333

[3 row(s)]

This query begins by grouping all of the ingredients together by vendor. Next, for each vendor, the subquery finds the vendors referred by that vendor. If the subquery returns any row, EXISTS returns true and the vendor ID and average inventory value are included in the final result.

Our last query in this section uses a derived relation in a subquery in the HAVING clause.

Query 7.44 Find the managers of stores with greater than average sales

```
SELECT manager
FROM stores s, orders o
WHERE s.storeid = o.storeid
GROUP BY s.storeid, manager
HAVING SUM(price) > (SELECT AVG(sales)
                        FROM (SELECT SUM(price)
                              FROM orders
                              GROUP BY storeid) AS d(sales));
```

manager
Greg Donahoo

[1 row(s)]

In Query 7.44, we need to find the average of the sales of all of the stores. We compute the store sales with a query similar to Query 4.11. As a derived table, we can now use this as any table and easily compute the average of the total sales. We use the HAVING clause to check the sales of the store against this average, and we return the managers for all above-average stores.

7.11 Subset Queries

One of the most challenging types of queries for SQL is one that compares two groups of rows to see if they are the same. These types of queries arise in many different applications. Some examples are as follows:

1. Has a student taken all the courses required for graduation?

2. List the departments and projects for which that department has all of the tools required for the project.

3. Find all the items that contain all of the ingredients provided by a vendor.

In each case, we are comparing two sets of values—the set of courses taken by a student and the set of courses required for graduation; the set of tools required for a project and the set of tools available to the department; and the set of ingredients supplied by a vendor and the set of ingredients in an item. We present two ways of answering these types of queries. In one approach, we use set operators (universal quantification), whereas the second approach uses set cardinality.

7.11.1 Subset Using EXISTS and EXCEPT

Suppose that you want to find all items and vendors such that all ingredients supplied by that vendor are in the item. Note that this is a subset query, since the set of ingredients supplied by a vendor is a subset of the ingredients used in the item. SQL does not provide a subset operator. Fortunately, we can combine SQL operators to evaluate subsets. One definition of a subset, $A \subset B$, is that there does not exist an element in A that is not in B. Looking at it this way, we can turn a subset query into an existence query followed by a set difference query. We must transform our subset query into an equivalent query following this pattern. Our new query is "Find all pairs of items and vendors such that there does not exist any ingredient provided by the vendor that is not used to make the item." As with all nested queries, the outer query must contain all desired attributes; therefore the outer query must be use the *items* and *vendor* tables. Here's a start on our outer query:

```
SELECT mi.name, companyname
FROM items i, vendors v
```

The reworded query also makes it obvious that we want to use the NOT EXISTS clause, but what does not exist? It is an ingredient provided by the vendor that is not in the item. The "not provided" is a clue we are looking for missing information, as in Query 6.8. In Query 6.8, we found all items that did not use cheese. Here, for any particular vendor, we want to find any particular item provided by the vendor but not used in the item. The fact we are looking at a particular vendor and a particular item gives us a clue that this is a correlated subquery.

For complex correlated subqueries, it is often helpful to examine a single case for the subquery. In our case, it would be Query 7.45.

Query 7.45 Find all ingredients supplied by Veggies_R_Us but not used in a Chicken Salad

```
    SELECT ingredientid -- ingredients supplied by Veggies_R_Us
    FROM ingredients i, vendors v
    WHERE i.vendorid = v.vendorid AND companyname = 'Veggies_R_Us'
EXCEPT
    SELECT ingredientid -- ingredients used in Chicken Salad
    FROM items it, madewith m
    WHERE it.itemid = m.itemid AND it.name = 'Chicken Salad';
```

ingredientid
PICKL
TOMTO

[2 row(s)]

Note that because Chicken Salads do not use pickles or tomatoes, then Chicken Salads do not use all ingredients provided by Veggies_R_Us.

Now we need to combine Query 7.45 with the earlier outer query fragment. However, because this is a correlated subquery, we need to remove *vendors* and *items* from the inner query. We want those references to be pulled from the outer query. We also need to remove the specific references to Veggies_R_Us and Chicken Salad. Query 7.46 is our result.

Query 7.46	Find all items and vendors such that all ingredients supplied by that vendor are in the item

```
SELECT name, companyname
FROM items it, vendors v
WHERE NOT EXISTS (
        SELECT ingredientid -- ingredients supplied by vendor
        FROM ingredients i
        WHERE i.vendorid = v.vendorid
    EXCEPT
        SELECT ingredientid -- ingredients used in item
        FROM madewith m
        WHERE it.itemid = m.itemid);
```

name	companyname
Chicken Salad	Don's Dairy
Chicken Salad	Flavorful Creams
Fruit Salad	Flavorful Creams
Garden Salad	Flavorful Creams
Millennium Salad	Flavorful Creams
Soda	Flavorful Creams
Water	Flavorful Creams
Fruit Plate	Flavorful Creams
Fruit Plate	"Fruit Eating" Friends
Fruit Plate	Ed's Dressings

[10 row(s)]

Notice that in the answer to this query every item contains all of the ingredients provided by Flavorful Creams. Flavorful Creams provides us with no ingredients. This means that every item contains all ingredients provided by Flavorful Creams. Another way to think about it is that the set of ingredients provided by Flavorful Creams is the empty set. Because the empty set is a subset of all sets, the set of items provided by Flavorful Creams is a subset of the ingredients used by every item.

Let's go through this query one step at a time, to see what happens.

1. Take the Cartesian product of the *vendors* and *items* tables.

2. For each vendor/item pair, perform the subquery.

3. If the inner query is empty, then that vendor/item pair is output.

The inner query consists of two parts.

1. The first part of the inner query finds all ingredients supplied by the vendor.

2. The second part of the inner query finds all ingredients used to make the item.

The result of the inner query is the rows from the first part not in the second part.

Subset queries are not easy to construct, but they have the same common pattern in the WHERE clause NOT EXISTS A EXCEPT B, where A is the subset and B is the superset. Query 7.47 is another example in which we answer the converse of Query 7.46.

Query 7.47 | Find all vendors and items such that all ingredients in the item are from the same vendor

```
SELECT i.name, companyname
FROM items i, vendors v
WHERE NOT EXISTS (
        (SELECT m.ingredientid -- ingredients used in item
         FROM madewith m
         WHERE i.itemid = m.itemid)
      EXCEPT
        (SELECT ingredientid -- ingredients supplied by vendors
         FROM ingredients i
         WHERE i.vendorid = v.vendorid));
```

name	companyname
Fruit Salad	"Fruit Eating" Friends
Garden Salad	Veggies_R_Us
Millennium Salad	Veggies_R_Us
Millennium Salad	Don's Dairy
Millennium Salad	Flavorful Creams
Millennium Salad	"Fruit Eating" Friends
Millennium Salad	Ed's Dressings
Millennium Salad	Spring Water Supply
Soda	Spring Water Supply
Water	Spring Water Supply

[10 row(s)]

In Query 7.47, the set of items in an ingredient is a subset of items provided by a vendor.

Subset queries are also called *for all* queries because the query is true *for all* rows in a table. In the case of Query 7.46, *for all* ingredients supplied by the vendor, the ingredient is used by the item. For the mathematically inclined, we translate that statement into "there does not exist an ingredient supplied by the vendor that is not used in the item."

7.11.2   Subset Using Set Cardinality

There is an alternative to the query mechanism in Section 7.11.1. This alternative uses the notion of set cardinality. The *cardinality* of a set is the number of elements in it. In other words, if we carefully allow only the elements in the set that we want, then if the sets have the same number of elements, they must be the same set. For example, if the number of ingredients in an item is equal to the number of ingredients in an item supplied by a vendor, then all of the ingredients in the item are supplied by the vendor. Compare Query 7.48 to Query 7.47.

Query 7.48	Find all items and vendors such that all ingredients in the item are supplied by that vendor

```
SELECT i.name, companyname
FROM items i, vendors v
WHERE
      (SELECT COUNT(DISTINCT m.ingredientid) -- number of ingredients in item
       FROM madewith m
       WHERE i.itemid = m.itemid)
    = -- number of ingredients in item supplied by vendor
      (SELECT COUNT(DISTINCT m.ingredientid)
       FROM madewith m, ingredients n
       WHERE i.itemid = m.itemid AND m.ingredientid = n.ingredientid
             AND n.vendorid = v.vendorid);
```

name	companyname
Fruit Salad	"Fruit Eating" Friends
Garden Salad	Veggies_R_Us
Millennium Salad	Veggies_R_Us
Millennium Salad	Don's Dairy
Millennium Salad	Flavorful Creams
Millennium Salad	"Fruit Eating" Friends
Millennium Salad	Ed's Dressings
Millennium Salad	Spring Water Supply
Soda	Spring Water Supply
Water	Spring Water Supply

[10 row(s)]

We count the number of ingredients in the item and compare that to the number of ingredients in that item provided by the specified vendor. If those two numbers are the same, then that vendor provides all of the ingredients for the item. Note that the Millennium Salad is present multiple times in the result. That is because the number of ingredients in a Millennium Salad is 0, and the number of ingredients in a Millennium Salad provided by each vendor is also 0.

Now compare the result of Query 7.49 with Query 7.46.

Query 7.49 | Find all items and vendors such that all ingredients supplied by that vendor are in the item

---

```
SELECT name, companyname
FROM items i, vendors v
WHERE -- number of ingredients in item supplied by vendor
     (SELECT COUNT(DISTINCT m.ingredientid)
      FROM madewith m, ingredients ing
      WHERE i.itemid = m.itemid AND m.ingredientid = ing.ingredientid AND
            ing.vendorid = v.vendorid)
  =
     (SELECT COUNT(DISTINCT ing.ingredientid) -- number of ingredients supplied by vendor
      FROM ingredients ing
      WHERE ing.vendorid = v.vendorid);
```

name	companyname
Chicken Salad	Don's Dairy
Chicken Salad	Flavorful Creams
Fruit Salad	Flavorful Creams
Garden Salad	Flavorful Creams
Millennium Salad	Flavorful Creams
Soda	Flavorful Creams
Water	Flavorful Creams
Fruit Plate	Flavorful Creams
Fruit Plate	"Fruit Eating" Friends
Fruit Plate	Ed's Dressings

[10 row(s)]

In this query, we count the number of ingredients in the item that are made by a specific vendor and compare that to the number of ingredients supplied by the vendor. Although in this query it does not matter, in general it is necessary to use COUNT(DISTINCT) instead of COUNT(*).

7.11.3 Comparing Set Cardinality and Subsets

With two very different approaches to subset queries, which should be used to answer these types of queries? There are three criteria to be weighed when making this choice:

Does your DBMS support the operation?
Although we can use NOT IN instead of EXCEPT if *NULL* values are not involved, some database systems cannot perform all of the operations needed for one of the two approaches. Usually, if a database only supports one option, it will be set cardinality.

Which is more efficient?

If a query is going to be executed many times, it is important that it execute as efficiently as possible. We can do a superficial analysis of Queries 7.47 and 7.48 to get an idea of the performance. Both queries require two subqueries to be performed for every row in the cross product of *items* and *vendors*. In each case, the work done in the first query is about the same: a join between the *items* and *madewith* table. However, the second query in the subset execution is a two-way join between *vendors* and *ingredients,* whereas the second query in the set cardinality approach is a four-way join between *items, madewith, ingredients,* and *vendors.* Clearly, Query 7.47 will execute the two-way join faster than Query 7.48 will execute the four-way join. However, the final step in Query 7.48 is a simple equality predicate, whereas the EXCEPT operation in Query 7.47 is much slower. How much slower depends on the size of the sets. If a set is very large, then this operation could dominate the time of the query execution. However, if the sets are both small, then the four-way join is likely to dominate the execution time. It is important to note that every DBMS performs query optimization to improve query performance. Query optimization is beyond the scope of this book, but it does mean that superficial analysis may be incorrect in determining the relative speed of query performance. Thus, you should execute both alternatives on real data to determine the relative speed of the queries. There are also many techniques (such as adding indexes, discussed in Chapter 9) that can greatly improve the speed of a query.

Which is easier to write?

If a query is not going to be executed a large number of times, then efficiency is not very important. As a result, generating a correct query quickly becomes important. Many programmers find the set cardinality approach easier to understand, so they will take that solution. Other programmers find the subset approach easier to ensure correct behavior (the subqueries tend to be more simple), so they prefer that method.

7.12 Subqueries in the SELECT Clause

We can include subqueries in the SELECT clause to compute a column in the result table. It works much like any other expression. You may use both simple and correlated subqueries in the SELECT clause as shown in Query 7.50.

| Query 7.50 | For each ingredient, list its inventory value, the maximum inventory value of all ingredients, and the ratio of the ingredient's inventory value to the average ingredient inventory value |

```
SELECT name, unitprice * inventory AS "Inventory Value",
     (SELECT MAX(unitprice * inventory)
      FROM ingredients) AS "Max. Value",
     (unitprice * inventory) / (SELECT AVG(unitprice * inventory)
                                FROM ingredients) AS "Ratio"
FROM ingredients;
```

Continued on next page

Query 7.50 (cont'd)

name	Inventory Value	Max. Value	Ratio
Cheese	4.50	3450.00	0.01266161140107764381
Chicken	54.00	3450.00	0.15193933681293172578
Crouton	4.00	3450.00	0.01125476568984679450
Grape	3.00	3450.00	0.00844107426738509588
Lettuce	2.00	3450.00	0.00562738284492339725
Pickle	32.00	3450.00	0.09003812551877435602
Secret Dressing	3.60	3450.00	0.01012928912086211505
Tomato	0.45	3450.00	0.00126616114010776438
Water	NULL	3450.00	NULL
Soda	3450.00	3450.00	9.7072354074928603
Watermelon	NULL	3450.00	NULL
Orange	0.50	3450.00	0.00140684571123084931

[12 row(s)]

This query uses uncorrelated subqueries to compute the average and maximum inventory value. Because we use uncorrelated subqueries, their values are the same for each row. These subqueries may be used as the terms of larger expressions as in our ratio column. Like other SELECT expressions, we can specify an alias.

Correlated subqueries in the SELECT clause work just like they do in the WHERE clause.

Query 7.51 List each ingredient and its supplier

```
SELECT name, (SELECT companyname
              FROM vendors v
              WHERE v.vendorid = i.vendorid) AS "supplier"
FROM ingredients i;
```

name	supplier
Cheese	Don's Dairy
Chicken	Don's Dairy
Crouton	Ed's Dressings
Grape	"Fruit Eating" Friends
Lettuce	Veggies_R_Us
Pickle	Veggies_R_Us
Secret Dressing	NULL
Tomato	Veggies_R_Us
Water	Spring Water Supply
Soda	Spring Water Supply
Watermelon	"Fruit Eating" Friends
Orange	"Fruit Eating" Friends

[12 row(s)]

In Query 7.51, the subquery is executed one for each ingredient. Like other expressions in the SELECT list, the subquery must return a single (scalar) value. Specifically, the result of the subquery must contain *exactly* one attribute and zero or one rows. If the inner query contains zero rows, the column value is *NULL.* Thus, Query 7.51 only works because we know that each ingredient is provided by at most one company.

Query 7.52 **ERROR!** Find the ingredients for each item

```
SELECT name, (SELECT name
              FROM ingredients JOIN madewith USING (ingredientid)
              WHERE items.itemid = madewith.itemid)
FROM items;
```

Query 7.52 generates an error because there are items with multiple ingredients. Of course, we can correctly answer Query 7.52 by using joins in the WHERE clause. Likewise, because aggregate functions return exactly one value (without a GROUP BY clause), they are good candidates for this technique, as in Query 7.53.

Query 7.53 Find the number of ingredients for each item

```
SELECT name, (SELECT COUNT(*)
              FROM ingredients JOIN madewith USING (ingredientid)
              WHERE items.itemid = madewith.itemid) AS "Ingredient Count"
FROM items;
```

name	Ingredient Count
Chicken Salad	4
Fruit Salad	2
Garden Salad	2
Millennium Salad	0
Soda	1
Water	1
Fruit Plate	6

[7 row(s)]

7.13 Wrap Up

Simple subqueries in the WHERE allow us to construct multitable queries by nesting one query inside another. We can connect an inner and outer query using any of the comparison operators. It is important to remember that subqueries compare a single row in the outer query to every row in the inner query. Forgetting this limitation can lead programmers to obscure errors.

Because these techniques are similar to the techniques in Chapter 5, it is important to know when the various approaches should be used. Here are some guidelines to help make the choice.

Possible:

As a result of the restrictions on the various techniques, some subquery approaches may not be able to answer the query. The derived relation technique will also always work, although it is not as widely supported.

Portable:

If the query is going to execute on different DBMSs, it must be supported on all of them.

Performance:

Assuming the query is going to be asked more than once, the time required to answer a query can be important. As a result, the various approaches should be optimized independently as much as possible, and then they should be compared on realistic data.

Preference:

If the query is going to be asked only once, or there is little difference in the performance, then choose the approach that you like the best. Not only will this be the easiest for you to write, but it will also be the easiest to maintain.

Review Questions

1. What is wrong with the following query?

```
SELECT name, companyname
FROM ingredients
WHERE vendorid IN
        (SELECT vendorid
          FROM vendors);
```

2. Consider the following query.

```
SELECT *
FROM ingredients
WHERE vendorid = (
     SELECT vendorid
     FROM vendors
     WHERE referredby = 'NWVID');
```

SQL will report an error if _____. If there are no rows in the *vendors* table with *referredby* of NWVID, the inner query returns _____ and the outer query returns _____. Make no assumptions about the data in *ingredients* or *vendors*.

3. If the inner query returns *NULL*, what will happen in the outer query if IN is used to connect the queries? NOT IN? > ANY? =? > ALL?

4. If a *NULL* value is in the outer query, what will happen when the inner query is evaluated with IN? NOT IN? > ANY? =? > ALL?

5. If the inner query is empty, what will happen in the outer query if IN is used to connect the queries? NOT IN? > ANY? =? > ALL?

6. Describe a query in which = ALL would be the correct predicate for a subquery.

7. Consider the following query:

```
SELECT companyname, (SELECT v2.repfname
                      FROM vendors v2
                      WHERE v1.referredby=v2.vendorid) as fname,
                     (SELECT v3.replname
                      FROM vendors v3
                      WHERE v1.referredby=v3.vendorid) as lname
        FROM vendors v1;
```

What does it return?

8. Write the previous query using (a) no subqueries and (b) derived tables. Which of the three approaches should be the fastest? Why? Determine an experiment to find out. Apply your experiment and see if you were correct.

9. Why are aggregate functions useful in subqueries?

10. What is the maximum number of subqueries on your DBMS?

11. Duplicate the results of Query 7.54 with the other operators. Hint: It can be done with a join, a UNION, a couple of derived relations, an EXCEPT, and several CAST statements.

Query 7.54 OUTER JOIN Review Question
```
SELECT *
FROM vendors v LEFT JOIN ingredients i ON v.vendorid = i.vendorid
```

---

12. What must be true of a subquery for it to appear in an expression?

13. Extend Query 7.12 to include meals.

14. Change Query 7.14 to find all ingredients not supplied by Veggies_R_Us.

15. Correct Query 7.15.

16. How many different ways can you combine joins and subqueries to generate the results of Query 7.20? Don't limit yourself to two levels of subqueries.

17. Under what conditions do > ANY and > ALL create the same results?

18. Can you modify Queries 7.31 and 7.32 so that they generate the same results on an empty table as well as a nonempty one? Which query do you consider to be correct?

19. How can you tell if a query is correlated or not?

20. A subset query compares _____ in one group to _____ in another group.

21. The basic structure of the WHERE clause in a subset query consists of _____ subquery A _____ subquery B, where subquery A finds the _____ and subquery B finds the _____.

22. The set cardinality approach requires two sets to be _____ in the number of rows.

23. Why does the set cardinality approach usually have more joins than the subset approach?

24. What is the difference between COUNT(*) and COUNT(DISTINCT) in set cardinality queries?

25. Can you simulate a cross product with subqueries in the SELECT clause?

Practice

For these exercises, we use the Employees Database presented at the end of Chapter 1. Answer each question with a single SQL statement. Your query must work for any set of data in the Employees Database, not just the set of data we provide.

1. Find the names of all people who work in the Consulting department.

2. Find the names of all people who work in the Consulting department and who spend more than 20% of their time on the project with ID ADT4MFIA.

3. Find the total percentage of time assigned to employee Abe Advice.

4. Find the names of all departments not currently assigned a project.

5. Find the first and last names of all employees who make more than the average salary of the people in the Accounting department.

6. Find the descriptions of all projects that require more than 70% of an employee's time.

7. Find the first and last name of all employees who are paid more than someone in the Accounting department.

8. Find the minimum salary of the employees who are paid more than everyone in the Accounting department.

9. Find the first and last name of the highest paid employee(s) in the Accounting department.

10. For each employee in the department with code ACCNT, find the employee ID and number of assigned hours that the employee is currently working on projects for other departments. Only report an employee if she has some current project to which she is assigned more than 50% of the time and the project is for another department. Report the results in ascending order by hours.

11. Find all departments where all of their employees are assigned to all of their projects.

12. Use correlated subqueries in the SELECT and WHERE clauses, derived tables, and subqueries in the HAVING clause to answer these queries. If they cannot be answered using that technique, explain why.

    (a) Find the names of all people who work in the Information Technology department.

    (b) Find the names of all people who work in the Information Technology department and who spend more than 20% of their time on the health project.

    (c) Find the names of all people who make more than the average salary of the people in the Accounting department.

    (d) Find the names of all projects that require more than 50% of an employee's time.

    (e) Find the total percentage time assigned to employee Bob Smith.

    (f) Find all departments not assigned a project.

(g) Find all employees who are paid more than someone in the Information Technology department.

(h) Find all employees who are paid more than everyone in the Information Technology department.

(i) Find the highest paid employee in the Information Technology department.

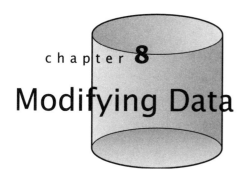

chapter **8**

Modifying Data

Our powerful query techniques do little good without data. We need some way to add, modify, and even delete data. SQL provides three statements for modifying data: INSERT, UPDATE, and DELETE.

8.1 INSERT: Adding New Rows

The INSERT statement adds new rows to a specified table. There are two variants of the INSERT statement. One inserts a single row of values into the database, whereas the other inserts multiple rows returned from a SELECT.

8.1.1 INSERTing a Row with VALUES

The most basic form of INSERT creates a single, new row with either user-specified or default values. The syntax of this INSERT statement is as follows:

```
INSERT INTO <table name>
[(<attribute>, ..., <attribute>)]
VALUES (<expression>, ..., <expression>);
```

INSERT creates a new row in *table name*. The new row contains the values determined by the expressions in the VALUES list. The expressions in the VALUES list correspond to the attributes in the comma separated following the table name. If no attributes are given, then the order of the attributes in *<table name>* is used. Insert 8.1 is a simple example. Note that we provide a query to show the modifications. However, the modifications will not actually be applied to the database. Thus, all of our updates will be on the database installed from the Web site.

Insert 8.1 Add new dressing

```
INSERT INTO ingredients VALUES
    ('EDSDR', 'Ed''s Vanishing Dressing', 'ounce', 0.1, NULL, DEFAULT, 'EDDRS');
```
See the results
```
SELECT name, unit, foodgroup, inventory, vendorid
FROM ingredients
WHERE vendorid='EDDRS';
```

name	unit	foodgroup	inventory	vendorid
Crouton	piece	Bread	400	EDDRS
Ed's Vanishing Dressing	ounce	NULL	0	EDDRS

[2 row(s)]

There are several things to note from this INSERT statement:

- This creates a *single,* new row in the *ingredients* table.

- The values of the row are specified by the value list. The items in the VALUES list are matched one-by-one, in order of the attributes in the *ingredients* table. For example, the first item in the values list (EDSDR) becomes the value for the first attribute (*ingredientid*) in the new row of the *ingredients* table. This means that the number, order, and data types of the items in the value list *must* match the number, order, and data type of attributes in the specified table. SQL attempts to implicitly convert each VALUE list expression result to the target column data type. You can also specify an explicit conversion using CAST.

- A *NULL* attribute value can be specified with the NULL keyword. All data types also have a default value (see Chapter 9). The default value for any attribute is *NULL* unless otherwise specified. Fields that are defined as NOT NULL do not have a default value unless one is explicitly specified.

What happens if somebody changes the order or number of attributes in the *ingredients* table? SQL may refuse to execute our INSERT statement. Even worse, if only the order of the attributes changes, SQL may put values in the wrong place without any warning. For example, if we reversed the ordering of the second and third attributes of the *ingredients* table, our INSERT statement will still execute; however, the *name* and *unit* values would be incorrect. In general, it is good to avoid this reliance on the attribute creation order by naming the attributes ourselves, as in Insert 8.2.

Insert 8.2 Add a dressing with attribute list

```
INSERT INTO ingredients
    (ingredientid, name, unitprice, unit, foodgroup, vendorid) VALUES
    ('EDSDR', 'Ed''s Vanishing Dressing', 0.1, 'ounce', NULL, 'EDDRS');
```
See the results
```
SELECT name, unit, foodgroup, inventory, vendorid
FROM ingredients
WHERE vendorid = 'EDDRS';
```

name	unit	foodgroup	inventory	vendorid
Crouton	piece	Bread	400	EDDRS
Ed's Vanishing Dressing	ounce	NULL	0	EDDRS

[2 row(s)]

Now the order of the values in the VALUES list is determined by the INSERT statement, not the table. In this example, we have reversed the order of *unit* and *unitprice* from the *ingredients* table in our attribute list, and we are missing the *inventory* attribute altogether. All columns not present in the INSERT statement are assigned their default value. The advantage of this form of the INSERT statement is that it will still work correctly if the attribute order in the *ingredients* table changes, if new attributes with default values are added, and even if attributes not listed in the INSERT attribute list are dropped. Of course, if attributes in the INSERT statement are dropped, the statement will fail.

For the spectacularly lazy, there is a special form of INSERT that creates a new row with *all* default values. You don't have to specify any data. Insert 8.3 is the lazy update.

Insert 8.3 Add a default slogan

```
INSERT INTO ads DEFAULT VALUES;
```
See the results
```
SELECT *
FROM ads;
```

slogan
Grazing in style
NULL
Bovine friendly and heart smart
Where the grazin's good
The grass is greener here
Welcome to the "other side"
NULL

[7 row(s)]

This inserts a row with all default values into the *ads* table. Recall that the *ads* table contains a single column, *slogan,* of type VARCHAR(50). Because we don't specify a default value for *slogan,* the default value is *NULL.*

Would this statement work on any other table in our database? Consider the *vendors* table. If we tried to insert a row using all default values, what would happen? Let's focus specifically on the primary key, *vendorid.* The default value for *vendorid* is *NULL*; however, the primary key constraint does not allow *NULL* values for any attribute of the primary key. If we attempted to insert a row of default values into *vendors,* the DBMS would reject it because it violates the primary key constraint. Our *ads* table is the only one in our schema with no primary key so it's the only table where we can use the DEFAULT VALUES form of INSERT.

8.1.2   INSERTing Multiple Rows with SELECT

The INSERT statement allows you to create new rows from existing data. It begins just like the INSERT statements we've already seen; however, instead of a VALUES list, the data are generated by a nested SELECT statement. The syntax is as follows:

```
INSERT INTO <table name>
[(<attribute>, ..., <attribute>)]
<SELECT statement>;
```

The SELECT form of INSERT is similar to the VALUES form except that it gets its new rows from a SELECT statement instead of a VALUES list. Unlike the VALUES form of INSERT that creates a single row, the SELECT form of INSERT allows creation of zero or more new rows. SQL evaluates this statement by first executing the SELECT and generating a result table. SQL then attempts to insert a new row in *<table name>* for each row in the SELECT result table. The attribute list of the SELECT result table must match the attribute list of the INSERT statement. The INSERT statement's attribute list is the same as the attribute list of *<table name>* unless an optional comma-delimited attribute list is specified. As with the VALUES form of INSERT, any unspecified attributes are assigned their default values. You may use any SELECT statement you wish as long as it generates a result table with a compatible attribute list.

Let's look at an example. Being the health-conscious restaurateur that you are, you decide to add water to every meal that doesn't already have it. You need some way to add a row to the *partof* table for each meal that doesn't already include water. Insert 8.4 does this.

Insert 8.4   Add water to every meal

```
INSERT INTO partof (mealid, quantity, itemid)
    SELECT mealid, 1,
        (SELECT itemid FROM items WHERE name = 'Water')
    FROM meals
    WHERE mealid NOT IN
        (SELECT mealid
         FROM partof p, items m
         WHERE p.itemid = m.itemid AND name = 'Water');
```

```
See the results
```
```
SELECT p.mealid, name, discount, p.itemid
FROM meals m, partof p
WHERE m.mealid = p.mealid AND p.itemid = 'WATER';
```

Insert 8.4 (cont'd)

mealid	name	discount	itemid
CKSDS	Chicken N Suds	0.00	WATER
VGNET	Vegan Eatin'	0.00	WATER

[2 row(s)]

The simple subquery nested within the WHERE clause finds the meals with water. Moving from inside out, using NOT IN the next SELECT statement finds the meal IDs for meals without water. The simple subquery in the attribute list provides the item ID for water. Because the *discount* attribute is not specified, each new row has the default value of 0.00.

8.2 DELETE: Removing Rows

You can remove rows from a table using DELETE.

```
DELETE FROM <table name> [[AS] <alias>]
[WHERE <condition>];
```

DELETE removes all rows from *<table name>* where *<condition>* evaluates to true. The WHERE is optional, but beware! If there is no WHERE clause, DELETE removes *all* rows. DELETE can only remove rows from a single table. Delete 8.5 is a simple example.

Delete 8.5 Remove items with a *NULL* price

```
DELETE FROM items
WHERE price IS NULL;
```

See the results

```
SELECT name, price
FROM items;
```

name	price
Chicken Salad	2.85
Fruit Salad	3.45
Garden Salad	0.99
Soda	0.99
Water	0.00
Fruit Plate	3.99

[6 row(s)]

To execute this statement, SQL goes row by row through *items* deleting any row satisfying the WHERE predicate. The WHERE clause can involve any number of tables. Consider the situation where you're just about to open your restaurant and you hear on the news that Don's Dairy is under investigation for unsafe food handling. Delete 8.6 removes any ingredients supplied by Don's from all items.

Delete 8.6 Remove all ingredients supplied by Don's Dairy

```
DELETE FROM madewith
WHERE ingredientid IN
      (SELECT ingredientid
       FROM ingredients i, vendors v
       WHERE i.vendorid = v.vendorid AND companyname = 'Don''s Dairy');
```

See the results

```
SELECT itemid, i.ingredientid, quantity, vendorid
FROM madewith m, ingredients i
WHERE m.ingredientid=i.ingredientid;
```

itemid	ingredientid	quantity	vendorid
CHKSD	LETUS	1	VGRUS
CHKSD	SCTDR	1	NULL
FRTSD	GRAPE	10	FRTFR
FRTSD	WTRML	5	FRTFR
GDNSD	LETUS	4	VGRUS
GDNSD	TOMTO	8	VGRUS
FRPLT	WTRML	10	FRTFR
FRPLT	GRAPE	10	FRTFR
FRPLT	CRUTN	10	EDDRS
FRPLT	TOMTO	8	VGRUS
WATER	WATER	1	SPWTR
SODA	SODA	1	SPWTR
FRPLT	ORNG	10	FRTFR

[13 row(s)]

Here we use a simple subquery to find the ingredients from Don's. The results of the subquery execution are then used in the WHERE clause to evaluate each row of *madewith*.

DELETE may also use correlated subqueries as shown in Delete 8.7. Remember that our updates are made on the original database, so Delete 8.6 has not been applied. However, the Millennium Salad has no ingredients.

Delete 8.7 Remove items with no ingredients

```
DELETE FROM items
WHERE NOT EXISTS
      (SELECT *
       FROM madewith
       WHERE items.itemid = madewith.itemid);
```

See the results

```
SELECT itemid, COUNT(ingredientid)
FROM items i FULL JOIN madewith mw USING(itemid)
GROUP BY itemid;
```

Delete 8.7 (cont'd)

itemid	count
SODA	1
GDNSD	2
FRPLT	6
FRTSD	2
WATER	1
CHKSD	4

[6 row(s)]

Like correlated SELECT subqueries in the WHERE clause, we can think of this statement as iterating over all of the rows in the *items* table, evaluating the WHERE clause to test if there are any rows in the *madewith* table for this item. Caveat: If any of the items to be deleted are included in a meal, the DBMS will reject this delete because of the foreign key constraint. We leave correcting this as an exercise for the reader. One solution is deferred constraint enforcement (see Chapter 11). Note that SQL allows table aliases in the FROM clause of DELETE statements if we need them to qualify an attribute.

When executing DELETE, we have to be careful with the WHERE clause. Using substring matching with LIKE or an inequality comparator can cause unexpected consequences. For example, if we decide we are never going to have the Millennium Salad, Delete 8.8 would be the *wrong* way to get rid of it.

Delete 8.8 **INCORRECT!** Delete Millennium Salad

```
DELETE FROM items
WHERE name LIKE '%Salad%';
```
See the results
```
SELECT *
FROM items;
```

itemid	name	price	dateadded
SODA	Soda	0.99	2003-02-06
WATER	Water	0.00	2002-05-19
FRPLT	Fruit Plate	3.99	2000-09-02

[3 row(s)]

8.3 UPDATE: Changing Row Values

You can change the values in existing rows using UPDATE.

```
UPDATE <table-name> [[AS] <alias>]
SET <column>=<expression>, ..., <attribute>=<expression>
[WHERE <condition>];
```

UPDATE changes all rows in *<table name>* where *<condition>* evaluates to true. For each row, the SET clause dictates which attributes change and how to compute the new value. All other attribute values do not change. The WHERE is optional, but beware! Like DELETE, if there is no WHERE clause, UPDATE changes *all* rows. UPDATE can only change rows from a single table.

Suppose your refrigeration unit failed overnight, forcing you to throw away all of your milk products. Update 8.9 modifies your milk ingredient inventory.

Update 8.9 Set the inventory to 0 for all ingredients in the milk food group

```
UPDATE ingredients
SET inventory = 0
WHERE foodgroup = 'Milk';
```

See the results

```
SELECT name, foodgroup, inventory
FROM ingredients
ORDER BY foodgroup;
```

name	foodgroup	inventory
Crouton	Bread	400
Grape	Fruit	300
Tomato	Fruit	15
Watermelon	Fruit	NULL
Orange	Fruit	10
Chicken	Meat	120
Cheese	Milk	0
Lettuce	Vegetable	200
Pickle	Vegetable	800
Secret Dressing	NULL	120
Water	NULL	NULL
Soda	NULL	5000

[12 row(s)]

UPDATE goes row-by-row through *ingredients* changing the *inventory* attribute value to 0 for any row satisfying `foodgroup = 'Milk'`. Whereas the updates can only apply to one table, the WHERE clause can involve any number of tables. Consider the situation where Don's Dairy offers a discount for customers who order more inventory. Update 8.10 reflects our database after we make a large purchase.

Update 8.10	Decrease the unit price by 20% and increase the inventory by 100 units for every ingredient provided by Don's Dairy

```
UPDATE ingredients
SET unitprice = unitprice * 0.8, inventory = inventory + 100
WHERE vendorid IN
      (SELECT vendorid
       FROM vendors
       WHERE companyname LIKE 'Don%');
```
See the results
```
SELECT name, unitprice, inventory, vendorid
FROM ingredients;
```

name	unitprice	inventory	vendorid
Crouton	0.01	400	EDDRS
Grape	0.01	300	FRTFR
Lettuce	0.01	200	VGRUS
Pickle	0.04	800	VGRUS
Secret Dressing	0.03	120	NULL
Tomato	0.03	15	VGRUS
Water	0.06	NULL	SPWTR
Soda	0.69	5000	SPWTR
Watermelon	0.02	NULL	FRTFR
Orange	0.05	10	FRTFR
Cheese	0.02	250	DNDRY
Chicken	0.36	220	DNDRY

[12 row(s)]

Note that our SET expressions can use old values to compute new values. SET expressions can be complex, including the use of subqueries. Consider the situation where a big freeze has caused a jump in tomato prices. You need to increase the price of every item by $0.05 for each slice of tomato. Update 8.11 makes this modification for you.

Update 8.11	Raise the price of all items by 5 cents per tomato slice in the item

```
UPDATE items
SET price = price + 0.05 *
            (SELECT quantity
             FROM madewith w
             WHERE items.itemid = w.itemid AND ingredientid='TOMTO')
WHERE itemid IN
      (SELECT itemid
       FROM madewith
       WHERE ingredientid = 'TOMTO');
```
See the results
```
SELECT name, price, quantity as tomatoes
FROM items i, madewith m
WHERE i.itemid = m.itemid and ingredientid = 'TOMTO';
```
Continued on next page

Update 8.11 (cont'd)

name	price	tomatoes
Fruit Plate	4.39	8
Garden Salad	1.39	8

[2 row(s)]

Here we use a correlated subquery in the SET expression to find the number of tomatoes used in each item.

8.4 Testing Your DELETE and UPDATE WHERE Conditions

Recall that the WHERE clause is actually optional for the DELETE and UPDATE statements. If the WHERE clause is omitted, DELETE removes and UPDATE changes *all* rows from the target table. This makes DELETE and UPDATE dangerous statements because you can easily forget to include the WHERE clause and remove or change all rows. Even with a WHERE clause, you may execute a DELETE or UPDATE that changes the wrong rows.

To reduce the danger of these statements, you should always test your WHERE clause in a SELECT before executing a DELETE or UPDATE. Develop your DELETE or UPDATE statement in a separate text editor and write the WHERE clause *before* adding DELETE or UPDATE. In Chapter 11 we'll see how to execute DELETEs and UPDATEs as part of a transaction that can be undone. Effectively, this provides a way to modify the data and evaluate the results before making the changes permanent. If we made incorrect data changes, we can discard the changes before anybody sees them.

8.5 Living within Constraints

SQL enforces a wide range of constraints on the data in a database. We are already familiar with the primary and foreign key constraints. We'll learn about specifying constraints in Chapter 9. Constraints are enforced by rejecting any conflicting insert, update, or delete. The implications of most constraint types are fairly obvious. You cannot put a *NULL* value in a column declared NOT NULL. A primary key cannot contain *NULL* and must be unique. Let's take a moment to consider the impact of foreign key constraints. A foreign key value must either be *NULL* or reference a specific value in the parent table. Say you just hired a new vendor, Hawaiian Munch, to provide pineapples. You need to insert a new row in both *vendors* and *ingredients.* As a reminder, the *ingredients* table is a child table containing a foreign key, *vendorid,* referencing *vendorid* in the parent table, *vendors.*

Does the insert order matter? Absolutely! If you try to insert into *ingredients* first, the new *ingredients* row will have a vendor ID that is not yet contained in the *vendors* table. This means that the DBMS will reject the insert of the new ingredient. You must insert the new vendor before inserting any new ingredients from that vendor. In general, when inserting you must insert into the parent table before inserting into the child table.

Insert 8.12 Insert satisfying foreign key constraints

```
INSERT INTO vendors
       VALUES ('HAWNM', 'Hawaiian Munch', 'Coco', 'Nut', NULL);
INSERT INTO ingredients
       VALUES ('PNAPL', 'Pineapple', 'cube', 0.10, 'Fruit', 50, 'HAWNM');
```

What about deletes? If we want to delete a vendor, say Ed's Dressings, we must first handle all of the referencing rows in *ingredients*. We have a couple of choices on how to handle this problem. First, we can delete the rows in ingredients that refer to this vendor. The statements to delete these rows would be Delete 8.13.

Delete 8.13 **ERROR!** Remove ingredients from former vendor

```
DELETE FROM ingredients
WHERE vendorid IN
       (SELECT vendorid
        FROM vendors
        WHERE companyname = 'Ed''s Dressings');
```

However, with our database design this will not work. The attribute *ingredientid* is part of another foreign key constraint with the *madewith* table. Besides, we may not want to get rid of the ingredients supplied by the vendor, just the vendor. So, we modify the *ingredients* table to indicate which ingredients no longer have a supplier by setting the vendor ID to NULL for all ingredients supplied by Ed's Dressings.

Update 8.14 Set the vendor ID to *NULL* in *ingredients* supplied by Ed's Dressings

```
UPDATE ingredients
SET vendorid = NULL
WHERE vendorid IN
       (SELECT vendorid
        FROM vendors
        WHERE companyname = 'Ed''s Dressings');
```

This solves the problems in the *ingredients* table, but deleting a vendor presents another problem. The *vendors* table has a foreign key relationship to itself using the *referredby* column. If some other vendor is referred by Ed's Dressings, we must also update that reference before deleting the vendor.

Update 8.15 Set *referredby* to *NULL* for vendors referred by Ed's Dressings

```
UPDATE vendors SET referredby = NULL
WHERE referredby IN
       (SELECT vendorid
        FROM vendors
        WHERE companyname = 'Ed''s Dressings');
```

Now we are able to delete the rows from the *vendors* table with the simple statement in Delete 8.16.

Delete 8.16 Delete former vendor

```
DELETE FROM vendors
WHERE companyname = 'Ed''s Dressings';
```

Note that if we wanted to delete the ingredients, we must delete the corresponding *made-with* entries. In general, you must delete from the child table before deleting from the parent table.

What about update? Say you wanted to change the vendor ID for *Hawaiian Munch* to HWNMC. You can't change the vendor ID in *vendors* because a row in *ingredients* references it. You can't change the vendor ID for the row in ingredients to HWNMC because that vendor ID doesn't exist yet. How do you fix this? It requires several steps to be executed together. SQL 8.17 shows one possible set of steps.

SQL 8.17 Changing a vendor ID

```
INSERT INTO vendors
  SELECT 'HWNMC', companyname, repfname, replname, referredby
  FROM vendors WHERE vendorid = 'HAWNM';

UPDATE ingredients SET vendorid = 'HWNMC' WHERE vendorid = 'HAWNM';

DELETE FROM vendors WHERE vendorid = 'HAWNM';
```

We use INSERT to copy the Hawaiian Munch row from the *vendors* table using the new vendor ID. Using UPDATE we change the ingredients vendor ID to the new ID. Finally, we remove the old Hawaiian Munch row with DELETE. If some other user generates a list of vendors after the INSERT but before the DELETE, they'll get an incorrect list. We'll present a solution to this in Chapter 11.

8.6 Wrap Up

SQL allows us to modify the data in a database. INSERT allows you to create new rows from expressions, default values, and existing data. It is not surprising that DELETE removes all rows where the WHERE conditional evaluates to true. UPDATE modifies all rows where the WHERE conditional evaluates to true according to the list of assignment expressions. A DELETE/UPDATE with no WHERE clause removes/modifies *all* rows. Finally, an INSERT, DELETE, or UPDATE that results in data that violate any constraint is rejected.

Review Questions

1. Unless otherwise specified, the default value for any data type is _____.

2. If the following INSERT statement is valid, what do you know about the table *things*?

   ```
   INSERT INTO things VALUES ('Magic Ring');
   ```

3. What happens if I try to insert a new vendor with ID VGRUS into the *vendors* table?

4. What happens if I try to delete the vendor with ID VGRUS?

5. A DELETE or UPDATE without a WHERE clause applies to _____ rows.

6. What happens when we execute this query?

   ```
   UPDATE items
   SET price = price + 0.05 *
           (SELECT quantity
            FROM madewith w
            WHERE items.itemid = w.itemid AND ingredientid = 'TOMTO');
   ```

7. The multi-row INSERT can be used to insert a single row of values. Write the INSERT-SELECT statement that is the same as the following:

   ```
   INSERT INTO madewith VALUES('GDNSD','CHESE',10);
   ```

8. Why is it a good idea to use the optional attribute list with an INSERT statement?

9. In the Restaurant Database, what happens when we execute the following statement:

   ```
   INSERT INTO vendors (vendorid) VALUES ('NEWVN');
   ```

10. In the Restaurant Database, what happens when we execute the following statement:

    ```
    INSERT INTO vendors (companyname) VALUES ('New Vendor');
    ```

11. In the Restaurant Database, does Delete 8.18 work as it claims?

    Delete 8.18 Delete the most expensive item

    ```
    DELETE
    FROM items
    WHERE price >= (SELECT MAX(price)
                    FROM items);
    ```

12. In the Restaurant Database, what does Update 8.19 do?

    Update 8.19 Review question

    ```
    UPDATE items
    SET price = (SELECT CASE
                        WHEN price < 1.00 THEN price * 1.05
                        WHEN price < 2.00 THEN price * 1.1
                        ELSE price * 1.2
                   END);
    ```

Practice

For these exercises, we use the Employees Database presented at the end of Chapter 1. Your query must work for any set of data in the Employees Database, not just the set of data we provide.

1. Give the single statement to create a new employee with ID 12 and name Ron Neuman. All other values should be the default.

2. Give the single statement to assign the employee with ID 12 to the department with code ADMIN.

3. Give the single statement to remove all employees from the project with ID ADT4MFIA.

4. Give the single statement to increase the revenue of all projects by 10% that have a project worked on by an employee with last name Hardware.

5. Give the single statement to assign the employee with ID 12 to the project(s) with revenue greater than $15,000. Each project should be assigned an equal portion of 100% time. For example, if there are 4 such projects, the employee with ID 12 should be assigned 25% time for each project.

6. Give the statement(s) to delete all employees of the Accounting department.

7. Harry Hardware's twin brother, Igor, has decided to join the company. He'll work for the same department and make the same salary as his brother. Pick an unused ID. Give the single statement to create this new employee. You never know when somebody else might be changing Harry's salary, department, or last name; therefore, your statement must derive these values from the database. In other words, you cannot look up Harry's last name and use the literal value in the creation statement for Igor.

8. You have created a new department named Shipping with code SHPNG. The new department is a subdepartment of ADMIN. To handle this new department, you have hired a new employee named Ed Fex with ID 20 to manage the department. Give the statement(s) to add this new information to the database. Make up any unspecified data yourself.

9. Give the statement(s) to remove the Administration department. Any responsibilities that the Administration department has (e.g., being a super department, owning projects) should be transferred to the department with code CNSLT. Don't peek at the data.

chapter **9**

Creating, Deleting, and Altering Tables

By now you can answer almost any query from a given set of tables, but where do tables come from? You create them using SQL. Tables and all other parts of a database (columns, keys, etc.) that are not data are collectively known as *metadata.* Metadata is data about data. Because SQL is great at handling data, it is not surprising that SQL is also great at handling metadata.

9.1 Creating Simple Tables

The basic table has a name and a set of columns, each with its own data type. We can create a table in SQL using (surprise!) CREATE TABLE.

```
CREATE TABLE <table name> (
<column name> <type> [<default value>] [<column constraints>],
...
<column name> <type> [<default value>] [<column constraints>],
<table constraint>,
...
<table constraint>
);
```

This creates a table named *<table name>*. The columns of the table are specified in a comma-delimited list of name/data type pairs. Optionally, you may specify constraints and default values. Before creating a table, most DBMSs require the creation of a database to hold the new table. For now we assume the database already exists. We discuss database creation later in the chapter. Let's create a simplified version of the *vendors* table.

DDL 9.1 Basic table creation

```
CREATE TABLE vendors (
  vendorid CHAR(5),
  companyname VARCHAR(30),
  repfname VARCHAR(20),
  replname VARCHAR(20),
  referredby CHAR(5)
);
```

There are several things worth noting from this CREATE statement:

- This creates a table named *vendors.*

- The new table contains five columns. Each column has a data type. For example, the first column of the *vendors* table is *vendorid* with data type CHAR(5). Section 1.2 explains SQL data types.

- The new table does not contain any data. We discuss inserting data in Chapter 8.

- As with SELECT, extra whitespace, such as line breaks, are ignored by SQL. This statement could have been written on a single line. We only break it up for readability.

- If we try to create a new table with the same name as an existing table, SQL returns an error. Later, we'll see how to delete and/or alter existing tables.

9.2 DEFAULT Values

Recall from our discussion of INSERT that when a new row is created, any columns without a specified value are assigned the default value. Unless otherwise specified, the default value of a column is *NULL*. SQL allows you to specify a default value for a column using the DEFAULT clause.

```
DEFAULT <value expression>
```

<value expression> is a simple expression of literals, functions, and values. *<value expression>* must evaluate to a data type that matches or can be implicitly converted to the column data type. The DEFAULT clause follows the attribute name and type declaration. Let's look at a few attributes from our Restaurant schema:

DDL 9.2 Specify attribute DEFAULT values

```
companyname VARCHAR(30) DEFAULT 'SECRET'
inventory INTEGER DEFAULT 0
dateadded DATE DEFAULT CURRENT_DATE
```

9.3 Constraints

Your DBMS can do much more than just store and access data. It can also enforce rules (called constraints) on what data are allowed in the database. Such constraints are important because they help maintain data integrity. For example, you may want to ensure that each meal costs at least as much its ingredients.

You may not realize it, but you're already using one form of database constraint. When you specify the data type of a column, you constrain the possible values that column may hold. This is called a *domain constraint.* For example, a column of type INTEGER may only hold whole numbers within a certain range. Any attempt to insert an invalid value will be rejected by SQL. This is a good thing because you wouldn't want an inventory of "abc" pickles. SQL allows the specification of many more constraint types.

SQL enforces constraints by prohibiting any data in the database that violate any constraint. Any insert, update, or delete that would result in a constraint violation is rejected without changing the database.

There are two forms of constraint specification:

Constraint Type	Usage
Column constraint	Declared with and applies to one particular column
Table constraint	Declared separately and may apply to one *or more* columns

Each type of constraint has a column and/or table constraint form.

9.3.1 NOT NULL

Remember the good old *NULL* value and all of the problems it can cause? By default, most DBMSs allow *NULL* as a value for any column of any data type. You may not be so keen on allowing *NULL* values for some columns. Fortunately, you can require the database to prohibit *NULL* values for particular columns by using the NOT NULL column constraint. Many DBMSs also include a NULL column constraint, which specifies that *NULL* values are allowed; however, because this is the default behavior, this constraint usually is unnecessary. Note that the NULL column constraint is not part of the SQL specification. Let's revisit our *vendors* table creation:

DDL 9.3 Create a table with DEFAULT values and NULL value constraints

```
CREATE TABLE vendors (
  vendorid CHAR(5) NOT NULL,
  companyname VARCHAR(30) DEFAULT 'SECRET' NOT NULL,
  repfname VARCHAR(20) DEFAULT 'Mr. or Ms.',
  replname VARCHAR(20),
  referredby CHAR(5) NULL
);
```

- Here we constrain *vendorid* to non-*NULL* values. Now the DBMS will not allow any row where *vendorid* is *NULL*. Because we have disallowed NULL values for *vendorid* and not specified a default value, we cannot insert a new row that doesn't specify a value for *vendorid*.

- We specify multiple column characteristics in a space-delimited list. For example, *companyname* must be non-NULL, and if no value is specified, the company name is SECRET.

- Although it is the default to allow *NULL* values, we specify a NULL constraint for *referredby*. Some DBMSs may require explicit specification of either NULL or NOT NULL.

9.3.2 UNIQUE

The UNIQUE constraint forces distinct column values. Suppose you want to avoid duplicate meal names. Just specify the UNIQUE column constraint on the *name* column as follows:

DDL 9.4 Specify a UNIQUE column constraint

```
CREATE TABLE meals (
  mealid CHAR(5) NOT NULL,
  name CHAR(20) UNIQUE
);
```

Now the DBMS will not allow any row with a duplicate *name* value. Note that UNIQUE only applies to non-*NULL* values. A UNIQUE column may have many rows containing a *NULL* value. Of course, we can exclude all *NULL* values for the column using the NOT NULL constraint with the UNIQUE constraint.

What if we want to make the values for a set of columns unique? For example, suppose we want to make sure that we don't have two vendor representatives with the same first and last name. We could try the following column constraint specifications:

DDL 9.5 **INCORRECT!** Specify a multi-attribute UNIQUE constraint

```
repfname VARCHAR(20) DEFAULT 'Mr. or Ms.' UNIQUE,
replname VARCHAR(20) UNIQUE,
```

Unfortunately, such column constraints apply independently. Under these constraints, we could not have two representatives with the first name "Bob", even if their last names differed, because the UNIQUE constraint for *repfname* only applies to that column. Fortunately, UNIQUE also has a table constraint form that applies to the entire table instead of just a single column. Table constraints are specified as another item in the comma-delimited list of table elements. Such table constraints apply to groups of one or more columns. Consider the following CREATE TABLE statement:

DDL 9.6 Specify a multi-attribute UNIQUE constraint

```
CREATE TABLE vendors (
  vendorid CHAR(5) NOT NULL,
  companyname VARCHAR(30) NOT NULL DEFAULT 'SECRET' UNIQUE,
  repfname VARCHAR(20) DEFAULT 'Mr. or Ms.',
  replname VARCHAR(20),
  referredby CHAR(5) NULL,
  UNIQUE(repfname, replname)
);
```

The UNIQUE(repfname, replname) table constraint allows multiple vendor representatives with the same first or last name. What it doesn't allow is more than one vendor with the same first *and* last name. Note that the table constraint form of UNIQUE may take a single column.

9.3.3 PRIMARY KEY

Recall from Chapter 1 that the primary key of a table is a column or set of columns that uniquely identifies a row in the table. For example, *itemid* is the primary key from the *items* table. We can declare a primary key using the PRIMARY KEY constraint. Here we show PRIMARY KEY used as a column constraint.

DDL 9.7 Specify a PRIMARY KEY column constraint

```
itemid CHAR(5) PRIMARY KEY
```

What about a primary key with multiple columns? For example, the primary key of the *partof* table contains two columns. You cannot simply add the PRIMARY KEY constraint to every column in the key because SQL will think you are trying to create multiple primary keys, which is not allowed. Instead, use the table constraint form of PRIMARY KEY.

DDL 9.8 Specify a PRIMARY KEY table constraint

```
CREATE TABLE partof (
  mealid CHAR(5),
  itemid CHAR(5),
  quantity INTEGER,
  discount DECIMAL (2, 2) DEFAULT 0.00,
  PRIMARY KEY(mealid, itemid)
);
```

Of course, it is perfectly legal for the the table constraint form of PRIMARY KEY to contain a single column. Keep the following in mind when specifying the PRIMARY KEY constraint:

- No values of the primary key columns may be *NULL,* so we don't need the NOT NULL constraint for *itemid* (although some DBMSs may require it). In the *partof* table, *neither itemid* nor *ingredientid* may have a *NULL* value for any row.

- Because the primary key uniquely identifies a row in the table, SQL will not allow two rows with the same value for all attributes of the primary key.

- SQL allows tables to be created without a primary key; however, this is usually a bad idea because we won't be guaranteed to have a way to specify a particular row.

- The PRIMARY KEY and UNIQUE constraints differ in two ways:

    1. UNIQUE allows *NULL* values for its columns.

    2. There can be at most one PRIMARY KEY constraint for each table. There is no such limit on the number of UNIQUE constraints for a table.

9.3.4 FOREIGN KEY

A foreign key restricts the values of a column (or a set of columns) to the values appearing in another column (or set of columns) or to *NULL.* In table *ingredients* (child table), *vendorid* is a foreign key that refers to *vendorid* in table *vendors* (parent table). We want all of the values of *vendorid* in the *ingredients* table either to reference a *vendorid* from *vendors* or to be *NULL.* Any other vendor ID in the *ingredients* table would create problems because you couldn't look up information about the vendor such as the company name or the representative.

In SQL, we specify a foreign key with the REFERENCES column constraint.

```
REFERENCES <referenced table>[(<referenced column>)]
```

A column with a REFERENCES constraint may only have a value of either *NULL* or a value found in column *<referenced column>* of table *<referenced table>*. If the *<referenced column>* is omitted, the primary key of table *<referenced table>* is used. Here is the *madewith* table with the appropriate foreign keys.

DDL 9.9 Specify a FOREIGN KEY column constraint

```
CREATE TABLE madewith (
  itemid CHAR(5) REFERENCES items(itemid),
  ingredientid CHAR(5) REFERENCES ingredients,
  quantity INTEGER DEFAULT 0 NOT NULL,
  PRIMARY KEY(itemid, ingredientid)
);
```

With both the primary key and references constraints, the DBMS will only accept column values for *itemid* in *madewith* if the following are true:

- The value exists in the *items.itemid* (foreign key constraint) AND

- The value is not *NULL* (primary key constraint)

Similar constraints hold on *ingredientid*.

What about a foreign key with multiple columns? You cannot simply add the FOREIGN KEY constraint to every column in the foreign key because SQL will treat each independently. Instead, use the table constraint form of FOREIGN KEY.

```
FOREIGN KEY (<column list>) REFERENCES
<referenced table>[(<referenced columns>)]
```

None of our tables have a multiple column foreign key. Here we demonstrate the table constraint form of FOREIGN KEY in the *partof* table creation statement.

DDL 9.10 Specify a multi-attribute FOREIGN KEY table constraint

```
CREATE TABLE partof (
  mealid CHAR(5),
  itemid CHAR(5),
  quantity INTEGER,
  discount DECIMAL (2, 2) DEFAULT 0.00,
  PRIMARY KEY(mealid, itemid),
  FOREIGN KEY(mealid) REFERENCES meals(mealid),
  FOREIGN KEY(itemid) REFERENCES items(itemid)
);
```

To create a foreign key reference, SQL requires that the referenced table/column already exist. For example, *items.itemid* must exist before you can specify the foreign key reference of *madewith.itemid*.

9.3.5 CHECK

We can specify a much more general type of constraint using the CHECK constraint. A CHECK constraint specifies a boolean value expression to be evaluated for each row before allowing any data change. Any INSERT, UPDATE, or DELETE that would cause the condition for any row to evaluate to false is rejected by the DBMS.

```
CHECK (<condition>)
```

A CHECK constraint may be specified as either a column or table constraint. In the following example, we specify two CHECK constraints on the *ingredients* table: a column CHECK constraint on the allowable *foodgroup* values and a table constraint over the inventory value of each ingredient.

DDL 9.11 Specify a column and table CHECK constraint

```
CREATE TABLE ingredients (
  ingredientid CHAR(5) PRIMARY KEY,
  name VARCHAR(30) NOT NULL,
  unit CHAR(10),
  unitprice NUMERIC(5,2),
  foodgroup CHAR(15) CHECK (foodgroup IN ('Milk', 'Meat', 'Bread',
                                          'Fruit', 'Vegetable')),
  inventory INTEGER DEFAULT 0,
  vendorid CHAR(5),
  CHECK (unitprice * inventory <= 4000),
  FOREIGN KEY(vendorid) REFERENCES vendors(vendorid)
);
```

Does an ingredient with a *NULL* food group violate the CHECK constraint? No. In this case, the CHECK condition evaluates to unknown. The CHECK constraint only rejects a change when the condition evaluates to false. In the SQL standard, a CHECK constraint condition may even include subqueries referencing other tables; however, many DBMSs do not implement this feature.

9.3.6 Naming Constraints

You can name your constraints by using an optional prefix.

```
CONSTRAINT <name> <constraint>
```

For example, we can name the foreign key constraint in our *ingredients* table. Here is an excerpt of that statement.

DDL 9.12 Name FOREIGN KEY constraint

```
CREATE TABLE ingredients (
  ingredientid CHAR(5) PRIMARY KEY,
  name VARCHAR(30) NOT NULL,
  . . .
  CONSTRAINT vidfk FOREIGN KEY(ingredientid) REFERENCES vendors
);
```

Why name your constraints? When you attempt an insert, update, or delete that violates a constraint, SQL rejects the operation and issues an error message. Many DBMSs include the name of the violated constraint in the error message. Also, we can delete constraints by name with ALTER TABLE (Section 9.9).

9.4 Creating a Table from Tables

SQL allows you to create and populate a new table from existing tables with one statement. You could create the new table yourself and populate it using INSERT, but that's a lot of work. Fortunately, SQL provides a version of CREATE TABLE to do it all for us.

```
CREATE TABLE <table name>
[(<column list>)] AS <subquery>
```

CREATE TABLE AS creates a new table named *<table name>* with the columns and rows returned by *<subquery>*. By default, the column names are determined by the subquery; however, you can override this with the optional column list. The data types of the columns are determined by the SELECT, and initially we have no constraints.

Suppose you wanted to have total sales for the stores stored in the database so you do not have to compute it every time. We can create the table with the aggregate data.

DDL 9.13 Create a new table using CREATE TABLE AS

```
CREATE TABLE sales(storeid, manager, total) AS
SELECT s.storeid, manager, SUM(price)
FROM orders o, stores s
WHERE o.storeid = s.storeid
GROUP BY s.storeid, s.manager;
```

This creates an actual table named *sales* populated with the data returned from the SELECT.

We can achieve the same results using SELECT INTO. This approach simply modifies the SELECT statement so that the output goes to a new table. To do this, add an INTO *<table name>* clause in the SELECT.

DDL 9.14 Create a new table using SELECT INTO

```
SELECT s.storeid, manager, SUM(price) as total
INTO sales
FROM orders o, stores s
WHERE o.storeid = s.storeid
GROUP BY s.storeid, manager;
```

In both cases, the data type of *sales.storeid* is CHAR(5), derived from the data type of *sales.storeid*. Similarly, the type of *sales.manager* is VARCHAR(30). The type of total is based on the results of the computation and will be a numeric type.

Remember Query 7.13? With our sales table it is very easy to answer.

Query 9.15 Find the managers of stores with more than $20 in sales

```
SELECT manager
FROM sales
WHERE total > 20;
```

manager
Greg Donahoo
Greg Speegle

[2 row(s)]

Note that both of these approaches create a completely new table. Any changes to orders or stores will have *no effect* on the *sales* table. An alternative approach that links the *sales* table and the underlying tables is called a *view*, which we discuss in Chapter 10.

9.5 CREATE DOMAIN

SQL allows the specification of user-defined domains based on existing data types. These domains work just like any other data type.

```
CREATE DOMAIN <domain name> [AS] <data type> [DEFAULT <value expression>]
[<CHECK constraint list>];
```

Let's try an example. Several columns in our restaurant schema are IDs (e.g., *itemid, vendorid,* etc.). For corresponding IDs, we must make sure we use the same data type in each table. To ensure such consistency, we create a domain for the ID data type.

DDL 9.16 Create an ID domain

```
CREATE DOMAIN idtype AS CHAR(5);
```

Now we can declare all of our ID columns as type *idtype.*

We can also associate a default value and a set of CHECK constraints with a domain. The syntax is identical to the DEFAULT and column-constraint CHECK in CREATE TABLE with one exception. Because we want the check constraint of the domain to work for any attribute with the user-defined domain, we use the VALUE keyword in place of the attribute name. Let's create a *pricetype* with a default value of 0 and a check constraint of a nonnegative price. We demonstrate its use on an abbreviated *ingredients* table.

DDL 9.17 Use domain attribute types

```
CREATE DOMAIN pricetype AS NUMERIC(5,2) DEFAULT 0 CHECK (VALUE >= 0);

CREATE TABLE ingredients (
  ingredientid idtype PRIMARY KEY,
  unitprice pricetype,
  vendorid idtype NOT NULL REFERENCES vendors(vendorid)
);
```

You can change a domain's default value and constraints using ALTER DOMAIN. You can delete a domain using DROP DOMAIN. Unfortunately, few DBMSs support any of the domain statements.

9.6 Referential Actions: The Autopilot of Foreign Key Maintenance

Maintaining foreign key constraints can be painful. To update or delete a referenced value in the parent table, we must make sure that we first handle all foreign keys referencing that value in the child table. For example, to update or delete VGRUS from the *vendors* table, we must first update or delete all *ingredients.vendorid* and *vendors.referredby* values. SQL allows us to specify the default actions for maintaining foreign key constraints for UPDATE and DELETE on the parent table by adding a referential action clause to the end of a column or table foreign key constraint:

```
ON UPDATE <action>
ON DELETE <action>
```

Any UPDATE or DELETE on the parent table triggers the specified *<action>* on the referencing rows in the child table. The possible actions are in Table 9.1.

Action	Definition
SET NULL	Sets any referencing foreign key values to *NULL*.
SET DEFAULT	Sets any referencing foreign key values to the default value (which may be *NULL*).
CASCADE	On delete, this deletes any rows with referencing foreign key values. On update, this updates any row with referencing foreign key values to the new value of the referenced column.
NO ACTION	Rejects any update or delete that violates the foreign key constraint. This is the default action.
RESTRICT	Same as NO ACTION with the additional restriction that the action cannot be deferred (see Chapter 11).

Table 9.1: Foreign key actions.

Let's look at an example. Each ingredient references the ID of the vendor that provides it. If a vendor changes its ID, we want the providing vendor ID to change for all ingredients the vendor provides. If a vendor is deleted, we want the providing vendor ID to change to our default vendor, Gene's Generic Gunk, with ID GEGEK for all ingredients the vendor provided. DDL 9.18 demonstrates this in an abbreviated *ingredients* table creation.

DDL 9.18 Specify CASCADE and SET DEFAULT referential actions

```
CREATE TABLE ingredients (
    ingredientid CHAR(5) PRIMARY KEY,
    vendroid CHAR(5) DEFAULT 'GEGEK' REFERENCES vendors ON UPDATE CASCADE ON DELETE
        SET DEFAULT
);
```

For a deletion to work, the GEGEK vendor must already exist in the *vendors* table. Instead of setting a default vendor ID, we could simply set *ingredients.vendorid* to *NULL*.

DDL 9.19 Specify SET NULL referential action

```
CREATE TABLE ingredients (
    ingredientid CHAR(5) PRIMARY KEY,
    vendorid CHAR(5) REFERENCES vendors ON DELETE SET NULL
);
```

The default referential action is NO ACTION so far the *ingredients* table created in DDL 9.19 updates to *vendors.vendorid* violating the foreign key constraint are rejected.

9.7 Indexes

So far we have assumed a simple model of reading tables where the database does the following:

1. Reads a row in the table

2. Evaluates the WHERE condition

3. If there is another row, goes to Step 1; otherwise, quits

This is called *sequential* processing because we are processing the table row-by-row. In general we have to read the entire table to make sure we have found all of the rows that satisfy the WHERE condition. For large tables, sequential processing can be very time-consuming. Furthermore, as rows are added to the table, it will tend to become *fragmented*. This means that parts of the table are not stored together on a disk; they are spread out on the disk. This slows down sequential processing even more.

There are many algorithms for faster lookup. The approach used in database systems is to have an additional data structure called an *index*. An index is usually defined over a single attribute. The database can use the index to quickly find all of the rows that contain a particular value of that attribute. Consider Query 9.20.

Query 9.20 Index example

```
SELECT companyname
FROM vendors
WHERE vendorid = 'VGRUS'
```

If we have an index on the *vendorid* column, the DBMS can use the index to find the location of the row containing the particular *vendorid* value instead of sequentially searching. As a result, the query will execute in almost exactly the same time whether we have six rows in our *vendors* table or 600,000. However, the sequential search method would take 100,000 times longer on the larger table.

9.7.1 CREATE INDEX

We can create an index using the CREATE INDEX command.

```
CREATE [UNIQUE] INDEX <indexname> ON <table name>(<column list>)
```

This creates an index on the values of the attribute in *<column list>* from table *<table name>*. Indexes are so important for query performance that some databases will automatically create an index on the primary key of a table. This index is particularly important for speeding up many types of queries. If a query, particularly one involving a join on a foreign key, is running slowly, adding a query on the primary key may help a great deal.

Notice that indexes do NOT have to be on unique domains. Nonunique attributes can also be indexed and provide similar query performance improvements, although an attribute with few distinct values (e.g., gender) will not benefit much from an index. If the attribute *is* unique, then we can add the keyword UNIQUE to create a unique index. Let's create the index for the *vendorid* of the *vendors* table.

DDL 9.21 Create index on *vendors.vendorid*

```
CREATE UNIQUE INDEX vendorindex ON vendors(vendorid);
```

It is an error to declare a unique index on a nonunique attribute.

With all of the great benefits of an index, you might be tempted to add an index on everything. There are two problems with this idea. First, if you are updating the table, every index must also be updated, slowing down the performance of the update. Second, if you add an index that is never used, you unnecessarily consume resources. This leads to the following benefit analysis for adding an index.

1. The primary key of the table should have an index.

2. The more times an attribute is used in a query, the better a candidate it is for an index.

3. The higher the ratio of queries to updates, the better the chances the index will improve overall performance.

9.7.2   DROP INDEX

We can remove an index using the DROP INDEX command.

```
DROP INDEX <index name>
```

This removes the specified index. It does not modify any data.

9.7.3   Indexes Are NOT in SQL 2003

Despite the importance of indexes to DBMS performance, indexes are not part of the SQL standard. The rationale behind this decision is that creating indexes is part of the physical storage and access of the data. The SQL standard is limited to the logical description of the data, so indexes are not included. However, any production-grade DBMS must have indexes, and most will have a mechanism for you to add your own. If the syntax presented here does not work for you, check your DBMS documentation.

9.8   DROP TABLE

You can remove a table using the following:

```
DROP TABLE <table name> [CASCADE | RESTRICT];
```

DROP TABLE deletes the table *<name>* along with its data from the database. Let's drop the *ads* table.

DDL 9.22 Drop table
```
DROP TABLE ads;
```

Be careful. Once you drop a table, it's gone, along with all of its data. You cannot undo a DROP TABLE. Let's compare this statement with one we saw earlier.

Delete 9.23 Delete all rows
```
DELETE
FROM ads;
```

The DELETE operation removes all of the rows from the table, but the table still remains. With DROP TABLE, the table itself is removed, along with all of its rows, all of its constraints, and everything else related to it. With the DELETE statement, the ON DELETE actions we discussed earlier can be applied, but when the DROP TABLE statement is executed, the constraints themselves may become invalid because the reference table is gone. Thus, DROP TABLE is even more extreme than DELETE without a WHERE clause.

In fact, SQL does not allow a table to be dropped if its removal invalidates any constraints. If you try to drop the *vendors* table, SQL will refuse because of the foreign key constraint on *ingredients.vendorid.* This is the default behavior or the result of using the RESTRICT option. To remove a table with constraints, we can specify CASCADE with DROP TABLE. This will cause any constraints referencing the table to be removed before the table is dropped. Let's try dropping the *vendors* table with cascading.

DDL 9.24 Drop table with CASCADE

```
DROP TABLE vendors CASCADE;
```

SQL begins by dropping the foreign key constraint from *ingredients.* Then, it can actually drop the *vendors* table.

According to the SQL specification, you must specify either CASCADE or RESTRICT with DROP TABLE. It is not optional. We present it as optional because most (if not all) DBMSs treat it as optional, with a default behavior of RESTRICT. For compliance with the SQL standard, it's a good idea to specify either CASCADE or RESTRICT.

9.9 ALTER TABLE

You can modify the columns and constraints of a table using the following:

```
ALTER TABLE <table name> <action>;
```

There are several types of actions:

ADD [COLUMN] *<column definition>*
Adds a new column to *<table name>*. The *<column definition>* may contain any of the elements of a column definition in CREATE TABLE, such as types and constraints.

ALTER [COLUMN] *<column name>*
[SET DEFAULT *<value expression>* | **DROP DEFAULT]**
Change or drop the specified default value from *<column name>*. Your DBMS will likely let you alter much more than just the default values.

DROP [COLUMN] *<column name>* **[CASCADE | RESTRICT]**
Delete *<column name>* from *<table name>*. If there are any external dependencies on this column, the drop will be rejected. If CASCADE is specified, the DBMS will attempt to eliminate all external dependencies before deleting the column. If RESTRICT is specified, the DBMS will not allow the DROP if any external dependencies would be violated. This is the default behavior.

ADD *<table constraint>*
Add a new constraint to *<table name>*. *<table constraint>* uses the same syntax as table constraints in CREATE TABLE.

DROP CONSTRAINT *<constraint name>* [**CASCADE** | **RESTRICT**]

Delete *<constraint name>* from *<table name>*. If there are any external entities that depend on this constraint, the drop could invalidate the entity. If RESTRICT is specified and an entity could be invalidated, the DBMS will not drop the constraint. This is the default behavior. If CASCADE is specified, the DBMS will attempt to eliminate all potentially violated entities before deleting the constraint.

Let's add a company Web page to the *vendors* table.

DDL 9.25 Add a column to a table

```
ALTER TABLE vendors
ADD COLUMN url VARCHAR(100) DEFAULT 'unlisted';
```

The new attribute, *url,* is added to the table. The url value for all of the existing rows is unlisted. If we hadn't specified a default, all of the existing rows would have a value of *NULL* for the *url* attribute.

What if we want to drop the foreign key constraint on *ingredients.vendorid?* The DROP CONSTRAINT syntax requires a constraint name. Usually, the DBMS names a constraint if you don't provide a name. Finding that name (if it exists) is DBMS specific. Let's assume that we heeded our earlier warning and created *ingredients.vendorid* as follows:

DDL 9.26 Name a FOREIGN KEY constraint

```
vendorid CHAR(5) CONSTRAINT vidfk REFERENCES vendors;
```

We can remove the constraint as follows:

DDL 9.27 Drop a constraint

```
ALTER TABLE ingredients
DROP CONSTRAINT vidfk RESTRICT;
```

According to the SQL specification, you must specify either CASCADE or RESTRICT with DROP COLUMN or DROP CONSTRAINT. It is not optional. We present it as optional because most (if not all) DBMSs treat it as optional, with a default behavior of RESTRICT. For compliance with the SQL standard, it's a good idea to specify either CASCADE or RESTRICT.

9.10 Generated Values

SQL will automatically generate data for you. Say you wanted to make a table of purchases, consisting of an order number, the ID of the vendor, and the time of the order. For a new order, the order number should be 1 more than the last order number.

SQL provides several mechanisms for autogeneration of data. Let's look at an example for the *purchases* table.

DDL 9.28 Create *purchases* table

```
CREATE TABLE purchases (
orderno INTEGER GENERATED BY DEFAULT AS IDENTITY,
vendorid CHAR(5) REFERENCES vendors,
ordertime TIMESTAMP DEFAULT CURRENT_TIMESTAMP
);
```

To insert a new order, we only really need the vendor ID.

DDL 9.29 Generated data example

```
INSERT INTO purchases (vendorid) VALUES ('VGRUS');
```

This will autogenerate an order number and set the order time to the current time. Pretty nice! Unfortunately, although most DBMSs have autogeneration, most have their own, DBMS-specific way of declaring autogenerated columns. Consult your DBMS documentation.

9.11 Sequences

Identity is one way of automatically generating values in SQL, but a more general approach is a sequence. A sequence is a database object that generates values. The values are numeric, but the sequence can be ascending or descending, can skip values, and can start at any valid value.

The 2003 standard defines a sequence as follows:

```
CREATE SEQUENCE <sequence name> [AS <data type>]
[START WITH <signed numeric literal>]
[INCREMENT BY <signed numeric literal>]
[MAXVALUE <signed numeric literal> | NO MAXVALUE]
[MINVALUE <signed numeric literal> | NO MINVALUE]
[CYCLE | NO CYCLE]
```

Effectively, each time a new value is generated by a sequence, the increment value is added to the current value. If the increment value is negative, then the current value decreases and the sequence is *descending.* If the increment value is positive, then the current value increases and the sequence is *ascending.* It is illegal for the increment value to be 0.

We may have many sequences in our database. For example, we can have a separate sequence for each store to generate order numbers. Whenever a customer places an order at that store, that sequence increases its value and returns a result. Because each store has its own sequence, we can have the same order number in different stores.

For example, the command

DDL 9.30 Create a default sequence

```
CREATE SEQUENCE castr_seq;
```

creates a sequence with default values for type (implementation defined), starting value (implementation defined), increment (1), maxvalue (implementation defined), minvalue (implementation defined), and cycling (NO CYCLE). If we only wanted even numbers between 100 and 1000 generated, we could create the following sequence:

DDL 9.31 Create a complex sequence

```
CREATE SEQUENCE even_numbers START WITH 100 INCREMENT BY 2 MAXVALUE 1000
                           MINVALUE 100;
```

The first value of the sequence *even_numbers* will be 100, the next will be 102, and so on.

To get a number from a sequence, we use the NEXT VALUE function. For an ascending function, the NEXT VALUE function returns the lowest valid value not already returned for the sequence. The syntax for the function is straightforward.

```
NEXT VALUE FOR <sequence name>
```

Unfortunately, there are many restrictions on where we can use the NEXT VALUE function. Among other places, it *cannot* appear in the following:

- Select list with DISTINCT (Chapter 3.2)
- WHERE condition
- ORDER BY (Section 3.5)
- Aggregate function (Chapter 4)
- CASE statement (Section 3.7).

That still leaves many places where we can use the NEXT VALUE function, including derived relations (Section 7.9) and cursors (Section 13.1).

One of the best places to use sequences is for inserting values into a table. We can automatically generate a new order number for the CASTR store.

DDL 9.32 Insert new order with sequence order number

```
INSERT INTO orders VALUES (NEXT VALUE FOR castr_seq, 1, 'CASTR','SODA', 0.99);
```

There are several important points to note about Insert 9.32. First, this only inserted one row into the *orders* table. If we inserted multiple lines for the same order, the NEXT VALUE function would increment the order number every time. Most DBMSs provide a function to return the current value of the sequence without incrementing it. This could be used for additional rows belonging to the same order. Second, *any* call to NEXT VALUE will increment the sequence. Thus, if a second cashier increments the sequence, even calling a DBMS-specific current value function will not work. A common practice is to use the sequence number outside of SQL (see Chapter 13) to ensure that it does not change.

We could also use a sequence to generate the line numbers for orders. In this case, the line numbers start over with each new order. The CYCLE option causes the values returned by the sequence generator to start over, but it has an effect only when the sequence exceeds the maximum value.

The SQL Standard specifies an ALTER SEQUENCE command to reset the current value of a sequence or to modify any of the other properties, such as MINVALUE or INCREMENT. Its syntax is as follows:

```
ALTER SEQUENCE <sequence generator name>
[RESTART WITH <signed numeric literal>]
[INCREMENT BY <signed numeric literal>]
[MAXVALUE <signed numeric literal> | NO MAXVALUE]
[MINVALUE <signed numeric literal> | NO MINVALUE]
[CYCLE | NO CYCLE]
```

To reset the line number when we start a new order, we could issue the following statement:

DDL 9.33 Alter sequence

```
ALTER SEQUENCE castr_line_seq RESTART WITH 1
```

Most DBMSs have other functions for modifying this value, and some do not use this statement to reset the value. Check your DBMS documentation.

Finally, it is easy to delete a sequence with the following command:

```
DROP SEQUENCE <sequence name> [CASCADE | RESTRICT]
```

As with the other DROP commands, if RESTRICT is specified, the sequence will not be dropped if it invalidates the database. In particular, if a trigger (Chapter 13.3) uses a sequence, the DROP SEQUENCE will fail. The CASCADE option will remove all dependent database objects.

9.12 Global and Local Temporary Tables

SQL allows the creation of temporary tables. Such tables might be used for storing results that were expensive and/or complex to compute. Temporary tables are created like any other table with the exception of the TEMPORARY keyword. GLOBAL and LOCAL determine the access scope of a temporary table. There are many restrictions on the use of TEMPORARY tables. Consult your DBMS documentation for specific details.

An example of declaring a LOCAL TEMPORARY TABLE follows:

DDL 9.34 Create temporary table

```
CREATE LOCAL TEMPORARY TABLE temp (
    key INTEGER,
    value VARCHAR(100)
);
```

9.13 Creating a Database

In SQL, databases are organized into a hierarchy of containers, as shown in Figure 9.1. You already knew that tables contained rows and columns. A *schema* contains a collection of tables, and a *catalog* contains a collection of schemas. Each catalog, schema, table, and attribute has a name. Names within a container must be unique, but other containers may contain objects with the same name. For example, we've already seen the names of the attributes within a table must be unique; however, two tables may both have attributes with the same name. Using the hierarchy, you can give a fully qualified name to a database object as follows:

```
<catalog>.<schema>.<table>.<column>
```

The mechanism for creating catalogs is system dependent. Schemas are created using CREATE SCHEMA.

```
CREATE SCHEMA <schema name>
```

Although all DBMSs support an object hierarchy, many define their own, nonstandard organization. See your DBMS documentation for details.

While it is not part of the standard, most DBMSs define a database container for holding tables (or schemas containing tables). A DBMS manages a collection of databases. We can create a database using either a DBMS-specific tool or a command similar to the following:

```
CREATE DATABASE <database name>
```

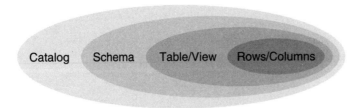

Figure 9.1: SQL container hierarchy.

9.14 Wrap Up

We can create a table in SQL by specifying a table name and a comma-delimited list of column name/data type pairs to CREATE TABLE. We may also specify a set of constraints to be enforced by the DBMS. Such constraints are key to maintaining the integrity of your data. Enforcement of these constraints is accomplished by not allowing an INSERT, UPDATE, or DELETE to execute if the results of the statement violate a constraint.

We can also change tables by using the ALTER TABLE command. This allows us to add or remove columns, constraints, and other metadata. We can even change how a DBMS will enforce the constraints. SQL provides for automatically generated values. Finally, we can create databases and schemas to hold our tables.

Review Questions

1. Insert a row into the projects table without a startdate or an enddate. What happened?

2. For each of the following columns, what is a reasonable DEFAULT value?

   - employees.firstname

   - projects.enddate

   - projects.revenue

   - workson.assignedtime

3. Consider the *person* table.

DDL 9.35 Create *person* table

```
CREATE TABLE person (
   pid INTEGER PRIMARY KEY,
   name VARCHAR(100) NOT NULL,
   age INTEGER DEFAULT 20 NOT NULL,
   badgeid INTEGER DEFAULT 1 UNIQUE
);
```

For each INSERT statement that follows, give a result of Accepted or Rejected. Provide all reasons for rejection. The statements are executed in the given order, and any rejected statements are ignored.

Statement	Result
INSERT INTO person DEFAULT VALUES;	
INSERT INTO person (pid, name) VALUES (1, DEFAULT);	
INSERT INTO person (pid, name) VALUES (2, 'Jack');	
INSERT INTO person (pid, name) VALUES (3, 'Jill');	

4. List all of the constraints that may apply to multiple attributes.

5. Give the SQL command to create a domain named *bloodtypedomain* as a CHAR(2). Restrict the possible values to A, B, O, AB.

   Complete the following table creation. Make sure that *bloodtype* cannot be *NULL* and *gender* can only be "M", "F", or *NULL*.

DDL 9.36 Patient table

```
CREATE TABLE patient (
  id INTEGER PRIMARY KEY,
  gender CHAR(1)
  bloodtype
);
```

6. Consider the *vehicle* table.

DDL 9.37 Vehicle table

```
CREATE TABLE vehicle (
  vehicleid CHAR(5) PRIMARY KEY,
  manufacturerid INTEGER NOT NULL REFERENCES manufacturer,
  productioncost NUMERIC(10, 2) CHECK (productioncost >= 0),
  retailprice NUMERIC(10, 2) CHECK(retailprice > productioncost)
);
```

For each INSERT statement, give a result of Accepted or Rejected. If rejected, name the violated constraint.

INSERT INTO vehicle VALUES	Result
('CAR01', 1, 15000, 25000);	
('CAR02', 1, NULL, 25000);	
('CAR03', NULL, 26000, 25000);	
('CAR04', 1, 26000, 25000);	
('CAR03', 1, NULL, -5);	

7. For the Restaurant Database, which attributes would benefit from an index?

8. For the Employees Database, add an index for employees.deptcode. Is this index unique or nonunique?

9. Create a table *test* with two attributes: value and key. Make value a VARCHAR(200). Make key an INTEGER and UNIQUE. Insert 100 rows into the table. Search for a random key value and time how long the search takes. Repeat with 10,000 rows. Repeat with 1,000,000 rows. Create an index on key and repeat the experiments. Do not insert any *NULL* values for key.

Practice

The local library has hired you to create a database containing books, authors, and patrons.

1. Give the SQL statements to create a database named library and add the following tables. Make sure you enforce all constraints and implement all defaults. Include all reasonable indexes.

Library

books—Books in the library

Column	Type	NULL Allowed	Default Value	Comments
bookid	INTEGER	No		Primary key
title	VARCHAR(200)	No		
pages	INTEGER	Yes		
sequelto	INTEGER	Yes	*NULL*	Foreign key to book(bookid) indicating the book that this is a sequel. If the book is not a sequel, the value is *NULL*

wrote—Pairs books with authors

Column	Type	NULL Allowed	Default Value	Comments
bookid	INTEGER	No		You figure out the primary key for this table
authorid	INTEGER	No		Does not allow an author to be listed multiple times on a single book
authororder	INTEGER	No	0	Determines author order on a book; do not allow multiple authors on the same book to have the same *authororder* value

authors—Authors of library books

Column	Type	NULL Allowed	Default Value	Comments
authorid	INTEGER	No		Primary key
name	VARCHAR(100)	No		Does not allow multiple authors with same name

checksout—Pairs books with patrons

Column	Type	NULL Allowed	Default Value	Comments
patronid	INTEGER	No		You figure out the primary key for this table; if a patron is deleted, all of her checksout records should be automatically deleted; if a patron's ID is changed, the patronid references should automatically change to the new value
bookid	INTEGER	No		A book may be checked out by a patron multiple times
dateout	DATE	No	Current date	
datein	DATE	Yes	NULL	If the book has not been checked in, *datein* should be *NULL*; make sure that the *datein* is on or after the *dateout* if it is not *NULL*

patrons—People that check out library books

Column	Type	NULL Allowed	Default Value	Comments
patronid	INTEGER	No		Primary key
name	VARCHAR(100)	No		
favoritebook	INTEGER	Yes		Foreign key to book(bookid) indicating this patron's favorite book; if the patron doesn't have a favorite book, the value is *NULL*

2. Give the SQL statements to populate the tables with 2 books (one a sequel of the other), 2 patrons (Ed and Earl with a favorite book), and 2 authors (Jane and Jill). Assign Jill to one book and both Jane and Jill to the other book. Check out both books to Ed. Make the remaining data up yourself.

3. Give the SQL statements to check in all checked out books and then checkout all books by Jill to Earl. Make no assumptions about the data.

4. Give the SQL statement to increase by 10 the number of pages for all books written by Jane. If the number of pages is NULL, do not change the value. Make no assumptions about the data.

5. Give the SQL statements to delete all information related to the author Jill including her author information, books she wrote, and the checkout records of those books. Make no assumptions about the data.

6. Give the SQL statement to remove the *pages* column from the *books* table.

7. Give the SQL statement(s) to successfully remove the *books* table.

8. Add an index for the *name* attribute of the *authors* table. Should it be a unique index?

9. Add an index for the *bookid* attribute of *checksout*. Should it be a unique index?

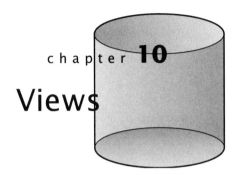

chapter 10
Views

A view is a virtual table defined by a query. It provides a mechanism to create alternate ways of working with the data in a database. A view acts much like a table. We can query it with a SELECT, and some views even allow INSERT, UPDATE, and DELETE. However, a view doesn't have any data. All of its data are ultimately derived from tables (called *base tables*) like those we created in Chapter 9. Views are similar to derived tables (see Chapter 7), except that views are defined once and can be used in many queries. We can create a view using the CREATE VIEW command.

```
CREATE VIEW <view name> [(<column list>)] AS <SELECT statement>
```

This creates a view named *<view name>*. The column names/types and data for the view are determined by the result table derived by executing *<SELECT statement>*. Optionally, we can specify the column names of the view in *<column list>*. The number of columns in *<column list>* must match the number of columns in the *<SELECT statement>*.

Let's create a view showing the ingredients (ingredient ID, inventory, and inventory value) supplied to us by Veggies_R_Us.

DDL 10.1 View vrs
_____

```
CREATE VIEW vrs AS
    SELECT ingredientid, name, inventory, inventory * unitprice AS value
    FROM ingredients i, vendors v
    WHERE i.vendorid = v.vendorid AND companyname = 'Veggies_R_Us';
```

This creates a view named *vrs*. Note that views may contain expressions and even simple literals. Let's take a look at the view.

DDL 10.2 Show *vrs* view

vrs

ingredientid	name	inventory	value
LETUS	Lettuce	200	2.00
PICKL	Pickle	800	32.00
TOMTO	Tomato	15	0.45

Our *vrs* view contains four columns with the names and types of the results from the SELECT statement. Note a view's SELECT statement may refer to other views.

Because the view is just a virtual table, any changes to the base tables are instantly reflected in the view data. For example, if we doubled the inventory for the Tomato ingredient, the *vrs* view would show a doubled inventory and inventory value, as in this example.

Update 10.3 Update the tomato inventory

```
UPDATE ingredients
SET inventory = inventory * 2
WHERE ingredientid = 'TOMTO';

SELECT * from vrs;
```

ingredientid	name	inventory	value
LETUS	Lettuce	200	2.00
PICKL	Pickle	800	32.00
TOMTO	Tomato	30	0.90

[3 row(s)]

10.1   Why Views?

There are several uses for a view.

Usability—We can use a view as a wrapper around very complex SELECT statements to make our system more usable.

Security—If we need to restrict the data a user can access, we can create a view containing only the permitted data. The user is given access to the view instead of the base table(s). See Chapter 12 for details.

Reduced Dependency—The database schema evolves over time as our enterprise changes. Such changes can break existing applications that expect a certain set of tables with certain columns. We can fix this by having our applications access views rather than base tables. When the base tables change, existing applications still work as long as the views are correct.

10.2 Querying Views

We can query views just like base tables.

Query 10.4 Find all ingredients provided by Veggies_R_Us with an inventory of more than 100

```
SELECT name
FROM vrs
WHERE inventory > 100;
```

name
Lettuce
Pickle

[2 row(s)]

Note that these are exactly the same results as Query 10.5.

Query 10.5 Rewrite as Query 10.4 using only base tables

```
SELECT name
FROM ingredients i, vendors v
WHERE i.vendorid = v.vendorid AND companyname = 'Veggies_R_Us'
      AND inventory > 100;
```

name
Lettuce
Pickle

[2 row(s)]

Let's create a new view called *menuitems* that lists all of the items we have for sale, including meals and items, and how much they cost. The actual view definition is quite complex.

DDL 10.6 Create *menuitems* view

```
CREATE VIEW menuitems (menuitemid, name, price) AS
  (SELECT m.mealid, m.name, CAST(SUM(price * (1 - discount)) AS NUMERIC(5,2))
   FROM meals m LEFT OUTER JOIN partof p ON m.mealid = p.mealid
        LEFT OUTER JOIN items i ON p.itemid = i.itemid
   GROUP BY m.mealid, m.name)
UNION
  (SELECT itemid, name, price
   FROM items);
```

Once this view is created, we can easily list our menu items.

Query 10.7 Find all menu items

```
SELECT *
FROM menuitems;
```

menuitemid	name	price
CHKSD	Chicken Salad	2.85
CKSDS	Chicken N Suds	3.68
FRPLT	Fruit Plate	3.99
FRTSD	Fruit Salad	3.45
GDNSD	Garden Salad	0.99
MILSD	Millennium Salad	NULL
SODA	Soda	0.99
VGNET	Vegan Eatin'	4.38
WATER	Water	0.00

[9 row(s)]

It is now easy to find the most expensive item on our menu.

Query 10.8 Find the most expensive menu item

```
SELECT name
FROM menuitems
WHERE price =
        (SELECT MAX(price)
         FROM menuitems);
```

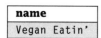

name
Vegan Eatin'

[1 row(s)]

It also is easy to find the number of items without a price.

Query 10.9 Find the priceless menu items

```
SELECT COUNT(*)
FROM menuitems
WHERE price IS NULL;
```

count
1

[1 row(s)]

Earlier, we presented similar queries, but we restricted our results to items and excluded the meals. Queries 10.4–10.9 would be much more complex without the views.

10.3 Updating Views

We can even perform INSERT, UPDATE, and DELETE on a view, which is propagated to the underlying tables; however, there are restrictions on the kinds of views that can be updated. Unfortunately, not all DBMSs allow updating through views and some DBMSs have other restrictions (such as only having one table in the query specifying the view). Even if your DBMS allows updates to views, you should be careful about using it, because some results may be unexpected.

According to the SQL 2003 standard, for a view to be *updatable,* the query defining a view must:

- Not contain DISTINCT
- Not reference the same column twice in the SELECT clause
- Not have a GROUP BY or HAVING clause
- Not contain UNION, EXCEPT, or INTERSECT
- Contain attributes from only one table
- Have exactly one row in a base table that corresponds to each row in the view

Furthermore, to insert values through a view, the view must:

- Contain the primary key of the table
- Contain all attributes of the table with NOT NULL constraints and no non-null default value

Finally, even if a view is updatable, not all columns within the view may be updatable. For example, derived columns such as *value* in the *vrs* cannot be updated.

Thus, our *menuitems* view cannot be directly updated because it contains attributes from the *items, meals,* and *partof* tables. The *vrs* view can be updated as if it were a base table.

Update 10.10 Updating through views

```
UPDATE vrs
SET inventory = inventory * 2;

SELECT *
FROM vrs;
```

ingredientid	name	inventory	value
LETUS	Lettuce	400	4.00
PICKL	Pickle	1600	64.00
TOMTO	Tomato	30	0.90

[3 row(s)]

It is important to note that updates through views can have unexpected consequences, depending on the behavior of your DBMS. For example, a DBMS might allow an INSERT on *vrs,* such as Insert 10.11. The underlying *ingredients* table would be updated with the provided values, but the *vendorid* would be set to the default value (in our case, *NULL).* Because the query specification for *vrs* requires the *vendorid* to be VGRUS, our new row does NOT appear in the view.

Insert 10.11 Inserting through a view

```
INSERT INTO vrs(ingredientid, name, inventory) VALUES
               'NEWIN','New ingredient',100);
```

As a result, updating through views should be treated with caution and tested thoroughly. In general, updates through views work best when the view is defined as a subset of a table and all attributes that determine if a row is in a view are updatable.

What if a view cannot be updated? We can still change the view by updating the underlying table. For example, to change the *menuitems* view, we have to update the underlying tables. Fortunately for us, the updates will be automatically reflected in the view, as in Update 10.12.

Update 10.12 Increase the discount for Fruit Salad in the Vegan Eatin' meal

```
UPDATE partof
SET discount = discount + 0.1
WHERE itemid = 'FRTSD' AND mealid = 'VGNET';
```
See the results
```
SELECT *
FROM menuitems;
```

menuitemid	name	price
CHKSD	Chicken Salad	2.85
CKSDS	Chicken N Suds	3.68
FRPLT	Fruit Plate	3.99
FRTSD	Fruit Salad	3.45
GDNSD	Garden Salad	0.99
MILSD	Millennium Salad	NULL
SODA	Soda	0.99
VGNET	Vegan Eatin'	4.03
WATER	Water	0.00

[9 row(s)]

10.4 DROP VIEW

We can remove a view with the DROP VIEW command.

```
DROP VIEW <view name> [CASCADE | RESTRICT]
```

This removes the specified view; however, it does not change any of the data in the database. SQL does not allow a view to be dropped if view is contained in the SELECT statement of another view. This is the default behavior or the result of using the RESTRICT option. To remove such a view, specify the CASCADE option. This will cause any dependent views to be removed before the view is dropped. According to the SQL specification, you must specify either CASCADE or RESTRICT with DROP VIEW. It is not optional. We present it as optional because most (if not all) DBMSs treat it as optional, with a default behavior of RESTRICT. For compliance with the SQL standard, it's a good idea to specify either CASCADE or RESTRICT.

10.5 Wrap Up

Views are virtual tables whose columns and data are defined by a SELECT statement. You may SELECT from views just like any other table. Some views even allow INSERT, UPDATE, and DELETE. Updates to the base tables that a view is built from are immediately reflected in the view.

Review Questions

1. A view can be defined over _____ tables and may contain _____ attributes.

2. How does SQL determine the data types of attributes in a view?

3. If the optional *<column list>* is used in creating a view, what are the restrictions on it?

4. How can you always update any view?

5. List one application for each of the three reasons for using views mentioned in Section 10.1.

6. Perform Queries 10.4, 10.8, and 10.9 without using any views.

7. According to the 2003 SQL specification, which of the following views are updatable? Which will allow inserts?

DDL 10.13 Review I

```
CREATE VIEW one AS
    SELECT DISTINCT manager
    FROM stores;
```

DDL 10.14 Review II

```
CREATE VIEW two AS
    SELECT storeid, SUM(price)
    FROM orders
    GROUP BY storeid;
```

DDL 10.15 Review III

```
CREATE VIEW three AS
    SELECT manager
    FROM stores
    UNION
    SELECT replname
    FROM vendors;
```

DDL 10.16 Review IV

```
CREATE VIEW four AS
    SELECT storeid, manager
    FROM stores
    WHERE manager LIKE '%Jeff%';
```

Practice

For these exercises, we use the Employees Database presented at the end of Chapter 1. Answer each question with a single SQL statement. Your query must work for any set of data in the Employees Database, not just the set of data we provide.

1. Create a view containing all of the employees assigned to the 'Robotic Spouse' project. Include the percent time they are assigned to the project.

2. Query your view created in the previous question to find the employee first and last name with the greatest amount of time assigned to 'Robotic Spouse'.

3. Create a view of employees with their department name.

4. Query your view to find all the first and last names of employees in the Consulting department.

5. Create a view showing all of the projects assigned to Abe Advice, including his percentage time on each project.

6. Query your view to find the total amount of time Abe is assigned to projects.

7. Create an updatable view showing employees and their salaries. Give everyone a 10% raise by updating the view.

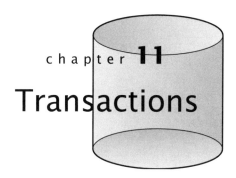

chapter **11**

Transactions

Databases are all about sharing data, so it is common for multiple users to be accessing and even changing the same data at the same time. The simultaneous execution of operations is called *concurrency*. Sometimes concurrency can get us into trouble if our changes require multiple SQL statements. Let's look at an example. We always want to make sure that we have all of the ingredients for every item before we submit a customer's order. Let's start with Query 11.1.

Query 11.1 Find the available and required ingredients for a Garden Salad

```
SELECT ingredientid, ing.name, quantity, inventory
FROM items itm JOIN madewith USING (itemid)
    JOIN ingredients ing USING (ingredientid)
WHERE itm.name = 'Garden Salad';
```

ingredientid	name	quantity	inventory
LETUS	Lettuce	4	200
TOMTO	Tomato	8	15

[2 row(s)]

Note that because of a tomato shortage, we only have enough ingredients for one Garden Salad. We could execute Query 11.1 each time an item is ordered. After verifying we have the necessary ingredients, we can make the item and update the inventory of the used ingredients. To remove the ingredients from the inventory, we perform Update 11.2.

Now consider the following scenario: Two customers, Bob and Mary, arrive at about the same time and each go to a different register. Bob orders a Garden Salad. Bob's register

Update 11.2 Remove the ingredients used in making a garden salad

```
UPDATE ingredients
SET inventory = inventory -
    (SELECT quantity
     FROM items itm JOIN madewith mw USING (itemid)
     WHERE itm.name = 'Garden Salad'
           AND ingredients.ingredientid = mw.ingredientid)
WHERE ingredientid IN
    (SELECT ingredientid
     FROM items itm JOIN madewith USING (itemid)
     WHERE it.name = 'Garden Salad';
```

```
See the results
```

```
SELECT ing.name, inventory
FROM items itm JOIN madewith USING (itemid)
    JOIN ingredients ing USING (ingredientid)
WHERE itm.name = 'Garden Salad';
```

Query Result

name	inventory
Lettuce	196
Tomato	7

[2 row(s)]

runs Query 11.1, which indicates that there are enough ingredients to make his order. While Bob decides if he wants to order a drink, Mary also orders a Garden Salad. Mary's register runs Query 11.1, which again indicates that there are enough ingredients to make her order. Mary immediately pays for her order, and her register executes Update 11.2. Bob finally decides against a drink, and his register executes Update 11.2. Of course, we only have enough ingredients to make one Garden Salad. This is a classic problem in database systems; it is called the *isolation* or *serializability* problem. In general, if two or more users access the same data and one or more of the statements changes the data, we have a conflict. If the users perform multiple steps, conflicts can cause incorrect results to occur.

To deal with this problem, databases allow the grouping of a sequence of SQL statements into an indivisible unit of work called a *transaction.* A transaction ends with either a commit or a rollback:

commit—A commit permanently stores all of the changes performed by the transaction.

rollback—A rollback removes all of the updates performed by the transaction, no matter how many rows have been changed. A rollback can be executed either by the DBMS to prevent incorrect actions or explicitly by the user.

The DBMS provides the following guarantees for a transaction, called the *ACID* properties:

Atomicity—Either all (commit) or none (rollback) of the changes within a transaction are made permanent.

Consistency—If a transaction executes on a consistent database, then when it terminates the database will still be consistent.

Isolation—A transaction can execute on a database as though it is the only transaction running.

Durability—Changes made by any committed transaction are permanent, even surviving system crashes and hardware failures.

ACID is a well-known database concept. Further details can be found in most database textbooks.

For Bob and Mary, Query 11.1 and the Update 11.2 are not two independent operations on the database but are actually part of a single order. The logical unit of work is *both* the query and the update. We use transactions to let Bob and Mary execute Query 11.1 and Update 11.2 as one unit of work. This avoids any conflicting updates to the database (either Bob, Mary, or neither gets the Garden Salad, not both), and we know that if a transaction commits, all of its changes are permanent.

11.1   Ending a Transaction—COMMIT and ROLLBACK

We begin with how to end a transaction. Recall that a transaction ends with either a commit or rollback. A commit is explicitly executed by the user using the COMMIT statement:

```
COMMIT [WORK]
```

COMMIT attempts to commit all of the changes made since the beginning of the transaction. If a problem is detected, COMMIT signals an error, and the transaction is rolled back. Once a commit successfully completes, the changes are permanent. Here's a situation where a fear of commitment can be healthy.

A rollback can be executed either by the DBMS (to prevent incorrect actions) or explicitly by the user using the ROLLBACK statement:

```
ROLLBACK [WORK] [TO SAVEPOINT <savepoint>]
```

ROLLBACK undoes all of the changes made since the beginning of the current transaction. We discuss savepoints in Section 11.4. Note that if you have an active transaction and you kill your query processor without executing a COMMIT, the DBMS should roll back all of your changes.

11.2   Starting a Transaction—START TRANSACTION

SQL starts a transaction automatically when a new statement is executed if there is no currently active transaction[1]. This means that a new transaction begins automatically with

---

[1] Technically, not all statements will signal the start of a transaction, but most that we care about do.

the first statement after the end of the previous transaction or the beginning of the session. A user may explicitly start a transaction using the START TRANSACTION statement.

```
START TRANSACTION [<transaction characteristics>]
```

Many DBMSs use BEGIN TRANSACTION instead of START TRANSACTION. We discuss transaction characteristics in Section 11.7.

While a transaction is running, all of the data accessed by the transaction are protected. For example, start a transaction and execute Query 11.1. Now, in a separate session try to execute Update 11.2. What usually happens is that Update 11.2 does not complete. The database has detected a possible conflict between Query 11.1 and Update 11.2. Whichever transaction tries to access the data second is blocked by the database. No operations can be submitted by that transaction until the block ends, and that won't happen until the first transaction terminates.

11.3 Auto-Commit

Most DBMSs include an *auto-commit* mode where a commit is automatically attempted after *every* SQL statement. With auto-commit, all transactions consist of only a single SQL statement. This breaks our solution to the simultaneous order problem because with auto-commit Query 11.1 and the Update 11.2 are executed in separate transactions. Usually auto-commit is the *default* mode. Changing to the *manual-commit* mode where a COMMIT statement must be executed to commit is DBMS-specific. Some DBMSs will temporarily suspend the auto-commit mode if the user enters a START TRANSACTION.

11.4 SAVEPOINTs

SQL allows you to create named placeholders, called *savepoints,* in the sequence of statements in a transaction. You can rollback to a savepoint instead of to the beginning of the transaction. Only the changes made after the savepoint are undone. To set a savepoint, use the SAVEPOINT command:

```
SAVEPOINT <savepoint name>
```

If we create a savepoint named sp, we can rollback to that savepoint with the following:

```
ROLLBACK TO SAVEPOINT sp <savepoint name>
```

Executing ROLLBACK without designating a savepoint or executing a COMMIT deletes all savepoints back to the start of the transaction. A rollback to a particular savepoint deletes all intervening savepoints.

How is this useful? Suppose Bob is ordering food for his entire soccer team, one player at a time, and the last player wants to change his order. ROLLBACK will undo the order for all players; however, if we created a savepoint before each player's order, we could easily rollback just the order of the last player.

Update 11.3 Setting and using savepoints in a transaction

```
START TRANSACTION;
-- Player 1 Order
SAVEPOINT player2;
-- Player 2 Order
...
SAVEPOINT player20;
-- Player 20 Order
ROLLBACK TO SAVEPOINT player20;
-- Player 20 New Order
```

We include all of the orders in a single transaction because we don't want to submit the team order unless everybody's order can be satisfied with the given inventory.

11.5 Immediate or Deferred Constraints

We learned in Chapter 9 that constraints may complicate data changes by forcing a particular ordering of inserts, updates, and deletes to avoid violation. Transactions provide a possible means for making it much easier. Recall that the ACID properties ensure that the database is consistent *when a transaction terminates.* During a transaction execution, the database may be *inconsistent.* In other words, we could violate the constraint for a little while, as long as we fixed it before the transaction terminates. Note that isolation ensures no other transaction will see the violated constraint.

SQL has two different modes for checking constraints: *DEFERRED* or *IMMEDIATE.*

IMMEDIATE—Constraint is checked after each statement.

DEFERRED—Constraint is not checked until the transaction attempts to commit.

In DEFERRED mode, a transaction can violate the constraint within the transaction as long as the violation is corrected before the commit. If you attempt to commit a transaction with changes that violate a constraint, the DBMS will rollback the transaction. Let's look at an example. We have a foreign key constraint for the *vendorid* in the *ingredients* table. If the constraint check mode for that constraint is DEFERRED, then we can execute a transaction that first deletes the vendor then deletes the ingredient supplied by the vendor. When the transaction performs a commit, the foreign key constraint is checked, and the constraint is satisfied.

If the constraint check mode is IMMEDIATE, however, then the constraint is checked when we attempt to delete the vendor, the constraint violation is detected, and a rollback is performed. This is exactly the situation as when we did not use transactions.

Why would we want to use IMMEDIATE constraints? Consider the case of a transaction performing a large number of insertions into the *ingredients* table. If the first ingredient inserted has a bad *vendorid,* a DEFERRED constraint would not discover this until all of the inserts had been performed, wasting a lot of work.

We can specify the default constraint check mode when we declare (or alter) the constraint. The possible constraint check times are INITIALLY DEFERRED or INITIALLY IMMEDIATE (default). We can even control whether a constraint can be deferred by specifying the constraint as DEFERRABLE or NOT DEFERRABLE (default) when we declare (or alter) the constraint. If a constraint is INITIALLY DEFERRED, then it is DEFERRABLE. If a constraint is NOT DEFERRABLE, we cannot specify its default constraint check mode to INITIALLY DEFERRED, and we cannot change it within a transaction.

To specify the default constraint check mode and/or constraint deferrability, we add the constraint characteristic on the end of a column or table constraint.

```
[[NOT] DEFERRABLE] [INITIALLY {DEFERRED |IMMEDIATE}]
```

Let's try an example using the *madewith* table.

DDL 11.4 Create deferred constraints

```
CREATE TABLE madewith (
  itemid CHAR(5) NOT NULL,
  ingredientid CHAR(5) NOT NULL,
  quantity INTEGER CONSTRAINT qtyck CHECK (quantity >= 0) NOT DEFERRABLE,
  PRIMARY KEY(itemid, ingredientid),
  CONSTRAINT itemidfk FOREIGN KEY(itemid) REFERENCES items(itemid) DEFERRABLE,
  CONSTRAINT ingidfk FOREIGN KEY(ingredientid) REFERENCES ingredients
                                             INITIALLY DEFERRED
);
```

The primary key constraint (by default) and the qtyck constraint are NOT DEFERRABLE INITIALLY IMMEDIATE so the mode for these constraints is always IMMEDIATE. The *itemidfk* constraint is DEFERRABLE INITIALLY IMMEDIATE so its default mode is IMMEDIATE, but we can change it within a transaction. The *ingidfk* constraint is DEFERRABLE INITIALLY DEFERRED so its default mode is DEFERRED, but we can change it within a transaction.

We change the constraint check mode with the SET CONSTRAINT command:

```
SET CONSTRAINTS {<constraint list> | ALL} {DEFERRED | IMMEDIATE}
```

If a list of constraints is given, then the constraint mode of each constraint is changed to the specified mode. We can use the ALL keyword to change the mode of all *deferrable* constraints.

The constraint modes are changed for only *one* transaction. If a transaction is currently active, that transaction will execute with the changed modes while all other transactions will execute with the default modes. If no transaction is active when a SET CONSTRAINTS statement is executed, then the next transaction performed within the same SQL context (e.g., the next transaction entered by the same user in a command line environment) will use the new constraint modes.

11.6 Testing Changes with Transactions

An incorrectly written INSERT, UPDATE, and DELETE can corrupt the database. For example, you could forget the WHERE clause in an UPDATE or DELETE or INSERT the wrong data. Because transactions provide the ability to rollback and isolation from other transactions, we can use them to test INSERT, UPDATE, and DELETE before we commit the changes. Let's look at an example. Suppose we wanted to remove all ingredients from the Chicken Salad (CHKSD) that are in the Milk food group. If we accidentally delete other ingredients, our menu system breaks. To avoid this, we can make the change and test the results within a transaction.

Transaction 11.5 Using the transactions to test DELETE

```
START TRANSACTION

-- Find the ingredients and their food group in Chicken Salad.
SELECT name, foodgroup
FROM madewith NATURAL JOIN ingredients
WHERE itemid = 'CHKSD'
```

Query Result

name	foodgroup
Cheese	Milk
Chicken	Meat
Lettuce	Vegetable
Secret Dressing	NULL

[4 row(s)]

```
-- Delete the milk ingredients from Chicken Salad
DELETE FROM madewith WHERE itemid = 'CHKSD' AND
ingredientid IN
(SELECT ingredientid
 FROM ingredients
 WHERE foodgroup = 'Milk');

-- Only the non-Milk ingredients should be left
SELECT name, foodgroup
FROM madewith NATURAL JOIN ingredients
WHERE itemid = 'CHKSD';
```

Query Result

name	foodgroup
Chicken	Meat
Lettuce	Vegetable
Secret Dressing	NULL

[3 row(s)]

```
-- Since update is correct, COMMIT. If not, then ROLLBACK
COMMIT;
```

Note that with isolation, you are the only person who can see the changes after the DELETE. If the test fails, you can rollback the entire transaction. If the test passes, execute a COMMIT so everybody else can see the changes.

11.7 Transaction Characteristics

The material in this section is rather advanced. We assume you already understand the consequences of changing the transaction characteristics. An explanation of these characteristics can be found in most introductory database texts. We can change the characteristics of a transaction with the SET TRANSACTION statement:

```
SET TRANSACTION <mode>[, <mode>]
```

One characteristic we can change is the access mode of the transaction. The two possible access modes are as follows:

READ ONLY—Only statements that do not change the data are allowed.

READ WRITE—Both statements that access and manipulate data are allowed.

We can also change the level of the transaction. The possible levels include the following:

SERIALIZABLE—Prevents all possible conflicts.

REPEATABLE READ—Allows a problem known as phantom read. A *phantom read* happens when a transaction reads a set of rows (such as an entire table). A second transaction then inserts a row into the table. If the first transaction repeats the read, the results will now be different.

READ COMMITTED—Allows the phantom read problem as well as what is known as the nonrepeatable read problem. A nonrepeatable read occurs when a transaction reads a single row. A second transaction updates that row, and the first transaction repeats the read operation, getting a different answer.

READ UNCOMMITTED—Allows the dirty read problem as well as the nonrepeatable and phantom read. This means transactions can interfere with each other and cause unexpected results. For example, suppose a test transaction put $1 million in our checking account. The testers are not worried about this because they are going to rollback the test transaction and undo all of the operations. A second transaction sees the $1 million and incorrectly approves a loan.[2] Now the test transaction performs a rollback. How do they correct the situation? Although this is an extreme example, similar problems can easily arise in such environments. Extreme care should be used in applications with read uncommitted isolation.

---

[2]Or worse, it allows us to withdraw the money. However, this requires even more relaxation of ACID.

SET TRANSACTION can only be performed once per transaction. If no transaction is active, SET TRANSACTION changes the characteristics of the next transaction. You can also specify the transaction characteristic in START TRANSACTION.

11.8 Locking Issues

When using a large database, there are a few important issues that arise as a result of the DBMS ensuring isolation. Specifically, we need to discuss *deadlocks* and *lock escalation.*

When a deadlock occurs in any computer system, progress cannot occur. For example, if two transactions execute Query 11.1 at the same time, the database will prevent any other transaction from changing the values read. Now suppose the first transaction tries to execute Update 11.2. The DBMS will "block" the transaction, preventing it from doing any work. If the second transaction commits, then the first transaction will be able to perform the update, and there will be no problems. However, if the second transaction also performs Update 11.2, then it will also be blocked.

In this case, neither transaction can make progress. They are deadlocked. What happens next depends on the database configuration. It is hoped that, the DBMS will detect this deadlock and rollback one of the transactions, allowing the other to make progress. However, sometimes the database will not detect such a situation for a long time. In these cases, user intervention is required to rollback one of the transactions. The exact user interaction will depend on the DBMS but requires one of the transactions to perform a rollback.

Lock escalation occurs as a result of a transaction updating a large amount of data in a single table. Usually, a DBMS will only lock as much of a database as needed for the transaction to perform its operations. However, if a transaction updates a large portion of a table, the DBMS may lock the entire table. This will help the performance of the update transaction, but it may cause serious performance problems for concurrent transactions, because they will not be able to read any of the table. The solutions to the lock escalation problem are application specific and include dividing the update transaction into independent transactions, running the transactions under a reduced isolation level, or accepting the reduced performance.

11.9 Wrap Up

A transaction is a logical unit of work. By combining multiple SQL statements into a single transaction we can execute many complex statements as though they are a single statement. This allows us to correctly update different tables at one time. Transactions can either commit, which means that all of the operations are saved to the database, or rollback, which means all of the operations are removed from the database.

Transaction processing in databases allows many transactions to execute at the same time with confidence. The theoretical properties ensured by a database are called the ACID properties. Providing these properties requires extra work on the part of the database. However, most applications consider the performance loss well worth the benefits gained.

The observant reader will have guessed by now that we are using transactions in reporting our results of database modifications. We perform the update and the query inside one transaction, then we abort the transaction. This allows us to show the result of the update without corrupting our database—exactly one of the roles of transactions.

Review Questions

1. A transaction may be started by (list two ways).

2. A transaction is ended by (list two ways).

3. A rollback is initiated by (list two ways).

4. A commit is initiated by (list two ways).

5. **True/False** A rollback only undoes the statement that causes a conflict or error.

6. If the DBMS is in auto-commit mode, a commit is attempted after every _____.

7. By default, a constraint is (circle those that apply)

   NOT DEFERRABLE INITIALLY IMMEDIATE DEFERRED

8. One of the problems that can happen with transactions is a situation called *deadlock.* Create a deadlock by executing the following:

   (a) Query 11.1 in one transaction

   (b) Query 11.1 in another transaction

   (c) Update 11.2 in the first transaction

   (d) Update 11.2 in the second transaction

   What happened on your DBMS?

9. Repeat the test with the isolation level set to READ UNCOMMITTED. What happened?

10. Repeat the test without transactions (auto-commit on). What happened?

11. Start a transaction with the characteristic of READ ONLY. Perform Query 11.1 and Update 11.2. What happened?

Practice

1. Consider a banking scenario. A customer wants to transfer money from Account 1 to Account 2. Write a transaction to first check the balance in Account 1, then to update Account 1, and then to update Account 2. Write an identical transaction to transfer money from Account 2 to Account 1. Use different amounts for each transfer. Without any concurrency control, interleave the steps of the two transactions in different ways. Is the final result correct? What would happen with serializable isolation?

2. In the Employees Database, the department table has a foreign key on itself. Make the following changes to the foreign key constraint and perform the updates. Do not delete subdepartments of subdepartments of the Administration department.

(a) Delete the Administration department and all of its subdepartments without using transactions.

(b) Using a transaction, delete the Administration department and all of its subdepartments.

(c) Change all of the foreign key constraints by adding the phrase INITIALLY DEFERRED. Delete the Administration department and all of its subdepartments with and without a transaction.

(d) Change all of the foreign key constraints by adding the phrase DEFERRABLE. Delete the Administration department and all of its subdepartments with and without a transaction. Use the SET CONSTRAINTS statement to make all constraints deferred. Delete the Administration department and all of its subdepartments with a transaction.

chapter **12**

Database Privileges

Databases are all about sharing data, so naturally a database is accessible to many users. Of course, not every user should be allowed to do everything. If we maintain employee information in our Restaurant Database, we might want to limit who can see salary information. We'd certainly want to limit who can give raises. The owner of the restaurant should be able to view and/or change any data. The restaurant accountant should be able to see, but not change, salary information. The employees should be able to see nonsensitive information, such as name and phone number, without being allowed access to salaries.

SQL allows us to assign different types of privileges to different users. A user is specified by a user identifier (e.g., Bob Smith is a user with the identifier bsmith). The creation and maintenance of users is DBMS specific. Some DBMSs use identifiers from the underlying operating system; others maintain their own set of users. Many DBMSs have a CREATE USER command for creating new users. Similarly, not all users are allowed to create tables, but this is not covered in the SQL standard. Consult your DBMS documentation.

The user that creates a database object, such as a table, is called the owner. The owner of an object can do just about anything he or she wants with that object, including determining the privileges of other users for that object. Let's see how SQL allows management of privileges.

12.1 GRANT

You can give privileges on an object to a user with the GRANT statement:

```
GRANT {ALL PRIVILEGES | <privilege>[, <privilege>...]}
ON <database object>
TO <grantee> [, <grantee>...]
[WITH GRANT OPTION]
```

GRANT gives the specified privilege(s) on the named object to the list of identified users. Specifying the WITH GRANT OPTION allows the identified users to grant their privileges to other users.

We only address privileges on tables and views here, but privileges can be granted on several types of objects. Available privileges include the following:

Privilege	Permits
SELECT[(<column list>)]	SELECT on the specified table. If *column list* is specified, the user may only access values for those columns; otherwise, the user may access all columns.
INSERT[(<column list>)]	INSERT for new row(s) on the specified table. If *column list* is specified, the user may only specify values for those columns; all other columns are given the default value. If *column list* is not specified, the user may specify values for all columns.
UPDATE[(<column list>)]	UPDATE on existing rows on the specified table. If *column list* is specified, the user may only update values for those columns; otherwise, the user may update all columns.
DELETE	DELETE of existing rows in the specified table.
REFERENCES[(<column list>)]	References to columns in the specified table including foreign key and CHECK constraints. If *column list* is specified, the user may only define references for those columns; otherwise, the user may reference all columns.
ALL PRIVILEGES	All privilege types.

Many people need different access to our tables. It is important that we grant exactly the privileges needed—no more, no less. Granting too many privileges opens the door for security holes. Being too restrictive prevents a user from doing their job.

Let's look at a access to the Restaurant Database users. We begin by granting access to John and Mary from the marketing department.

DCL 12.1 Give SELECT privileges

```
GRANT SELECT(storeid, itemid) ON ORDERS TO john, mary;
GRANT SELECT ON STORES TO john, mary;
```

John and Mary may only view which stores sold which items and the information about the stores. This is enough for them to handle a mass mailing advertising campaign.

DCL 12.2 Give SELECT privileges with GRANT OPTION
```
GRANT SELECT ON ORDERS TO ed WITH GRANT OPTION;
```

Ed, the company auditor, can now see the orders placed, and he can also allow others to see this information as well.

We restrict the creation and deletion of stores to our vice-president, Rachel. However, she cannot add an address for the store.

DCL 12.3 Give INSERT/DELETE privileges
```
GRANT INSERT(storeid, manager), DELETE ON stores TO rachel;
```

When Rachel inserts a new store, default values are used for the attributes other than *storeid* and *manager.* Note that if Rachel did not have access to the primary key, then any inserts attempted by Rachel would be rejected. Do you know why?[1] We allow our managers, Jeff and Greg, to update the locations of the stores. However, they cannot change the store ID or the name of the manager.

DCL 12.4 Give UPDATE privileges
```
GRANT UPDATE(address, city, state, zip) ON stores TO jeff, greg;
```

Our purchasing director, Jane, creates a purchase order to restock our inventory. Because purchase orders may be complex, Jane creates a new table for each order. These tables must refer to vendor IDs.

DCL 12.5 Give REFERENCE privileges
```
GRANT REFERENCES(vendorid) ON vendors TO jane;
```

This allows Jane to create a *purchases* table with a foreign key or CHECK constraint referencing *vendors.* If we didn't restrict the allowable references, an unscrupulous user could use references to discover sensitive information (e.g., create a table with references and insert guessed values until one works) or limit your ability to control your own table (e.g., create a table with a dependency, such as foreign key reference, to prevent deletion of rows from the referenced table).

---

[1] There is no default value for storeid, so *NULL* would be used. *NULL* is not an allowed value for a primary key.

Finally, we give all privileges to the owner of our company, Jack.

DCL 12.6 Give ALL privileges

```
GRANT ALL PRIVILEGES ON stores TO jack WITH GRANT OPTION;
GRANT ALL PRIVILEGES ON orders TO jack WITH GRANT OPTION;
...
```

Jack can give any privilege to any other user he wishes.

12.2 REVOKE

You can remove privileges on an object from a user using REVOKE:

```
REVOKE [GRANT OPTION FOR]
{ALL PRIVILEGES | <privilege>[, <privilege>...]}
ON <database object>
FROM <grantee> [, <grantee>...]
[CASCADE | RESTRICT]
```

REVOKE removes the specified privilege(s) on the named object from the list of identified users. Specifying the GRANT OPTION FOR option revokes the ability of the identified users to grant the specified privilege(s) to other users; it does not revoke the privilege itself. If we fire Greg, a manager, we need to revoke his privileges.

DCL 12.7 REVOKE privileges

```
REVOKE UPDATE ON stores FROM greg;
```

Consider Ed, our auditor to whom we granted SELECT privileges on *orders* with the ability to grant that privilege to other users. If Ed has granted privileges to other users, our attempt to revoke his privileges will be rejected because to delete Ed's privileges we must also delete the privileges Ed granted. The RESTRICT option disallows any REVOKE where there are any dependent privileges, which is the default behavior. We can fix this by using the CASCADE option to delete the specified privilege and any dependent privileges. According to the SQL specification, you must specify either CASCADE or RESTRICT with REVOKE. It is not optional. We present it as optional because most DBMSs either don't include CASCADE/RESTRICT or treat it as optional, with a default behavior of RESTRICT. To be compliant with the standard, it's a good idea to specify either CASCADE or RESTRICT if allowed by the DBMS.

12.3 PUBLIC

We can grant a privilege to all users by assigning it to PUBLIC. Of course, this means we should be very careful with any privileges granted to PUBLIC. One possibility is that we would want everyone to see all of the items on our menu. We do not have a table with that information, but we do have a view. We can assign privileges to views just as with tables.

DCL 12.8 Give PUBLIC privileges

```
GRANT SELECT(name, prices) ON menuitems TO PUBLIC;
```

Note that the privileges are assigned to PUBLIC, not to individual users. Therefore, we cannot deny any user any privilege that is assigned to PUBLIC. In other words, DCL 12.9 has no effect on the privileges allowed to Jane. Of course, we can revoke the privilege from PUBLIC.

DCL 12.9 REVOKE SELECT privileges

```
REVOKE SELECT(name) ON menuitems TO jane;
```

12.4 Creating a Set of Privileges Using ROLEs

User-based privilege maintenance can quickly become a nightmare. If a cashier is promoted to manager, you must remove the cashier privileges and add the manager privileges. If you want to add or revoke a privilege for all cashiers, you must remember all of their IDs. Fortunately, SQL has a solution. We can create a *role* that represents a type of database user and assign privileges to that role. Assigning a role to a user gives that user all of the privileges granted to the role.

We can create a role using the following:

```
CREATE ROLE <role name> [WITH ADMIN OPTION]
```

If WITH ADMIN OPTION is specified, the role grantee may grant the role to others. We grant and revoke privileges to roles just as we assigned them to users. Let's create our cashier role and assign the appropriate privileges.

DCL 12.10 Create a ROLE and GRANT privileges

```
CREATE ROLE cashier;
GRANT INSERT ON orders TO cashier;
```

We assign a role using GRANT.

```
GRANT <role name>, [, <role name>...] TO <grantee> [, <grantee>...]
[WITH ADMIN OPTION]
```

Now we can assign the *cashier* role to Abe and Sara.

DCL 12.11 Grant ROLE to users

```
GRANT cashier TO abe, sara;
```

Now Abe and Sara have all of the privileges of a cashier. Any new privileges assigned to the *cashier* role are now available to Abe and Sara. Any privilege revoked from the *cashier* role becomes unavailable to Abe and Sara, unless they are granted that same privilege by their user ID or some other role.

We use REVOKE to remove a role.

```
REVOKE [ADMIN OPTION FOR]
<role>[, <role>...]
FROM <grantee> [, <grantee>...]
[CASCADE | RESTRICT]
```

This works like the privilege form of REVOKE, except that it revokes roles. What do we do if Abe is no longer a cashier? We simply REVOKE his role.

DCL 12.12 Revoke user ROLE

```
REVOKE cashier FROM abe;
```

Abe no longer gets any privileges from his *cashier* role. Of course, he may have privileges from elsewhere.

We can delete a role altogether.

```
DROP ROLE <role>
```

The treatment of roles differs from DBMS to DBMS. Most DBMS either have roles or an analogous construct such as groups. Consult your DBMS documentation.

12.5 Using Privileges and Views

We saw that we can grant and revoke privileges to views, just like a table. Previously, we have granted privileges for all rows of the *orders* table. However, it makes more sense for cashiers to only have access to the orders for their store. We begin by creating a view for the FIRST store.

DDL 12.13 Create firststore view

```
CREATE VIEW firststore AS
SELECT * FROM orders WHERE storeid = 'FIRST';
```

The *firststore* view is updatable and can support inserts (if your DBMS allows that). Next, we create a ROLE that allows the cashiers at our first store to access the orders for that store.

DCL 12.14 Create ROLE for view privileges

```
CREATE ROLE firstcashier;
GRANT firstcashier to abe, sara;
GRANT SELECT ON firststore TO firstcashier;
GRANT INSERT ON firststore TO firstcashier;
```

Abe and Sara can now enter orders into our database as they sell lots of items to our customers. Note that if your DBMS does not support updates on views, then you can grant the privilege to the underlying table. Also note that Abe and Sara do NOT have the privilege to change any order placed in the system.

12.6 Wrap Up

Databases usually are accessed and manipulated by many different users. SQL allows us to control the kinds of operation each user is permitted to perform including SELECT, INSERT, UPDATE, DELETE, and even external references. GRANT adds new privileges to a user, whereas REVOKE removes existing privileges.

Controlling privileges on a user-by-user basis is very tedious. SQL provides a special identifier, PUBLIC, that allows us to determine privileges available to all users. In addition, we can create and assign privileges to database roles. We can then grant or revoke roles to or from users and other roles.

Review Questions

1. For each of the Queries 12.15 through 12.18, which of the privileges 12.19 through 12.22 would allow the operation? Assume the username is USER and they have role DBUSER.

Query 12.15   Query 1

```
SELECT *
FROM vendors;
```

Query 12.16   Query 2

```
SELECT vendorid
FROM vendors
WHERE companyname = 'Veggies_R_Us';
```

Query 12.17   Query 3

```
UPDATE vendors
SET companyname = 'Bad Vendor'
WHERE vendorid = 'VGRUS';
```

Query 12.18   Query 4

```
INSERT INTO vendors (vendorid) VALUES ('NEWVN');
```

DCL 12.19   Set privilege 1

```
GRANT ALL ON vendors TO PUBLIC;
```

DCL 12.20   Set privilege 2

```
GRANT SELECT(vendorid) ON vendors TO USER, DBUSER;
```

DCL 12.21   Set privilege 3

```
GRANT INSERT ON vendors TO DBUSER;
```

DCL 12.22   Set privilege 4

```
GRANT UPDATE(vendorid) ON vendors TO nobody;
```

2. We should be careful assigning privileges to _____.

3. _____ is used to remove privileges.

4. **True/False** Privileges can be assigned to views.

5. _____ are used to assign privileges to multiple users at one time.

Practice

For these exercises, we use the Employees Database presented at the end of Chapter 1. Your query must work for any set of data in the Employees Database, not just the set of data we provide. Assume we have users tom and sue.

1. Give everyone the privilege of seeing all employee information except salary.

2. Give sue the privilege of updating the revenue of projects.

3. Give tom the privilege of adding new projects but not end dates. Allow him to grant this privilege to someone else.

4. Create a role called dept_head for tom and sue. Allow dept_head to delete departments.

5. Create a view of project descriptions belonging to the Consulting department. Include all employees names and the amount of time each is assigned to the project. Let tom see this view.

6. Assuming the previous questions have been successful, revoke all of the privileges granted to tom, but allow sue to keep all of her privileges. Allow tom to keep all PUBLIC privileges.

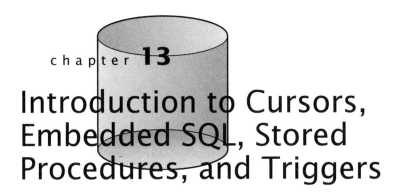

chapter **13**

Introduction to Cursors, Embedded SQL, Stored Procedures, and Triggers

SQL is powerful, but we need other capabilities to make it truly useful. Such capabilities include executing SQL and accessing results in other programming languages, scripting procedures, and reacting to changes in the database.

We present a basic introduction to some of these topics. Our objective is to inform you that such things exist, not to teach you how to use them. Each topic can be a book by itself, and the use and even existence of these capabilities differ wildly between DBMSs.

13.1 CURSORs

An SQL query returns an entire set of rows. In some instances, we may wish to process a result one row at a time instead of all at once. For example, we may wish to process a result from within a programming language and make decisions row-by-row. We can do this with a cursor. A cursor is basically a pointer to some position within the rows of a result set. We can use the cursor to iterate over the result rows.

Follow these steps to use a cursor:

1. **Declare Cursor**—A cursor declaration specifies the cursor name and the SELECT statement to generate the results.

```
DECLARE <cursor name> CURSOR FOR
<SELECT statement>
[ORDER BY <sort criteria list>]
```

Note that we may optionally specify the order of the cursor's traversal of the result.

2. **Open Cursor**—Opening a cursor executes the associated SELECT statement and positions the cursor at the beginning of the result.

```
OPEN <cursor name> CURSOR
```

3. **Fetch Rows**—Each fetch retrieves the next row in the result. After the last row has been fetched, subsequent calls to FETCH signal that there are not more data to fetch.

```
FETCH [FROM] <cursor name>
INTO [<target list>]
```

The *<target list>* specified the destination of the row values. Usually, these values are placed into host variables.

4. **Close Cursor**—Closing a cursor deallocates associated system resources.

```
CLOSE <cursor name>
```

Suppose you wanted to print the name and price of all menu items in descending order by price. Here's some example pseudocode:

Code 13.1 Menu prices code

```
DECLARE menuitem CURSOR FOR
SELECT name, price
FROM menuitems
ORDER BY price DESC;

OPEN menuitem CURSOR;

FETCH NEXT FROM menuitem
INTO :name, :price;

WHILE fetch returned data

  print name and price;

  FETCH NEXT FROM menuitem
  INTO :name, :price;

END WHILE

CLOSE menuitem;
```

The exact coding depends on the host language. Because the cursor syntax is part of SQL, many SQL interpreters will let you execute cursor commands directly. Experiment with declaring, opening, fetching from, and closing your own cursor.

Cursors are actually much more powerful than what's presented here. You can create scrollable cursors that allow random access to rows. Cursors can also be used to update and delete referenced rows.

13.2 Programming with SQL

Sometimes single SQL statements are not sufficient for what you need to do. There are several ways to create a sequence of SQL statements to solve a problem.

13.2.1 Stored Procedures

SQL allows the creation of scripts, called *stored procedures,* within the database. These scripts may contain one or more SQL statements. Stored procedures may take parameter values as input and even return results. The scripting language also includes loops, conditionals, variables, and so on. You may use cursors within stored procedures to process result sets one row at a time.

What purpose do stored procedures serve? They allow you to write a sequence of operations once and use it repeatedly. You only have to write the implementation of a process once when using a stored procedure. Stored procedures can also insulate users from changes to the underlying schema. When table changes occur, you only have to update the affected stored procedures. As long as the interface of the stored procedure doesn't change, nobody calling the stored procedure needs to know about the table changes.

As you might have guessed, writing stored procedures is a complicated topic that deserves a book of its own. In addition, there is little consistency between DBMSs on stored procedure syntax. Consult your DBMS documentation for specific information on creation and use of stored procedures.

Let's look at an example. You have a new customer that really, really loves your restaurant, but she's extremely allergic to tomatoes. You need to generate a special menu for her listing all items that contain no tomatoes. You consider writing a query just for her. Unfortunately, you'll have to rewrite this query every time she visits, and if you make an error just once, she may end up in the hospital (or worse). In addition, once she's told her friends about how accommodating your restaurant is to people with food allergies, you're going to have lots of new customers with all kinds of food allergies. Looks like what you need is a stored procedure that takes the name of an allergen and returns a list of eatable items.

Code 13.2   Create stored procedure

```
CREATE PROCEDURE AllergyMenu @allergen VARCHAR(30) AS
SELECT name, price
FROM items IT
WHERE NOT EXISTS
  (SELECT *
   FROM madewith m JOIN ingredients ig ON (m.ingredientid = ig.ingredientid)
   WHERE it.itemid = m.itemid AND ig.name = @allergen);
```

Code 13.2 creates a stored procedure named AllergyMenu that takes a single parameter, allergen, and finds the items that do not contain the specified allergen. The syntax here is specific to Microsoft SQL Server; however, the syntax will be similar for other DBMSs.

We can call this procedure using EXECUTE.

```
EXECUTE AllergyMenu('Tomato');
```

Again, the exact method of calling a stored procedure differs by DBMS.

13.2.2   Executing SQL in Other Programming Languages

Consider your favorite online store. They could tell everybody their schema and allow customers to use SQL to find and purchase merchandise. The complexity of searching and ordering in this manner would drive most users to find somewhere else to shop, even those who have read this book and are now SQL experts. In practice, databases work in the background, and applications provide the front-end interface. Such applications are responsible for driving user interaction through menus, dialog boxes, web pages, and so on. Applications query and update the database in response to user interaction. For your restaurant, if a customer requests a menu, your application should query the database for menu items and output them in a form the user can easily access. If a customer submits an order, the application should update the *orders* table.

Programming languages usually interact with relational databases by constructing SQL queries, sending them to the database, and processing the results. Communication between the application and the database is implemented by a library. In most cases, the results are made available through a cursor or cursorlike interface, allowing the application to process one row at a time.

Most programming languages support the use of SQL through libraries. Some even support many different libraries. Unfortunately, these libraries differ greatly between languages and DBMSs. To give you a general idea of how you might connect a programming language with a DBMS using SQL, we present a Java example. Even if you don't know Java, this should give you a general idea of how other approaches work.

To talk to databases using SQL, Java provides JDBC. JDBC uses a DBMS-specific driver that serves as a bridge between Java and the specific DBMS. Java applications speak JDBC, and the driver translates that to DBMS-specific speak, as shown in Figure 13.1. With minor changes to the code, a Java application can switch the underlying DBMS it is accessing by picking the JDBC driver of the new DBMS.

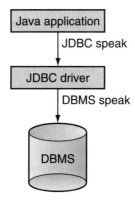

Figure 13.1: Java application using JDBC to talk to a DBMS.

Let's look at an example JDBC program.

```
import java.sql.*;

/**
 * JDBCExample accesses the database identified by the connection URL using the
 * specified driver for the given user. The ingredient ID and inventory value
 * (unitPrice * inventory) is printed to the console for the specified ingredient
 * name
 */
public class JDBCExample {

    public static void main(String[] args) throws Exception {

        // Test for appropriate parameters
        if (args.length != 5) {
            System.out println("Usage: <Driver Class> <Connection URL> <User Name> " +
                               "<Password> <Ingedient>");
            System.exit(1);
        }

        String driverClass = args[0]; // JDBC driver class to load
        String connectionURL = args[1]; // Database URL
        String userName = args[2]; // Database user name
        String password = args[3]; // Database password
        String ingredient = args[4]; // Name of ingredient

        Class.forName(driverClass); // Load JDBC driver

        // Create connection to database
        Connection conn = DriverManager.getConnection(connectionURL, userName,
                          password);
```

```
    // Create statement
    Statement stmt = conn.createStatement();

    // Construct string containing SQL query
    String sql = "SELECT ingredientid, unitprice * inventory AS invValue " +
                 "FROM ingredients WHERE name = \'" + ingredient + "\'";

    // Execute query and return result set
    ResultSet rs = stmt.executeQuery(sql);

    // Fetch rows until next() return false
    while (rs.next()) {
      System.out.println(rs.getString("ingredientid") + " " +
      rs.getString("inValue"));
    }

    // Deallocate resources
    rs.close();
    stmt.close();
    conn.close();
  }
}
```

JDBCExample prints the name and inventory value (unitprice ∗ inventory) of a specified ingredient. This program expects five parameters. Four of them are common to JDBC programs, whereas the fifth is application specific.

Driver Class—The class containing the DBMS-specific driver implementing the JDBC interface to talk the DBMS. Naturally, this value will be driver specific. Some example values include "org.postgresql.Driver" for a Postgres JDBC driver and "com.mysql.jdbc.Driver" for a MySQL JDBC driver.

Connection URL—A URL describing the database. The URL is of the form jdbc:*<subprotocol>*:*<subname>*. Both of these values will vary depending on your DBMS. Often, the subprotocol is related to the DBMS and the subname is the name of the database. Some example values include "jdbc:postgresql://databasehost.org/restaurant", where databasehost.org is the name of the machine hosting the DBMS and restaurant is the name of the database.

User Name—Name of the user with permission to access the Restaurant Database.

Password—Password of the user with permission to access to Restaurant Database.

Ingredient—Name of the ingredient to find.

JDBCExample begins by loading the specified JDBC driver. Remember that the drivers are DBMS specific, so you must use a JDBC driver that can talk to your DBMS. The driver documentation will include the driver class name. Next, a connection is created by the loaded driver. See your driver documentation for the specific syntax of the connection URL. The specified database user must have permission to access the specific database (see Chapter 12). Once the connection is created, JDBCExample creates a statement. The SQL query is constructed using basic string concatenation and submitted through the statement. The results are returned in a result set, which acts much like a cursor. Finally, all of the system resources are deallocated.

Accessing a database from a programming or scripting language is a powerful concept. Using JDBC, we've shown you an example of accessing a database from Java. Access from other languages using other libraries, although syntactically different, is often conceptually similar. Most dynamic Web page technologies nest scripting languages (e.g., JSP, ASP, PHP, etc.) inside hypertext markup language (HTML). In turn, these scripting languages can access databases using SQL to construct a Web page tuned to one particular user—even one allergic to tomatoes.

13.3 Triggers

A trigger is a SQL statement that is automatically executed whenever a table is modified. Specifically, a trigger can be set to fire whenever a row is inserted, updated, or deleted from a specified table. The trigger can be set to fire either before or after the operation.

13.3.1 CREATE TRIGGER

We can create a trigger using the CREATE trigger command:

```
CREATE TRIGGER <trigger name>
{AFTER | BEFORE}
{DELETE | INSERT | UPDATE [OF <column list>]}
ON <table name>
[REFERENCING <reference list>]
[FOR EACH {ROW | STATEMENT}]
<triggered SQL statement>
```

Usually, a trigger that fires before an operation will make sure the operation can execute correctly. A trigger that fires after the table modification usually will cause another action to take place. Triggers are added to the database using the CREATE TRIGGER command. For example, let's assume that we always have a 100% markup on the price of items. In other words, the price of an item is always twice the cost of the sum of the ingredients. We can create a trigger to update the price of a meal when the ingredient costs are modified.

DDL 13.3 Triggers

```
CREATE TRIGGER markup
AFTER UPDATE OF unitprice ON ingredients
UPDATE items SET price =
   (SELECT 2 * SUM(quantity * unitprice)
   FROM madewith m, ingredients i
   WHERE m.ingredientid = i.ingredientid AND items.itemid = m.itemid)
```

There are several important items to note about this trigger.

■ The trigger only fires when the *unitprice* column of the *ingredients* table is updated. This means it will not fire if we change the name of an ingredient.

■ The trigger does not fire when we change the *quantity* in the *madewith* table. We can solve that problem by adding a second trigger for updates on the *madewith* table.

■ The trigger will update every row in the *items* table (assuming the item is made with some ingredients) every time it fires. We will fix this problem with *row-level* triggers.

Another use of triggers is to log deletes from the database. For example, we might want to remember whenever we delete from the *items* table. We want to use the *logs* table to hold the date of the delete and the *itemid* that was deleted. To log the changes of a row, we must know when a particular row is updated. This functionality is provided by row-level triggers.

We can indicate that a trigger is row-level by adding the clause, FOR EACH ROW. Any trigger without that clause is considered a *statement-level trigger*. A *row-level trigger* fires once for every row that is changed. Thus, an update of many rows would fire many row-level triggers but only one statement-level trigger.

This performance disadvantage allows a tremendous computation capability. Because only one row is being updated, SQL allows us to access the value of that row before and after the update. Note that INSERT operations do not have old values and DELETES do not have new values. The SQL standard defines the following syntax for accessing these values:

```
<reference list> = <reference element>[<reference element> ...]

<reference element> =
OLD [ROW] [AS] <identifier> |
NEW [ROW] [AS] <identifier> |
OLD TABLE [AS] <old table> |
NEW TABLE [AS] <new table>
```

The trigger to log changes to the *items* table to the *logs* table would look like this.

DDL 13.4 Logging trigger

```
CREATE TRIGGER logging
BEFORE DELETE ON items
REFERENCING OLD ROW AS oldrow
FOR EACH ROW
    INSERT INTO logs VALUES (CURRENT_DATE, oldrow.itemid);
```

Finally, triggers can also be used to ensure integrity constraints. Whenever an update is made to the database, the trigger can check to make sure the update is allowed. If it is not, the trigger can generate an error and cause the transaction to perform a rollback. The details of this require DBMS-specific commands.

13.3.2 Trigger Firing Rules

Row-level triggers and statement-level triggers do not fire at the same time. For example, assume row-level trigger, *row,* and statement-level trigger, *statement,* are defined on the same table. The triggers would fire in response to the modification as follows:

1. *statement* triggers with BEFORE clause.
2. *row* triggers with BEFORE clause.
3. Database modification is performed.
4. *row* triggers with AFTER clause.
5. *statement* triggers with AFTER clause.

If there are multiple triggers of the same type that fire from the same update, the SQL standard defines them to fire in the order they were added to the database.

Caution is required when a trigger contains a reference to the table that fired the trigger. Row-level operations may not be seen by the trigger, even if the AFTER clause is used. There is no similar problem with statement-level triggers. Also, if a trigger modifies a table that contains a trigger, that trigger is also fired. It is possible for these updates to form a loop, resulting in an infinite number of triggers to fire. Most DBMSs prevent this by limiting the number of triggers that can be fired. This limit is high enough to handle ordinary transaction processing, but it will prevent infinite trigger chains.

13.3.3 DROP TRIGGER

We can remove a trigger using the DROP TRIGGER command:

```
DROP TRIGGER <trigger name>
```

13.3.4 Using Triggers

Triggers are very powerful operations, but they can consume large amounts of system resources. As such, they should be used with care. It is possible for a trigger to cause itself to fire, thus creating an infinite chain of triggers. As a result, all DBMSs have a limit to the depth of these trigger calls. The more common problem with triggers is causing multiple updates whenever a single update is requested. This will slow the system down and hurt performance. As a result, whenever simple integrity constraints such as domain constraints and foreign key constraints can be used to ensure the correctness of the database, triggers should be avoided.

13.4 Wrap Up

DBMSs support several mechanisms for programming with SQL. In this chapter, we introduced several of these mechanisms. Cursors allow iteration over query results, which may be useful for result processing in programming languages. Stored procedures allow you to write scripts that can be executed within SQL. Stored procedures can take parameter values and return computed results. You can access a relational DBMS from most programming languages by submitting SQL and processing results. Finally, using triggers, you can react to critical changes to the database.

Review Questions

1. SQL queries return _____, but we can use _____ to process results one row at a time.

2. The SQL associated with a cursor is actually executed by the _____ _____ statement.

3. **True/False** A trigger can fire when a SELECT statement is executed on a table.

4. What is the name of the driver class for a JDBC driver that can talk to your DBMS?
   _____

5. Give the SQL command to execute a stored procedure named `ListEmployees` that takes a department name as the only parameter.

6. If a statement-level trigger and row-level trigger are both declared on the same operation, which is executed first? Does the operation matter? Does the declaration matter?

7. For the Restaurant Database, write a trigger to update the *ingredients* table whenever a vendor is deleted. For all ingredients supplied by that vendor, set the *vendorid* to NULL.

8. Write a trigger that would cause an infinite number of triggers to fire. What did your DBMS do?

Practice

1. Declare a cursor to list the vendor ID and company name of all vendors.

2. Execute the JDBCExample on your DBMS.

3. Add a column to the projects table that is the duration of the project. Write a trigger to update this value whenever the projects table is updated.

4. Add a column to the projects table that is the duration of the project. Write a stored procedure to update this value whenever it is called. Use pseudocode, or the stored procedure language for your DBMS.

5. Add a column to the projects table that is the duration of the project. Write a Java program to update this value every day.

6. Download and execute an example program in your favorite programming language from the Internet that accesses your favorite DBMS. Have fun!

Index